Constructive Guidance and Discipline: Preschool and Primary Education

MARJORIE V. FIELDS
University of Alaska Southeast

CINDY BOESSER

Merrill, an imprint of
Macmillan Publishing Company
New York

Maxwell Macmillan Canada
Toronto

Maxwell Macmillan International
New York Oxford Singapore Sydney

Cover art: Tiarra Dean
Editor: Linda A. Sullivan
Production Editor: Laura Messerly
Art Coordinators: Lorraine Woost, Vincent A. Smith
Photo Editor: Anne Vega
Cover Designer: Thomas Mack
Production Buyer: Jeff Smith
Electronic Text Management: Ben Ko, Marilyn Wilson Phelps

This book was set in Zapf Calligraphic 801 by Macmillan Publishing Company and was printed and bound by R. R. Donnelley & Sons Company. The cover was printed by Phoenix Color Corp.

Macmillan Publishing Company
866 Third Avenue
New York, NY 10022

Macmillan Publishing Company is part of the
Maxwell Communication Group of Companies.

Maxwell Macmillan Canada, Inc.
1200 Eglinton Avenue East, Suite 200
Don Mills, Ontario M3C 3N1

Library of Congress Cataloging-in-Publication Data
Fields, Marjorie Vannoy.
   Constructive guidance and discipline : preschool and primary
   education / by Marjorie V. Fields and Cindy Boesser.
        p.   cm.
   Includes bibliographical references and index.
   ISBN 0-02-337285-0
   1. School discipline. 2. Behavior modification. 3. Educational
   counseling. 4. Education, Preschool. 5. Education, Primary.
   I. Boesser, Cindy. II. Title.
   LB3012.F54 1994
   371.5—dc20   93-14777
                                        CIP

Printing: 1 2 3 4 5 6 7 8 9 Year: 4 5 6 7

Photo credits: Cindy Boesser, pp. 104, 172, 252, 256, 259, 261, 264; Jean-Claude Lejeune, pp. 8, 21, 43, 49, 107, 183; Macmillan Publishing Company, p. 201; Sunrise Photos, p. 27; all other photos by Marjorie V. Fields.

Illustration credits: Roz Cruise, p. 3; Dana Lyon, p. 19; Tracy Hillhouse Price, p. 37; Katherine Eiford, p. 57; Jon M. Choate, p. 77; Joshua Buffington, p. 99; Kimberly Spicher, p. 117; Jessica McCoy, p. 139; Jennifer J. Morse, p. 159; Jason Ginter, p. 181; Carly Craig, p. 197; Matthew Greely, p. 217; Shalom Schrader, p. 235; Christi Scott, p. 249; Rachel Bernstein, p. 267.

For the cause of
worldwide peace and harmony.

May it begin in the
hearts of children
and spread.

FOREWORD

This is a practical book with many examples and contrasts. It is not, however, a mere collection of recipes, but is a book full of instructive examples based on sound theoretical reasons. It also communicates a way of thinking about young children and attitudes of empathy.

The approach the authors recommend is good because it solves problems in positive ways and promotes the development of healthy personalities. In addition, though, the authors have a vision of autonomy as the aim of education that goes far beyond the development of healthy personalities. Since this vision has perhaps not been articulated as forcefully as it could have, I would like to take this opportunity to discuss autonomy as intended by Jean Piaget as the aim of education.

Autonomy in Piaget's theory means something different from its common meaning. Autonomy usually means the *right* to make decisions for oneself, and many people mistakenly think that it means the *right* to do whatever one pleases. In Piaget's theory, autonomy means not the right but the *ability* to make decisions for oneself about right and wrong, independent of reward and punishment, by taking relevant factors into account. When one takes relevant factors into account, one is not free to lie, steal, break promises, disturb other people, or be irresponsible.

Parents and teachers have traditionally tried to teach right and wrong by using reward and/or punishment. Reward and punishment give the appearance of working but the result in the long run is either blind conformity or susceptibility to manipulation through reward and/or punishment. The Watergate coverup affair, for example, happened because the men under President Nixon expected to be rewarded for doing what they knew to be morally wrong. As far as the effects of punishment are concerned, we all know how the possibility of punishment leads to calculation of risks.

A clear example of moral autonomy is Martin Luther King's struggle for civil rights. He took relevant factors into account, concluded that the laws discriminating against African Americans were unjust, and fought to put an end to these laws. Many people tried to stop him with incarceration, dogs, water hoses, and threats of assassination, but he could not be manipulated by reward or punishment.

The important question for parents and teachers is: How can we raise children to become morally autonomous adults, who make decisions based on what is right, rather than on what is rewarded or punished? Piaget's answer to this question was that we foster the development of autonomy first by refraining from using reward and punishment. By giving stickers to children for completing worksheets, for example, we unwittingly teach them to become susceptible to manipulation by reward. If we punish children for lying, to cite another example, children can learn only to avoid being punished. Piaget would suggest that, instead of punishing a child for telling a lie, we might look him or her straight in the eye and say with affection and skepticism, "I can't believe what you are saying because. . . . I want you to sit down and think about what you might do next time if you want me to believe you." This appeal to the human relationship between the child and the adult and to the direct consequence of the act has the effect of motivating the child to construct *from within*, over time, the value of honesty. Children who are thus supported in building their own conviction about the importance of honesty cannot tell lies even for a president who might dangle rewards.

A discussion of specific techniques is beyond the scope of the present context, and the reader is urged to read this book. I also recommend *The Moral Judgment of the Child* (chapters 2 and 3) by Piaget.

Today's children live with many serious potential problems such as drug abuse, AIDS, teenage pregnancies, and guns in schools. Although these may all look like separate problems, they are actually all symptoms of the inability to make decisions for oneself by taking relevant factors into account. Children who can take relevant factors into account do not take drugs, for example.

The belief that rules and values must be put into children from the outside through lectures, rewards, and punishment is outdated. Rules and values must be constructed (made) by children *from the inside* if they are to become children's own. Only when children have convictions of their own do they have the moral courage to say "No" to drugs, sex, and violence. Children need the same strength of internal conviction Martin Luther King had when he stood up to the punishment heaped upon him.

The time to start fostering the development of autonomy is at an early age. Through building strong human relationships, exchanging points of view with children, and allowing them to learn from their own mistakes, we can help them develop the capacity to take relevant factors into account. Autonomy is a complicated goal, and I congratulate the authors for going beyond the perspective of what seems to work in the short run. What seems to work in the short run often defeats our long-range goal of turning out adults who can decide for themselves between right and wrong.

Constance Kamii
Birmingham, Alabama
February, 1993

PREFACE

This book attempts to bring together the best of what is known about helping young children become happy, responsible, and productive people. We present guidance and discipline concepts within a framework of child development, developmentally appropriate practices, and constructivist education. Thus, only discipline approaches consistent with all three aspects of this framework are recommended here. We do take a stand about what is best for young children, rather than merely present an impartial overview of various approaches.

MAJOR THEORETICAL INFLUENCES

The information and ideas presented in this text come from a number of respected sources. We see four theorists as having major influences on child guidance concepts in this century: Alfred Adler, Carl Rogers, B. F. Skinner, and Jean Piaget. Rudolf Dreikurs's recommendations about logical and natural consequences extend Adler's concepts, Thomas Gordon has popularized Rogers's ideas through his Parent Effectiveness Training work, widespread behavior modification techniques are based on Skinner's work, and Piagetian scholars such as Constance Kamii and Rheta DeVries are spreading the word about constructivism and Piaget's views on the development of morality. Though we reject Skinner's approach, for reasons explained in chapter 9, we believe that the other three theorists have compatible views. Adler, Rogers, and Piaget all perceive the child as actively seeking understanding. This contrasts with the Skinnerian view, which sees education as something that happens to a child from outside sources. Adler and Rogers, as well as Piaget, respect the child's personal rate and style of developing social understanding. All three perceive the proper adult role as facilitating rather than controlling the child's gradual development as a constructive member of society. Piaget's theoretical framework is much broader than that of Rogers or Adler; it includes all of moral development as well as intellectual development. Thus, Adlerian and Rogerian concepts can be included as part of a Piagetian perspective, though the reverse is not true.

The research and writing of Jean Piaget and Constance Kamii on intellectual and moral autonomy are central to the message in this book. We have adapted Thomas Gordon's recommendations for effective communication and interpreted Rudolf Dreikurs's concept of logical and natural consequences into our discussion of a constructivist approach to discipline. We have also drawn on Erik Erikson's emotional development studies, referred to guidelines from the National Association for the Education of Young

Children, and quoted Lilian Katz. Many other sources are used in this book and are listed at the end of each chapter.

We look at guidance and discipline as teaching activities; therefore, the principles of effective early childhood education apply as much to this realm as to academics. In addition, we discuss the ways in which effective early-childhood education practices prevent or alleviate many common discipline problems.

Like any other aspect of teaching, guidance must acknowledge diversity among youngsters. In our recommendations, we have attempted to consider individual differences due to innate temperament as well as to culture, class, and gender.

We also recognize that teachers must increasingly deal with youngsters whose lives are in crisis. These youngsters create major new challenges in guidance and discipline. Two chapters are devoted to providing background and support for teachers as they meet these challenges. Although parent involvement is crucial to all aspects of education and for all children, we emphasize the home-school link most in the chapters about children with special needs.

ORGANIZATION OF TEXT

The first three chapters of the book constitute the foundations section. Chapter 1 begins to explain a view of discipline as a way of teaching autonomy and self-discipline while promoting self-esteem. Concepts introduced in chapter 1 are more fully addressed throughout the book. Chapters 2 and 3 consider stages in children's physical, emotional, intellectual, and social development as they relate to discipline problems and solutions. We consider a clear definition of discipline plus knowledge of child development to be the basic understandings for a discussion of discipline.

The second section of this text presents information about various approaches to discipline in descending order: from most positive to negative. Chapter 4 discusses how to prevent behavior problems by matching the child environment to developmental stages. Chapter 5 explains the role of developmentally appropriate programs in preventing discipline problems. Chapters 6 and 7 emphasize both prevention of problems and intervention when problems do occur. Chapter 6 explains how the adult example influences child behavior and shows how to help children use those examples during conflict situations. Chapter 7 presents effective ways to communicate with children both to prevent conflict and to address problems that arise. This subject of effective communication includes how to negotiate solutions to existing problems. Chapter 8 explains how to change unproductive behaviors by using related consequences to help children understand why certain behaviors are unacceptable. Chapter 9 discusses the pros and cons of behavior modification to change behavior. The dangers of punishment are presented in chapter 10.

Chapters 11 through 15 constitute the final section, building on the previous two parts. Child development knowledge from part 1 is used to help determine the cause of behavior problems; then information about guidance approaches from part 2 is used to select an appropriate response. Part 3 analyzes typical causes of discipline problems and relates them to the relevant approaches. These chapters emphasize the necessity of dealing with the cause of problems rather than just the symptoms. Chapter 11 discusses the relationship between maturational level and acceptable behavior, and chapter 12 looks at how unmet emotional needs cause problem behavior. Chapters 13 and 14 explore serious problems with causes outside the classroom and suggest help for the teacher or caregiver. Chapter 15 presents an overview of the possible causes of discipline problems and provides assistance in identifying which causes pertain to a particular situation. This chapter also provides a guide for matching causes with the particular approaches to discipline most likely to be effective.

PROVIDING EXAMPLES

Because we want to balance theoretical explanations with real-life examples, we use typical scenarios to illustrate ways of facilitating self-discipline and moral autonomy through approaches to discipline. Many of these examples are quite long in an effort to provide the context surrounding the situation. This is congruent with our message that teachers must not respond just to the behavior, but instead consider the many factors possibly relating to its cause. These stories proved extremely helpful to the college students who used this book in draft form. They reported that when they were struggling with an abstract concept, the example would help them understand.

Meet the cast of characters: Dennis, Maureen, Sheri, and the rest of the staff of the Midway Children's Center, a composite preschool/child-care center in the suburbs, provide examples of discipline with three- and four-year-olds. Mrs. Jensen's children and the staff of a typical inner-city school demonstrate the same concepts with primary grade children. We use first names for child-care staff and last names for public school staff, not to imply more respect for the latter but to reflect common practice.

Because contrasting desirable practices with undesirable ones often helps us define the desirable, we have also provided examples of common practices that we do not recommend. For this purpose, mythical preschool teacher Joanne and first-grade teacher Miss Wheeler are described in some very real situations.

Although the examples refer to preschoolers and first graders, we emphasize that the guidance concepts refer to preschool, kindergarten, and all other primary grades. Using just one grade level for primary-grade examples merely simplifies the book's cast of characters.

Examples from readers' own experience will be the most instructive. We believe that significant time with youngsters, preferably enough to establish an authentic relationship with them, is necessary for internalizing theories about guidance and discipline. We believe that personal observation and experience are crucial to learning—both in preschool and adulthood.

We use the term *teacher* throughout the book to refer to caregivers as well as to other teachers because any adults who guide children are teaching them. We firmly believe that adults working with children in child care must be as knowledgeable about child development as any other teachers. Because youngsters are so profoundly influenced by the adults in their lives, it is essential that all teachers have a solid understanding of how to influence youngsters in positive directions.

You see a child's picture of herself on the cover of this book and child self-portraits at the beginning of each chapter. Children's visions of themselves are extremely relevant to the primary messages of the book: (1) guidance and discipline approaches must always protect the child's self-esteem; (2) Self-discipline and moral autonomy are the only valid goals of discipline.

THE AUTHORS

The first author, Marjorie V. Fields, is a professor of early childhood education. As such, she has had the luxury of studying and reflecting extensively on the research and theoretical issues surrounding child guidance and discipline. Marjorie's role in the development of this book was to make sure that it reflected a clear and defensible theoretical base.

Both authors of this book are not college professors, as is typical. The second author, Cindy Boesser, wrote from the front lines, so to speak. She was recently director of a child-care center and has worked in a one-room multiage school. During her work on this manuscript, she held positions in child care and as a public school aide. Cindy's role was to make sure that the book reflected the real world.

ACKNOWLEDGEMENTS

We wish to acknowledge the reviewers of this text, whose opinions we appreciate: Becky Bailey, University of Central Florida; Kathryn Castle, Oklahoma State University; Christine Chaille, Portland State University; Mary Anne Christenberry, College of Charleston; Richard Elardo, The University of Iowa; Stephanie Feeney, University of Hawaii; Craig Hart, Brigham Young University; Randy Hitz, Montana State University; Constance Kamii, University of Alabama at Birmingham; Sherrill Richarz, Washington State University; Francine Stuckey, Eastern New Mexico University; Rodney Warfield, Frostburg State University; Stan Wollock, William Paterson College.

Marjorie Fields

I wish to express my deepest gratitude for assistance with this book to Constance Kamii. Connie has been my mentor as I struggled to understand constructivism and then to relate it to the subject of discipline. My colleagues, Stephanie Feeney and Randy Hitz, also made generous contributions to this project. Their suggestions plus their thorough, and sometimes stinging, criticism made this a much better book. Thanks also to Kathi Wincman for helping me express ideas more accurately and to Deborah Hillstead for her clear visions of classroom reality. I probably learned the most from children themselves, however. All the youngsters in all the classrooms where I have spent time over the last two decades helped me to understand what I read about child development and guidance. Raising my own two sons also taught me a lot, and I must thank them for being the subjects of my longitudinal research. Ruth Ryan and Sue Ogden made major contributions toward getting the manuscript in final form. I also owe a debt of gratitude to the many teachers who allowed me to take photographs in their classrooms and then assisted with parental permission forms.

Cindy Boesser

I owe the fullest measure of thanks for many invaluable years experiencing positive guidance to my mother, Mildred Boesser. Each moment of understanding, each act of respect, each word of encouragement helped me to grow in the belief that I was a capable, responsible, accepted human being. She consistently fostered my self-discipline, even allowing me to learn from my own sometimes-painful-to-watch mistakes. I also am very grateful for being able to observe my sister, Kate Boesser, raise my beautiful nieces. She is obviously using the guidance skills she constructed in her childhood with our mother, and is building upon them with her own growing awarenesses. And I am exceedingly thankful for the hundreds of teachers I have worked with in my adult life: the children. No one could have taught me better about their needs, their struggles and their unique ways of learning. Co-workers Lauren Gallagher and Nettie Lessman were most helpful in the sharing of ideas, honest feedback, brainstorming, and caring enough to try and try and try again, in one of the most demanding and rewarding of occupations: early childhood education. Last but not least, I would like to sincerely thank Dr. Marjorie Fields for inviting me to co-author this textbook, toward our common goal of more appropriate guidance and discipline for children everywhere.

BRIEF CONTENTS

CONTENTS

Chapter 8
Helping Children Understand Rules and Limits   139

Chapter 9
Controlling Behavior Externally   159

Chapter 10
Punishment vs. Discipline   181

PART 3   MATCHING DISCIPLINE CAUSES TO
DISCIPLINE APPROACHES   195

Chapter 11
Immaturity   197

1

Discipline Foundations

The first three chapters of this book provide the basic information necessary to study the topic of discipline. In the first chapter we define discipline as discussed in this text, comparing the concept of constructive discipline with authoritarian and permissive discipline. As part of this definition, we examine discipline in terms of the goals or outcomes desired. Chapter 1 also introduces the two basic premises of the book. One of these is working toward long-term discipline goals rather than only immediate concerns. The other is matching the discipline approach to the cause of the problem behavior.

Chapters 2 and 3 focus on child development issues that directly impact discipline in preschools and primary grades. Understanding how children grow, learn, and think helps adults to live more harmoniously with youngsters. This understanding not only creates more tolerance for normal childish behaviors, but it also reduces inappropriate adult expectations. Adults who lack this understanding often unknowingly create discipline problems. We believe that effective discipline approaches must be based on knowledge of child development.

Chapter 1

Thinking about Discipline

Teachers, parents, politicians, and ministers all express great interest in the topic of discipline. Better discipline is seen as the cure for a number of educational and societal ills. People often seem to believe that they are experts on discipline simply because they have experienced it. Many advocate simplistic views of how to reach complex goals: methods that usually focus on how to force young people into compliance. These recommendations ignore evidence about the results of such efforts. Statistics on delinquency, dropouts, and pervasive violence suggest that much discipline is missing its mark.

What is your view of discipline? Do you tend to think of it as punishing a child for doing something wrong? Many people think that discipline is a smack on a child's bottom. You may have heard a joke that refers to a paddle as the "board of education." This book defines discipline differently: helping children learn personal responsibility for their behavior and to judge between right and wrong for themselves. The emphasis is on teaching as we help youngsters learn responsible behaviors rather than merely stopping unproductive actions. Instead of just enforcing rules about what not to do, we want to help children learn to make wise choices about what they should do.

Most adults have strong ideas about how children should be disciplined. These ideas are often based on adults' own experiences of discipline as children. You may have heard someone say, "My dad beat me when I did wrong, and I turned out fine." Another might report a total lack of adult controls, expressing either resentment or pleasure at the memory. Rarely do people start from scratch and think about discipline on an analytical rather than emotional basis. We invite you to begin this exploration.

THE GOALS OF DISCIPLINE

Start by asking yourself, "What is the purpose of discipline?" If your answer is to get kids to be "good," then you need to define acceptable behavior. You will find that not everyone agrees on what is acceptable. One teacher may want students to be quiet in school, while another may accept and even encourage talking among students. If acceptable behavior is defined as helping children to be "good," expectations will also vary. Some adults value teaching youngsters to dutifully say "please" and "thank you" or "I'm sorry." However, many adults consider those empty and even hypocritical words unless they are genuine, arising from increased understanding about the feelings of others. In the absence of consensus about good behavior, how do we decide on discipline goals?

Long-term Goals

Whenever you teach something, you need to start by clarifying your long-term educational goals. Teaching discipline without long-term goals is like trying to plan a trip route without knowing where you are headed. In order to examine long-term goals, you may find it useful to ask yourself what kind of people you value. Notice that the word is *people* not *children*. Is there a difference? Look at the

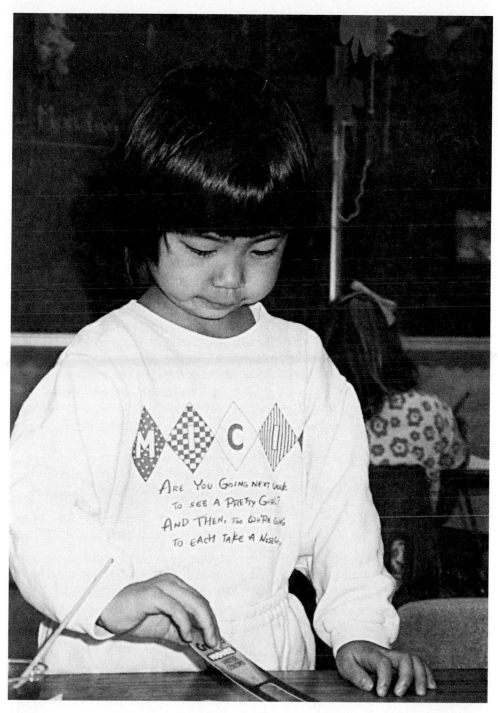

Discipline goals need to focus on what kind of people function best in society rather than merely what kind of children are best to manage.

list that follows and choose the three most desirable characteristics. If you are thinking about children, you might be attracted to the label *obedient*; however, you are not likely to choose that label for an adult characteristic. Keep in mind that early discipline influences character for a lifetime; therefore, it is essential to think about what kind of people function best in society rather than merely considering what kind of children are easiest to manage.

adventurous	considerate	innovative
assertive	curious	kind
athletic	determined	obedient
caring	energetic	popular
cautious	friendly	sensitive
competitive	happy	versatile
confident	intuitive	visionary

Common goals for youngsters are *confident, kind*, and *happy*. Parents may choose *assertive* and *curious* for their children, too. Some adults might choose both *assertive* and *obedient* or both *curious* and *cautious*. It is helpful to be aware that some combinations such as these may not be compatible. What do you really want? How can you best help children develop the skills and attitudes for happy, responsible, and productive lives? What character traits will best serve the person and society?

Positive Self-concept

There is general agreement that we want youngsters to grow up with a positive self-concept (Sternberg & Kolligan, 1990). While almost everyone voices this goal, many still use discipline methods that damage self-esteem. Children are routinely treated with much less respect than adults are. They are lectured, ignored, bullied, and bribed in ways no adult would ever put up with. Children often aren't really listened to, either. Later chapters will discuss how punishment and other coercive tactics—even rewards—can damage a person's self-esteem.

Self-discipline

Nearly everyone also agrees that self-discipline is a goal for children. Most approaches to discipline describe themselves as promoting self-discipline. Disagreements center around what leads to this goal. Some people believe that keeping a youngster away from all temptation will create self-discipline. Such an approach assumes that behavior is learned through force of habit. Others believe that rewards for acceptable behavior and punishments for unacceptable behavior will lead to self-discipline. Such viewpoints do not recognize that being manipulated by reward and punishment is vastly different from learning to decide what is right. The authors of this book have come to a very different conclusion. We are among those who believe that children can't learn to regulate their own behavior as long as others are regulating it for them. We see children's own experiences as their best learning tool.

Moral Autonomy

A more sophisticated version of self-discipline is called moral autonomy. This is a concept presented in Jean Piaget's work *The Moral Judgment of the Child* (1932, p. 65), and elaborated for modern audiences by Piagetian scholar Constance Kamii (1984). According to these sources, *autonomy* means being governed and guided by *oneself*. The opposite is *heteronomy*, which means being governed or ruled by someone else.

Some people misinterpret this concept and get worried when they hear about autonomy. They think that being governed by yourself means doing whatever you want. It is, however, a person *without* moral autonomy or self-discipline who is likely to act irresponsibly when there are no external controls. In fact, that description fits some young college students away from home for the first time. College dormitory life testifies to the fact that some well-meaning parents and teachers deny young people adequate opportunity to develop inner controls. Inexperienced at self-regulating their work, play, and sleep, some first-year college students find themselves unable to achieve a workable balance.

Autonomy does not mean lack of controls; rather, it refers to the *source* of control. Autonomous people carry those controls within. They are never without them, even when alone. Heteronomous people, by contrast, experience control only when someone else is present. They depend on an external judge to reward or punish their behavior. When you help youngsters develop moral autonomy, you affect how they behave, even when misbehavior isn't likely to be caught. Autonomous people don't need policing to keep them on the right path.

LONG-TERM VS. QUICK-FIX SOLUTIONS

Are teachers responsible for keeping children safe and orderly and also for helping them develop positive self-esteem, self-discipline, and moral autonomy? That's a tall order! Don't forget teachers have to teach, too. Can they really be blamed if they have a hard time thinking about long-range discipline goals? After all, teachers usually have a child for just one year. Parents, on the other hand, are generally aware that they will be dealing with this child through the teen years and beyond. One mother reports that she was powerfully motivated to help her son Michael learn self-discipline when she thought about his getting a driver's license in ten years. While Michael was little, she could protect him from harm by watching over him herself; but she doubted that she could ride along to make sure he was driving safely when he was sixteen. She knew that inner controls would stay with Michael long after she couldn't. Therefore, she focused on discipline approaches that foster inner control.

Nevertheless, even parents are sometimes tempted to ignore the future and concentrate on making their lives easier for now. Teachers may be under the added pressure to present a "well-disciplined" class, in the old sense of appearing quiet and controlled, which can make a difference at evaluation time with some principals. As a result, discipline methods that boast quick, short-term results at the expense of children's self-esteem and autonomy remain popular. You will read about some of these methods in chapter 9.

Fortunately, many teachers care too much about children to give in to temptation. They resist quick-fix approaches and work on positive alternatives. They know that helping children live peacefully together now and preparing them for the future can be compatible goals. Skillful teachers know how to work toward long-term discipline goals while maintaining a peaceful and productive learning environment. They know they don't have to make a choice between protecting children's self-esteem and keeping order. With the guidance of these knowledgeable and caring teachers, children can learn from experience to make wise decisions. In the process, they also can develop the positive self-esteem and moral autonomy necessary for self-discipline.

CONSTRUCTIVE DISCIPLINE

Common approaches to discipline vary from the very authoritarian, in which the adult makes all the rules and punishes any deviation, to the very permissive, in

Constructive discipline helps children develop the positive self-esteem and moral autonomy necessary for self-discipline.

which the child makes all the decisions. Too many people think they have to choose one or the other of those models. One teacher says she plays the "heavy" until she can't stand herself; then she switches to the opposite until she can't stand the kids. Too few adults (teachers or parents) are even aware of any other options. However, there is lots of room in between those extremes for approaches that balance the power of adult and child. The needs and views of both the adult and the child can be accommodated when discipline is viewed as teaching.

Discipline Models Compared

Many terms have been used to describe the different approaches to discipline. Authoritarian and permissive are commonly understood terms and concepts. Alternatives to these extremes have been harder to define and to understand. Baumerind (1967) wrote about authoritative discipline and explained how it differed from the authoritarian model. However, many people were confused by the similarities between the two labels. Another approach was to compare the forms of discipline with forms of government. The autocratic holding of power by the adult might be compared to a dictatorship. Anarchy might be an appropriate label for the overly permissive style that grants too much power to the child. The shared power approach could reasonably be called democratic (Greenberg, 1992b). But the democratic concept of majority rule doesn't work for discipline. Clearly the teacher would always be outnumbered.

Because we view discipline as teaching, we prefer to compare discipline models to learning theories. The authoritarian style is consistent with the *behaviorist* philosophy of education, with its emphasis on molding behavior via reward and punishment. The permissive style is compatible with the *maturationist* philosophy of education, with its belief in time as the best teacher. We believe that the best alternative to these philosophies reflects the Piagetian-based *constructivist* approach to education. Constructivism helps children learn from their experiences and from reflecting on those experiences (DeVries, Zan, Reese-Learned, & Morgan, 1991). Through this process, the learner gains increasingly sophisticated levels of understanding. Thus, children gradually develop the ability to take many relevant factors into consideration when deciding what action is best for all concerned.

THREE PHILOSOPHIES OF DISCIPLINE

Behaviorist: Molds behavior via reward and punishment
Maturationist: Believes that time is the best teacher
Constructivist: Helps children learn from experience

Discipline Goals Compared

In general, each discipline style has the same motive: love and/or concern for the child. However, each has very different goals. Obedience is the target behavior in the autocratic model, preferably unquestioning and immediate obedience. The permissive model emphasizes individual freedom. The constructivist goal for discipline is self-determined, responsible behavior. Responsible behavior reflects concern for the good of others and for oneself as well. This approach acknowledges the complexity of the ever-changing world; therefore, it teaches children to think for themselves about desirable or undesirable actions rather than tells them predetermined answers to current dilemmas.

Discipline Forms Differ

Not surprisingly, each model uses very different forms of discipline. Punishment and reward are used almost exclusively in the obedience model. Lack of any discipline is the distinguishing feature of the permissive model. Between these two clear-cut extremes, the constructivist model offers a multifaceted set of discipline options that will be explained in this text. These options focus on teaching and, like all good teaching, begin with good human relationships. Mutually caring and respectful relationships with adults and peers encourage youngsters to ponder the effects of their behavior on other people. Discipline strategies are aimed at helping children construct behavior rules and values for themselves.

Results Differ Also

Which model is best? What are the results of each? We can never be certain about research findings concerning human beings because we cannot ethically control the variables in a person's life. Each person is a unique blend of genetics, family dynamics, societal influences, and individual experiences. However, certain trends occur frequently enough to suggest a relationship. The authoritarian model is associated with anger and depression as well as low self-esteem and the inability to make self-directed choices. Likewise, those people with an overly permissive background demonstrate low self-esteem and difficulty getting along with others. The shared power model results in high self-esteem, good social skills, general competence, and self-discipline (Ramsey, 1992).

Research provides evidence that youngsters who have the opportunity for choice and self-direction in preschool are more able to make wise choices as teenagers. They are less likely to use drugs, to become pregnant, or to drop out of school (Schweinhart, Weikart, & Larner, 1986). You don't have to wait for ten years, however, to see the results of helping children become morally autonomous. Children in constructivist classrooms quickly learn to negotiate solutions to problems and to resolve their own conflicts (DeVries et al., 1991).

TEACHING FOR MORAL AUTONOMY

Certain basic concepts are central to a constructivist approach to discipline. They include providing age-appropriate choices for youngsters and assisting them in solving their own problems. You are always striving to help children understand, rather than making them merely obey. When undesirable behavior occurs, your discipline efforts must address the cause of the behavior for effective teaching to take place. Respect is also integral to constructivist teaching (Kamii, 1982). It is just as important for you to treat the child with respect as it is for the child to treat you with respect. Now let's examine these concepts in more detail.

Guiding Choices

Constructive discipline encourages children to make as many of their own decisions and choices as possible, which helps children to learn from their mistakes as well as their successes. In other words, you help children learn how to make wise choices instead of making all the choices for them. In the process of learning to regulate their own behavior, children make both good and bad choices for themselves. It is hard but necessary to let youngsters make the poor choices as well as the good ones. No matter what their age, people tend to learn best the lessons learned through their own experience— especially from analyzing their mistakes.

   Of course, children don't have the choice of putting their fingers in an electrical socket to experience a shock. But they do have the choice of not eating their snack and getting a little hungry, or the choice of not cooperating in play and subsequently being rejected by peers. Teachers whose goal is helping children learn to think for themselves don't help by thinking and acting for their students. They do not instantly step in and solve conflicts for youngsters. Instead, conflicts and problems are seen as potential learning situations. The children work at problem solving. The teacher's job is to facilitate the process as needed.

Teaching Problem Solving: An Example

For example, when preschoolers Sara and Christie were tugging on the same doll bed, each screaming, "I had it first!" Dennis, their teacher, resisted coming over and immediately taking the toy away, although it might have been simple to say, "If you can't play nicely, I'll have to put this away." Nor did he start the usual inquisition trying to determine which child had it first so that he could make the fairest decision. Instead, he facilitated decision making on the part of the children. He helped the girls to clarify the problem by stating what it appeared to be: "You both want a bed for your dolls." He further identified the dilemma: "There's only one of these beds and two sleepy babies." Then Dennis asked them what *they* thought they could do to solve their problem. In this way he helped the girls learn to think about fairness for both sides.

   Problem solving takes practice, just as other complex skills do. It is also dependent on levels of maturity. Young children have limited reasoning ability, but they

It is just as important for you to treat the child with respect as it is for the child to treat you with respect.

become more capable when encouraged to discuss their different views. The teacher works with children at their levels of maturation, demonstrating ways of expressing their feelings and suggesting possible approaches to solutions. The teacher may ask questions, such as "Where else could a baby doll sleep in this house?" This method still leaves the children in charge of a search for alternatives. Even if they aren't immediately successful, Dennis doesn't take over. However, if the children's frustration and anger appear to be getting beyond their ability to control, he might resort to taking the doll bed and putting it out of reach. He then would assure the girls that they could have it as soon as they come up with a solution.

Helping Children Understand

Dennis's approach to the doll bed dilemma was aimed at helping Sara and Christie begin to think about a viewpoint other than their own. Learning to consider the viewpoints of others in making decisions is part of learning moral autonomy. According to Piaget, we also teach moral autonomy and the necessary understanding of others' views when we help children see the consequences of their behavior rather than merely punishing it.

You can teach without punishing by asking ask Aaron to mop up the puddle he made by splashing water on the floor during exuberant water play. Similarly, you can help Kenji learn by briefly removing him from the block area until he chooses to stop knocking over other children's buildings. The teacher's role in developing moral autonomy is to help children figure out why their behavior is causing a problem, while providing them with the opportunity to help resolve the problem.

Mutual Respect

Constructive discipline involves respect and affection for the child. The quality of the relationship between child and adult is crucial to the success of any discipline approach. This means investing time in getting to know children as individuals and attempting to understand them. Spending time with a youngster and listening to that child not only helps an adult understand the child, but also demonstrates respect. Respecting children and their viewpoints helps them to respect our viewpoints (Kamii, 1984). Mutual respect is an essential ingredient of effective discipline. Any response can turn into punishment if accompanied by put-downs. For instance, to call a child sloppy for spilling or mean for knocking down the blocks would destroy the educational value of discipline teaching. The child would focus on self-defense rather than on the problem behavior. It is also important to be aware of how your attitude is projected. Anger or disgust in your tone of voice can override even the most carefully chosen words.

Treating the Cause Rather Than the Symptom

No amount of respect will make discipline effective unless your approach deals with the reason why the behavior occurred. If you only stop the behavior without treating the cause, the behavior problem will probably continue to be repeated. Discipline is like weeding a garden: If you don't get the roots out with the weeds, the weeds will be back in a few days. Effective approaches to discipline work to get at the root of the problem.

It isn't easy to figure out why children do the things they do. You certainly can't determine the cause simply by seeing the behavior. For instance, there are several reasons for why Aaron might have spilled water during water play. Perhaps he was just having such a good time that he didn't think about where the water was going. It is also possible that he spilled because of immature coordination, which made it hard for him to pour the water where he intended. Then again, maybe he knew what he was doing and did it on purpose. He might have spilled to get attention or to alleviate boredom.

Don't overlook the possibility that *you* may have caused a discipline problem. Chapters 2 and 3 illustrate how a mismatch between child development and teacher expectations can cause discipline problems. Chapters 4 and 5 discuss how inappropriate school environments and programs often cause behavior problems. Chapters 6 and 7 raise the issue of undesirable adult examples and communication styles as sources of undesirable child behavior. Chapters 9 and 10 explain how coercive and punitive discipline approaches backfire and create worse behavior problems.

Each different cause, whether originating with the child or the adult, points to a different solution. Yet there are many teachers and caregivers who have one solution for any and all infractions of the rules. Think about the commonly used time-out bench as it would affect Aaron in the case of each possible cause. How would the time-out bench affect his feelings about preschool fun if the spill was caused by his eagerness to explore? How would time-out affect his feelings about himself if the spill was caused by poor coordination? If attention-getting or boredom was the cause, would time-out keep Aaron from spilling again?

Observing to Discover the Cause

The best way to determine the cause of a child's behavior is to observe the child carefully and record your observations. You need to know a lot about a child to plan effective discipline. You need to know whether this is usual or unusual behavior and also under what circumstances it occurs. Are certain activities likely to trigger it? Is there a pattern of when, where, or with whom behavior problems are most likely? What do you know about the child's home routine, health, or family situation that might provide some clues? Communicating with parents and keeping careful records of child behavior are both indispensable parts of determining the cause of problems. You assess the child's social learning needs through this process of finding causes for behavior problems. This assessment is an essential guide for effective teaching.

As you read this text, you will be guided to match probable causes of behavior with appropriate approaches to discipline. Selecting the right approach requires that you understand many different approaches and also that you understand children and the many different reasons for their actions.

Don't overlook the possibility that a discipline problem was caused by inappropriate teacher expectations.

CONCLUSION

This chapter has attempted to stimulate your thinking about your values as they relate to guidance and discipline. Our discussion and comparison of definitions

Selecting the right discipline approach requires that you understand children and the many different reasons for their actions.

and goals of discipline resulted in the recommendation of a middle-ground approach with constructivist goals, rather than an authoritarian or a permissive approach. We began an introduction to ways of implementing constructivist approaches to discipline, with more complete explanations to come in the following chapters.

We hope that you will supplement what you read here with further reading from the recommended reading lists. We also hope that you will spend significant time with young children, proving guidance and discipline concepts to yourself through your own observation and experience. If you haven't read the preface to this book, you might want to do so. It provides further explanation about the intent of the authors. The preface also gives an overview of the three-part organization of the text: (1) Discipline Foundations, (2) Discipline Approaches, and (3) Matching Discipline Causes to Discipline Approaches.

FOR FURTHER THOUGHT

1. Reexamine and add to the list of desirable characteristics on page 6. Compare your list with those of others. Select the three characteristics you would most want to encourage through child guidance. Explain your choices and compare them with a friend's.
2. Think about your own parents' approach to child rearing. What characteristics do you think they most valued? How did those values influence your own childhood? Do your choices reflect those of your parents or are they different?
3. How would you rate yourself on a continuum from heteronomy to autonomy? How does this rating reflect the discipline approaches of your parents and teachers?
4. A problem to solve: Carlos is using the doll buggy. Betsy wants it and grabs it away. Carlos hits Betsy, and the battle is on.
    a. Describe a response that solves the problem without teaching autonomy or self-discipline.
    b. Describe a response that solves the problem and *does* teach autonomy and self-discipline.

REFERENCES AND RECOMMENDATIONS FOR READING

Books

CURWIN, R. L., & MENDLER, A. N. (1990). *Am I in trouble? Using discipline to teach young children responsibility*. Santa Cruz, CA: Network Publications.

CURWIN, R. L., & MENDLER, A. N. (1988). *Discipline with dignity*. Alexandria, VA: Association for Supervision and Curriculum Development.

DAMON, W. (1988). *The moral child: Nurturing children's natural moral growth*. New York: The Free Press.

DEVRIES, R., & KOHLBERG, L. (1987). *Constructivist early education: Overview and comparison with other programs*. Washington, DC: National Association for the Education of Young Children.

GORDON, T. (1989). *Teaching children self-discipline: At home and at school*. New York: Random House.

GROSSMAN, H. (1990). *Trouble-free teaching: Solutions to behavior problems in the classroom.* Mountain View, CA: Mayfield.

JOHNSON, D. W., JOHNSON, R. R., HOLUBEE, E. J., & ROY, P. (1984). *Circles of learning: Cooperation in the classroom.* Alexandria, VA: Association for Supervision and Curriculum Development.

KAMII, C. (1982). Autonomy as the aim of education: Implications of Piaget's theory. In C. Kamii, *Number* (pp. 73–87). Washington, DC: National Association for the Education of Young Children.

PIAGET, J. (1932). *The moral judgment of the child.* London: Routledge & Kegan Paul.

PIAGET, J. (1965). *The moral judgment of the child.* New York: The Free Press.

RAMSEY, P. G. (1991). *Making friends in school: Promoting peer relationships in early childhood.* New York: Teachers College Press.

STERNBERG, R. J., & KOLLIGAN, J.(EDS.). (1990). *Competence considered.* New Haven: Yale University Press.

Periodicals

BAUMERIND, D. (1967). Child care practices anteceding three patterns of preschool behavior. *Genetic Psychology Monographs, 75,* 43–88.

DEVRIES, R., ZAN, B., REESE-LEARNED, H., & MORGAN, P. (1991). Sociomoral atmosphere and sociomoral development: A study of interpersonal understanding in three kindergarten classrooms. *Moral Education Forum, 16*(2), 5–20.

GOFFIN, S. G. (1989). How well do we respect the children in our care? *Childhood Education, 66*(2), 68–74.

GREENBERG, P. (1992a). Ideas that work with young children. How to institute some simple democratic practices pertaining to respect, rights, responsibilities, and roots in any classroom (without losing your leadership position). *Young Children, 47*(5), 10–17.

GREENBERG, P. (1992b). Why not academic preschool? (Part 2) Autocracy or democracy in the classroom? *Young Children, 47*(3), 54–64.

HONIG, A. (1985). Research in review. Compliance, control and discipline. *Young Children, 40*(2), 50–58.

KAMII, C. (1984). Obedience is not enough. *Young Children, 39*(4), 11–14.

KATZ, L. (1989). Family living: Suggestions for effective parenting. Urbana, IL: ERIC Clearinghouse Document, ED313168.

LEVIN, R. A. (1991). The debate over schooling: Influences of Dewey and Thorndike. *Childhood Education, 68*(2), 71–75.

MILLER, C. S. (1984). Building self-control: Discipline for young children. *Young Children, 40*(1), 15–19.

SCHWEINHART, L., WEIKART, D., & LARNER, M. (1986). Consequences of three preschool curriculum models through age 15. *Early Childhood Research Quarterly, 1,* 15–45.

Papers

GARTRELL, D. (1988). *Developmentally appropriate guidance of young children.* St. Paul: Minnesota Association for the Education of Young Children.

Chapter 2

Physical and Emotional Development Affect Child Behavior

Child care and teaching become much easier when you are knowledgeable about child development and can match your expectations of children to their individual maturation levels. Each stage of development brings its own set of needs, abilities, and perspectives. This knowledge of children's physical, emotional, intellectual, and social development will guard against adult-caused behavior problems. Knowledge of child development will also help you to understand when inappropriate behavior is caused by a child who is working on a developmental task and does not mean to be "naughty" at all. Such information will provide useful guidelines for approaches to discipline. In this chapter and the next, we provide an overview of child development only as it pertains directly to discipline issues. These chapters are not intended to be a comprehensive coverage of child development.

PHYSICAL DEVELOPMENT

It is obvious that young children's physical needs and abilities are different from those of adults. Young children are not as strong or well coordinated as adults or older children; they also require more rest and more frequent nourishment. Additionally, they are unable to sit still for very long. Teachers sometimes forget this last fact and cause trouble for themselves and their students.

Devon and several of his classmates in Miss Wheeler's first-grade class routinely upset their teacher's day. They simply won't sit still and listen during group time. They are always getting up and wandering around when they are supposed to be working in their seats. Miss Wheeler constantly reminds them to sit still or to go back to their seats. She just doesn't understand that most young children have difficulty sitting still for very long. Next door, in Mrs. Jensen's first-grade room, children are free to move around between learning centers. There is very little enforced sitting in that room, and very little need for the teacher to reprimand anyone. Miss Wheeler feels like a police officer instead of a teacher, but she thinks it is the children who are at fault. Matching her expectations to the children's level of development would make her life much easier as well as eliminate a lot of needless tension for her students.

Not only do young children have a need to exercise their large muscles regularly, but they are also not very adept yet at small-muscle work. It is a fact of physical development that fine motor coordination lags behind gross motor coordination. Therefore, Beau, who is a fast runner and a great climber, may not be able to tie his shoes yet; and Yaisa, the best rope jumper in her first-grade class, may not be able to make a pencil do her bidding. Placing pressure on these children to perform above their current level of development will result in frustration and feelings of failure. Negative behaviors will surely follow. Matching your expectations to the children's abilities will avert some potential discipline problems.

Young children also have a need for adequate food and rest in order to work and play cooperatively at school. Children need these energy boosters at more frequent intervals than adults do. Sometimes Kelsey can't play cooperatively in the morning preschool session, and Dennis, her teacher, figures that she didn't eat much breakfast today. When this happens, he allows her to have her mid-morning snack a little early. Dennis is taking into consideration Kelsey's individual needs as well as the group's needs. The standard practice of snack time acknowledges the fact that little people in general can't eat much at one time and can't go as long between meals as big people can.

The practice of rest time at the preschool level acknowledges a need at that age, but formal rest periods tend to disappear once children enter the public schools. Yaisa attends the before- and after-school child care program at Lincoln Elementary. She gets to school at 7:30 in the morning and doesn't go home until 5:30 in the evening. Sometimes she gets crabby and picks a fight or bursts into tears for no apparent reason. Fortunately her teacher understands that Yaisa needs a break, not punishment for being difficult. Mrs. Jensen sees Yaisa's need and encourages her to find a comfortable pillow and a good book in the secluded classroom book nook. After a short rest, Yaisa is able to participate with the group again. Mrs. Jensen is trying to teach Yaisa and others with similar needs how to take a break when they need it rather than push themselves beyond their limits.

A child's need for rest is one of many physical needs that can cause behavior problems.

Her classroom offers several soft, seclusive spots, and her schedule offers the flexibility to use them.

EMOTIONAL DEVELOPMENT

Children come into this world with unique characteristics and then encounter a unique set of people and influences. Each child experiences the world in different ways. The combination of biological and experiential factors work together to form individual personalities.

Temperament

The temperament a child is born with is a primary influence on emotional development. It determines much not only about how the child behaves, but also how others react to the child. This interactive process between youngsters and those around them shapes emotional development and self-concept in positive or negative directions. The challenge for the caring adult is to respond positively to the more difficult child.

Research on newborns has identified distinct differences in several characteristics (Thomas & Chess, 1977). Some of these characteristics make children easier to live with than others do. Those children who are more regular in their patterns of eating and sleeping obviously make life easier for their parents. More responsive babies can be more fun to play with; however, negative responses may also be more intense with these children. Those who easily adapt to new situations and respond favorably to a new toy or a visiting relative are likely to elicit more favorable responses from others. Some youngsters seem to be born friendly, pleasant, and joyful, while others seem to start out life as the opposite. These individual differences influence the child's interactions throughout life and certainly are a factor in behavior and discipline.

Some of the personality characteristics identified by Thomas and Chess have direct bearing on school behaviors. Babies seem to be born with a certain level of activity, with the more active infant becoming the more active child. Individual attention span and distractibility factors are also evident in newborns. Children who are born with a high energy level and a low attention span and who are easily distracted are often in trouble in school settings. Teachers will find it more productive to help children channel those traits positively instead of trying to change the child's nature.

Developmental Stages

Children go through various stages in their emotional development, according to Erik Erikson's widely respected theory (1963). Each of these stages has a particular focus, or developmental task, that influences the child's responses at this time. We find Erikson's explanation of emotional development especially relevant to discipline issues. Understanding child behavior in terms of the stages that

Erikson describes can guide both prevention of discipline problems and intervention when problems do occur. We will discuss only the stages relevant to early childhood, although Erikson's stage theory continues through adolescence, adulthood, and old age.

These stages are roughly correlated to ages, but individual differences and diversity of experience create variations from the norm. Theoretically, a child completes one stage and goes on to the next, but in actuality people seem to continue working on all previous stages as they proceed to the next. Teachers and parents also may notice a child under duress regressing to a former stage. Some serious problems, such as family crises and how they affect learning, will be discussed in chapter 13.

ERIKSON'S STAGES OF CHILD DEVELOPMENT

❑ Trust vs. mistrust: Babies learn to trust or mistrust the world around them

❑ Autonomy vs. shame: Toddlers learn to define themselves as individuals or feel shame about their independent urges

❑ Initiative vs. guilt: Children learn to test their individual powers and abilities or feel guilty about making "mistakes"

❑ Industry vs. inferiority: Children extend their ideas of themselves as workers or learn to feel inferior and incapable

Trust vs. Mistrust

Even if you never plan to work with babies, you need to know about the *trust vs. mistrust* stage of development, which Erikson relates to infancy. This is the time when babies are making their first discoveries about what kind of a world they have entered. Many are welcomed into homes where they are the center of attention, and their slightest protest is met with efforts to alleviate distress. These babies begin early to trust that they are important and that the world is a safe and friendly place. Some babies aren't so lucky. Their parents may be overwhelmed with personal problems and the baby is just one more worry, or their caregivers may be overworked and untrained. These babies may cry from hunger or other discomfort without any response. What a different image of themselves and their world these babies get!

About fifty years ago, parents were told that picking up babies when they cried would spoil them. Dutiful mothers and fathers fought their natural urges to respond to the cries of their infants. Instead, they attended to feeding and chang-

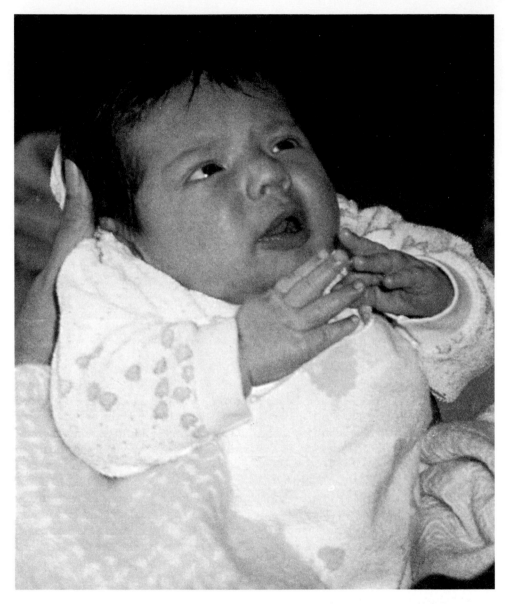

Babies are making important discoveries about what kind of world they have entered.

ing needs on a set schedule, to which the child was expected to conform. Remnants of this theory persist in the culture today, threatening the healthy development of trust in infancy. Parents and caregivers need to know how important it is to respond to a baby's cries. These beginning efforts to communicate needs deserve our attempts to reply. Responsive adults are essential to a child's trust development.

Children continue to actively work on trust during preschool and beyond. They are looking for evidence that they can trust their larger world. The reassurance of caring and consistent adults in their daily lives helps youngsters develop trust. Some have had negative past experiences that lead them to expect continued disappointments from people they encounter (Jacobsen & Willie, 1986). Like Christie in the following example, they expect rejection and are constantly checking to see if someone is still their friend. They also frequently seek the reassurance of the teacher's attention.

> Crying, Christie sat holding the guinea pig. Sheri, the preschool aide, came over to her, asking, "Did Perky bite you?" Ignoring her question, Christie burst out, "Amy says Perky stinks! She won't play with me. She only likes Michael! Nobody wants to play with me! I want to go home." Sheri settled down on the pillow next to Christie to give her some comfort. Together they petted the guinea pig for a minute. Gazing across the room at Amy, the "offender," Sheri commented, "Amy and Michael are building quite a tall tower!" Sheri was hoping to help Christie learn to enter the play situation, so she suggested, "Christie, would you like to build with the Legos, too? Do you think there are enough Legos?" Certain of her outcast role, Christie wailed, "It doesn't matter. They won't play with me!"

If a child's experiences lead to a lesson in mistrust rather than trust, that person's whole life can be affected. Future friendships and even marriages suffer from this lack of trust. It first appears as insecurity with friends and excessive demands on teachers. Later in life, an inability to trust co-workers and the suspicion of spouses can undermine relationships. As relationships fail to withstand the pressure, a vicious cycle of self-fulfilling prophecy is perpetuated. We have all known children and adults who fit this pattern: They expect others to reject them, so they behave in ways that invite rejection. Your challenge is to help children have experiences that reverse this cycle before it is too late.

Autonomy vs. Shame

The toddler years are the time for development of *autonomy*, as Erikson defines it. (Erikson's use of the term to describe emotional development is different from Piaget's concepts of intellectual and moral autonomy, which were discussed in chapter 1.) Erikson's autonomy stage is the period when youngsters work at defining themselves as separate from the adults they have, until now, completely depended on. As infants, they were so dependent that they actually felt themselves a part of their parents or caregivers. But toddlers suddenly begin to see that they are separate people, with ideas and wills of their own. They need to test this new revelation to make sure it is true and to convince themselves of their independence. This period is known as the "terrible twos" and can create serious discipline problems for the unwary adult. The formerly docile child suddenly says an emphatic "No!" to your suggestions and tests the limits you set.

Andrew is so caught up in his ability to say no that he sometimes says no to things he really wants. "Do you want some ice cream?" his mother asks. "No," says Andrew proudly. Because Andrew is her sixth child, Debbie has been through this behavior before. She knows that right now her two-year-old is focusing on his power to say yes or no, not on whether or not he really wants some ice cream. When Andrew inevitably changes his mind and does decide to have ice cream, Debbie doesn't lecture him about the fact that saying no means he doesn't get any. Instead, she encourages his new independence by respecting his decisions, either way.

Additionally, Debbie gives Andrew as many opportunities as possible to make decisions and choices. These opportunities not only help him feel proud of his independence, but they also help him cooperate during times when there is no choice. Children who routinely have a chance to exercise their personal power are more able to accept times when adults must make the decisions. Conversely, children who don't get ample opportunity for making choices can be incredibly stubborn. In other words, Debbie knows that letting Andrew make decisions such as whether to have ice cream or which shirt to wear will make it easier when he *doesn't* get to decide what time he goes to bed. The following example also demonstrates how giving children choices helps them to accept adult limits when they are required.

> Out for a fall cranberry hunt, Jeffrey bounded along the trail ahead of the group. He squealed with delight as he came upon the first icy puddles of the season. What an inviting challenge! His teacher resisted warning him and the other youngsters away from the adventure. Dennis, an experienced teacher of young children, reminded himself of the extra little socks tucked in his daypack, just in case. Besides, the children were sure to come across hundreds of puddles this winter. Why not let them learn? These shiny-topped, slimy-bottomed pools were irresistible. No amount of adult warnings about hidden depths and wet feet would discourage any naturally inquisitive child from testing that ever-so-thin layer of brittle, frozen skin. If denied, they would probably just sneak ahead and try it out of sight. So Dennis let the children choose which puddles to test. He enjoyed watching the individual youngsters pounce from one shattering splash to the next. Soon the inevitable happened, and Jeffrey yelped! He had almost lost his boot to an ice-hidden mud bog's sucking grip. Impressed by its strength, he investigated the next puddle with a bit more respect. He was learning! Later that afternoon a cloud bank stole the sun's warmth. The teacher approached Jeffrey matter-of-factly and said, "It's time to put your knit hat on." Because he had made plenty of his own choices already, Jeffrey easily accepted that this one was not his.

Children don't suddenly get over the need to assert themselves when they turn three. If you understand this need and learn to give lots of choices, it is often

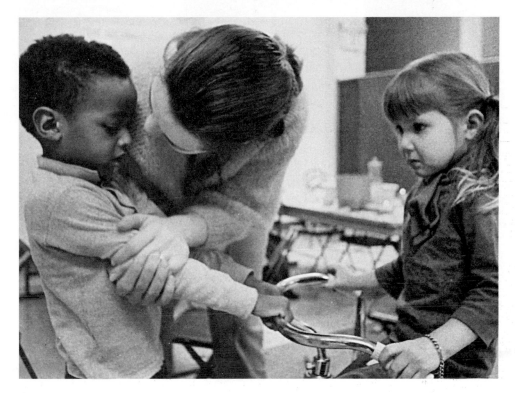

Giving children choices meets their need for independence and helps them to cooperate.

incredibly easy to get children to cooperate. Kimberly's child-care teacher, Dennis, used this understanding to solve a problem that Kimberly was having at her child-care center. It seemed that Kimberly was asserting herself by refusing to cooperate when getting ready to go home, antagonizing her tired and hurried father. Dennis didn't give attention to the undesirable behavior by wheedling and bribing her to get her boots and coat on, nor did he take away her independence by forcing her to put them on. Instead, he gave Kimberly some choices. The choice was not *whether* to get ready to go home, but rather *how* to get ready. "Do you want to put on your boots first or your coat first?" asked Dennis. "Would you like me or your daddy to help you with your zipper?" was the next question. "Can you put on your own boots, or would you like help?" was another. In no time at all, Kimberly was ready to go *and* feeling proud of herself.

Erikson's theory says that when children do not develop emotional autonomy, they develop a sense of shame instead. Shame can be caused by their experiences with adults who don't understand what is happening when children assert themselves; these adults think that their job is to stamp out "naughtiness." Unfortunately, they may only be successful at making children believe they are being bad, when really the children are just working at being grown-up. As a result, the children develop feelings of shame about the natural urges of independence.

Initiative vs. Guilt

The next stage of emotional development is called *initiative vs. guilt*, according to Erikson. Most preschool children are in this stage. You will see them further testing their individual powers and abilities. Their physical and intellectual abilities are increasing rapidly as they joyfully try out new skills.

Developmental tasks now include the need to participate in real work. Megan is always right there when it is time to prepare the afternoon snack. She takes great satisfaction in setting the table or spreading peanut butter on celery sticks. She practices small motor coordination and even math skills as she meticulously places five raisins on each celery stick. Her feelings of accomplishment and confidence are also growing. Megan and her classmates are invited to assist with many necessary jobs in the afternoon session of preschool. They care for the guinea pig, cleaning her cage and feeding her. They water the plants, sweep up under the sand table, and organize the dress-up clothes on hooks. They take pride in this work because the afternoon teachers, Dennis and Nancy, communicate their belief in the children's abilities. The teachers accept the children's levels of ability and don't make a fuss if a job isn't done perfectly or if a little something is spilled in the process.

Whenever the afternoon staff thinks about developing a new learning center, they first discuss the plan with the students. Dennis knows from his classes in early childhood education, as Nancy knows from raising four children, that children will learn much from the planning process and that their involvement will help ensure that new materials are used constructively. After a field trip to a bank, the children want to play bank in the pretend play area. Instead of looking all weekend for materials, Dennis and Nancy invite children to bring things from home that could be used in a bank. The weekly newsletter explains the plan to parents and asks them to contribute. On Monday, the children arrive with old checkbooks, deposit slips, canceled checks, a real cash box, and play money. Aaron's mom works in a bank, so she contributes a pad of loan application forms.

As the interested youngsters work to arrange these materials in a way meaningful to them, they cooperate in problem solving and planning. They are willing to invest effort to resolve disagreements in *their* bank. Before long, things are set up to their satisfaction, and several youngsters are busily scribbling on the checks, making important banking transactions. These children are feeling good about the work they have done, and it shows in their behavior.

In the morning session at Midway Children's Center, the teacher makes the snack in advance and pours juice for each child. Joanne discourages the children's offers to help, telling them that they will only spill if they try to pour their own juice. Joanne spends long hours after school and on weekends preparing materials and rearranging the classroom. She prides herself on always having everything ready for her students when they arrive. She wouldn't dream of using class time to set up a new activity; everything is strictly preplanned and scheduled. She doesn't have pets in her class because she doesn't have time to care for them and the children "are too young to do it properly." Everything is under control: hers.

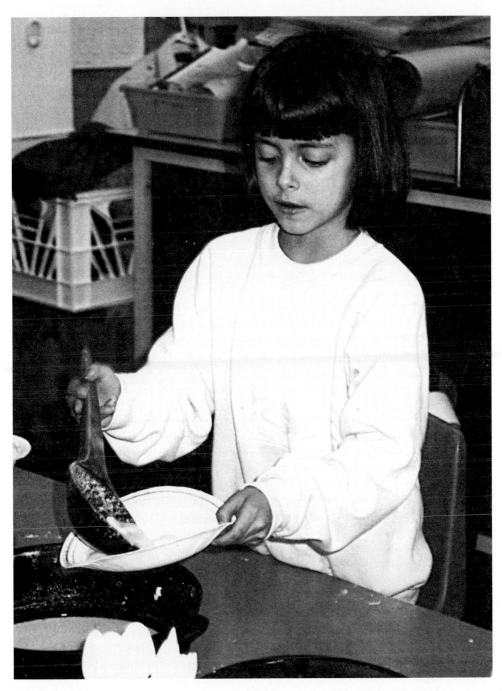

Children need to participate in real work in order to feel confident and competent.

In spite of all her careful planning, Joanne has many more discipline problems than the afternoon staff does. The students often seem disinterested in what Joanne has planned for them. They frequently "misuse" the materials, pursuing their own ideas instead of copying the model at the art table. When the children don't follow Joanne's plans, she tells them how disappointed she is.

Josh and his friends feel ashamed when they disappoint their teacher. They don't understand that it is their healthy curiosity and energy that is getting them into trouble. They only know that what they are interested in doing is "bad." They assume that they are bad children. Because Joanne's training is with older children, she isn't familiar with this stage of child development. Thus, she often misinterprets the children's actions. What a different kind of experience this teacher and her young students would have if Joanne only knew how to harness their constructive energy into activities that would develop their sense of initiative.

Of course, things don't always go perfectly when you give children real responsibility. But when there is a problem, teacher response makes the difference between an experience that assists healthy emotional development and one that damages it.

It was a warm spring day that seemed just right for a warm-weather snack. Dennis told the snack helpers that they could make frozen juice bars out of the juice today. They were excited about this special treat and eagerly set to work. Megan carefully counted and poured three cans of water into the frozen grape juice concentrate. Kimberly stirred and stirred until it was completely mixed. Meanwhile, Sam was getting the ice cube trays and toothpicks out. All three children took turns at the sloppy task of pouring the juice into the ice cube trays. They discussed at length the problem of getting the toothpicks to stand up and became frustrated in their efforts. Finally, they decided to take Dennis's advice and wait until the bars were a little bit frozen before inserting the toothpick handles.

Sam was feeling extremely proud of his work in making such a special snack. Every few minutes he would check to see if the juice bars were getting hard yet. Suddenly his arm bumped one of the trays, staining the inside of the freezer purple and spilling grape juice down the front of the refrigerator to puddle on the floor. Sam was horrified, unable to move.

Dennis joined him, placing a gentle hand on Sam's shoulder. The teacher calmly asked, "What do you want to use to clean up, a sponge or a rag?" Sam relaxed a little and grabbed a sponge. Dennis kept him company, commenting, "That sure surprised you." Sam agreed with a tremulous smile but continued to be upset about the ruined juice bars. Dennis asked Sam if he'd like to mix some more juice to refill the ice trays. Eagerly Sam set about the task of making amends for his mistake.

It would be understandable if the teacher were very cross about the incredible mess Sam had made. Under the circumstances, you might start to say things like "How can you be so clumsy!" or even "Just get away from there so you don't spill the rest!" Those words would certainly create feelings of shame and inadequacy.

Your knowledge about children coupled with your concern for their feelings should stop the words before they come out. You know that Sam's impatience and his lack of coordination are both normal for his age. You want Sam to develop positive feelings about himself and his abilities. Therefore, you would respond as Dennis did and help Sam correct his error rather than making the child feel bad about himself. The result may be a later snack if the refilled ice tray doesn't freeze in time, but what a small price to pay for Sam's emotional health.

Industry vs. Inferiority

School-age youngsters are working through an emotional development stage that builds on the preschool stage of *initiative vs. guilt*. Erikson calls this next stage *industry vs. inferiority*. During this phase, children are extending their ideas of themselves as workers and contributing members of society. Their tasks now focus on earning recognition by producing things and mastering the tools to do so. In a subsistence society, this stage means learning to hunt, fish, cure skins, gather berries, and preserve food. In our current society, it means learning to read, write, think quantitatively, and work cooperatively. Once again, children need to have opportunities for *real work* that is meaningful to them and that they are allowed to do on their own.

Mrs. Jensen's first graders were planting seeds this morning as part of their study to learn how things grow. There were a variety of fast-growing seeds available: beans, radishes, carrots, and alfalfa. Children also had access to a variety of planting materials and containers. Some were interested in the idea of watching bean sprouts grow in a jar of water. Others liked the idea of growing an alfalfa crop in a paper cup filled with dirt. The prospect of actually growing a carrot to eat was attractive to many. The youngsters had the opportunity to explore as many of the options as they wished. They also had the freedom to do their planting in their own way. The parent helper was worried because some of the seeds weren't being planted at the recommended depth. Mrs. Jensen reassured him that the variety of planting approaches and the varying results were an educational experience. The children certainly weren't worried. They felt very important to know that they were starting the process of making something grow.

When the seeds were planted, the youngsters began making journals for recording the growth of their plants. The children made the books themselves, counting out the agreed-on number of pages, choosing a cover color, and then folding and stapling them into booklet form. The parent helper noticed that the children could not keep the pages lined up as they stapled. He offered to help with folding

Children need to feel successful as they work at reading and writing, or they lose confidence in themselves as learners.

and stapling. Mrs. Jensen explained to the well-meaning father that the children took pride in doing this work themselves. Sure enough, the children all *loved* their books, crooked and crumpled as they were. Everyone felt like a success.

Too many children are labeled failures at this stage. You certainly have seen the devastating consequences for the child who fails to begin reading on society's schedule. This is the child whom others shun for being dumb. This is the child who disrupts class out of frustration and anger. This is the child the teachers are eager to send off to the reading specialist. Many students who eventually become school dropouts begin dropping out in first grade (Schorr, 1989). Lifelong inferiority complexes begin early.

Shelley had a narrow escape. She came home in tears saying she was dumb. Her teacher had given up on her progress with reading skills and wanted to send her out to the reading specialist. Fortunately this step couldn't be taken without a parent conference. Miss Wheeler explained to Shelley's mom that Shelley didn't seem able to do the daily phonics worksheets; therefore, she obviously needed special help. Shelley's mother was puzzled by this report because her daughter was already reading at home and wrote wonderful stories, too. Her teacher was surprised to hear about Shelley's success at home. She couldn't figure out how a child could read and write but not be able to do phonics sheets. Miss Wheeler was new to first grade after teaching in the upper grades and wasn't knowledgeable about beginning reading. She didn't realize that phonics sheets are much more abstract than actual writing is and that most children learn phonics through meaningful writing experiences. Miss Wheeler listened to the child's mother, however, and did not further damage Shelley's belief in herself as a learner.

Blake not only couldn't do worksheets, but also really wasn't interested in writing when he was a first grader. Mrs. Jensen met with his parents and decided that Blake just wasn't ready yet. They knew he was a bright child and would become a reader and writer in time. They made sure that he had plenty of opportunity to experience books and many purposes for writing, but they made no demands for a certain level of performance from him. Most of all, they made sure that he never felt like a failure. They knew that not reading in first grade wasn't fatal but that feeling like a failure could endanger his self-esteem and his future ability to learn. This child was supported as he negotiated the *industry vs. inferiority* stage in his own time.

CONCLUSION

Some lucky kids have parents and teachers who know that there is no magical time by which every child must be reading or doing any other specific task. These children are accepted and encouraged to work and grow in their own way. Some lucky kids have parents and teachers who help them develop trust in others and belief in their own abilities. Some youngsters are born with difficult temperaments and yet encounter acceptance for who they are. *These* children do not develop poor self-concepts and become discipline problems that worsen each year. Some children are not so lucky. Their healthy emotional development is thwarted by parents or teachers who do not understand child development.

FOR FURTHER THOUGHT

1. Observe in an early childhood setting, watching for examples of young children's inability to sit still for very long. What problems do you see when adults forget this aspect of child development?
2. As you observe young children, try to identify different temperaments as described in this chapter. What is the difference between a person's current mood and that person's temperament?
3. Think about people you know well. Do any of them exhibit signs suggesting they may not have developed trust as described in this chapter? How does that problem affect their social interactions?
4. Observe toddlers, watching for expressions of developing emotional autonomy as described in this chapter. How do adults respond? Do you recommend any different responses based on your understanding of this aspect of emotional development?
5. Observe preschoolers, watching for expressions of their desire for real work. Does their environment meet this need? What changes could be made to assist their development of initiative?
6. Observe young children in public school, looking for the difference between those who are succeeding with school tasks and those who are not. In what ways do the youngsters express their feelings about their abilities?
7. A problem to solve: Jeremy isn't working on his writing assignment. He is fooling around and bothering others instead.
    a. What are some possible causes of this behavior?
    b. How would you address the various causes?
    c. How might the problem have been avoided?

REFERENCES AND RECOMMENDATIONS FOR READING

Books

Bredekamp, S. (Ed.). (1987). *Developmentally appropriate practice in early childhood programs serving children from birth through age 8, expanded edition.* Washington, DC: National Association for the Education of Young Children.

Edwards, C. (1986). *Promoting social and moral development in young children.* New York: Teachers College Press.

Erikson, E. (1963). *Childhood and society* (2nd ed.). New York: Norton.

Greenspan, S., & Greenspan, N. T. (1986). *First feelings.* New York: Penguin.

Harris, J., & Liebert, R. (1991). *The child* (3rd ed.). Englewood Cliffs, NJ: Prentice-Hall.

Maccoby, E. (1980). *Social development: Psychological growth and the parent-child relationship.* New York: Harcourt Brace Jovanovich.

Mize, J., & Ladd, G. W. (1990). Toward the development of successful social skills training for preschool children. In S. R. Asher & J. D. Cole (Eds.), *Peer rejection in childhood* (pp. 338–361). New York: Cambridge University Press.

RAMSEY, P. G. (1991). *Making friends in school: Promoting peer relationships in early childhood.* New York: Teachers College Press.

RUBIN, K., & EVERETT, B. (1982). Social perspective-taking in young children. In S. G. Moore & C. R. Cooper (Eds.), *The young child: Reviews of research* (Vol. 3). Washington, DC: National Association for the Education of Young Children.

SCHORR, L. (1989). *Within our reach: Breaking the cycle of disadvantage.* New York: Anchor Books/Doubleday.

THOMAS, A., & CHESS, S. (1977). *Temperament and development.* New York: Brunner/Mazel.

YAMAMOTO, K. (1972). *The child and his image: Self concept in the early years.* Boston: Houghton Mifflin.

Periodicals

CROCKENBERG, S., & LITMAN, C. (1990). Autonomy as competence in 2-year-olds: Maternal correlates of child defiance, compliance, and self-assertion. *Developmental Psychology, 26*(6), 961–971.

DODGE, K. A. (1983). Behavioral antecedents of peer social status. *Child Development, 54,* 1386–1399.

HARTUP, W. W., & MOORE, S. G. (1990). Early peer relations: Developmental significance and prognostic implications. *Early Childhood Research Quarterly, 5*(1), 1–18.

HENDRICK, J. (1992). Where does it begin? Teaching the principles of democracy in the early years. *Young Children, (47)*(3), 51–53.

KEMPLE, K. M. (1991). Research in review. Preschool children's peer acceptance and social interaction. *Young Children, 46*(5), 47–54.

LADD, G. W. (1983). Social networks of popular, average, and rejected children in school settings. *Merrill-Palmer Quarterly, 29,* 283–308.

LEAVITT, R. L., & POWER, M. B. (1989). Emotional socialization in the postmodern era: Children in day care. *Social Psychology Quarterly, 52*(1), 35–43.

Papers

GARTRELL, D. (1988). *Developmentally appropriate guidance of young children.* St. Paul: Minnesota Association for the Education of Young Children.

HONIG, A. S., & WITTMER, D. S. (1987). *Socialization and discipline for infants and toddlers.* Presented at the annual meeting of the National Association for the Education of Young Children, Chicago, IL. Urbana, IL: ERIC Clearinghouse Document, ED291484.

JACOBSEN, J., & WILLIE, D. (1986). *The influence of attachment pattern on peer interaction at 2 and 3 years.* Presented at the International Conference on Infant Studies, New York.

PHILLIPS, S. (1988). Toddlers. In *Selected papers* (No. 58). Kensington, Australia: Foundation for Child and Youth Studies.

SROUFE, L. A., & EGELAND, B. (1989). *Early predictors of psychopathology and competence in children.* Urbana, IL: ERIC Clearinghouse Document, ED308019.

Chapter 3

Intellectual and Social Development Affect Discipline

Young children are not miniature adults. That idea is central to early childhood education and basic to the constructivist view of learning. It reminds us that children have unique needs that must be considered in their care and education. The statement also cautions us against adult egocentricity in assuming that children's thinking is the same as ours. In this chapter we examine some ways in which children's ways of thinking influence their behavior and impact your discipline decisions. Information about young children's intellectual and social development will not only help you immeasurably in the areas of guidance and discipline, but it will also help you be a more effective teacher.

INTELLECTUAL DEVELOPMENT

Piaget's writing (1965) and observation of youngsters say that a child's view of the world and reality is different from an adult's. Children's limited reasoning ability coupled with their limited experience often bring them to conclusions inconsistent with adult logic. This situation often gets children into trouble. Teachers and parents get angry at youngsters for what adults perceive as disobeying rules, telling lies, being selfish or inconsiderate, and behaving in totally irrational ways. To make matters worse, the children don't think that they have done anything wrong. For a parent or teacher who doesn't understand what Piaget (1964) has explained about intellectual development, this behavior can be totally infuriating. However, it is often just a normal part of child development.

Breaking Rules

Part of Jean Piaget's famous and extensive studies of children's thinking involved their understanding of rules in games (1965). He focused on rules in the game of marbles, finding out that child views of rules differ with age. The younger children weren't able to follow the rules but believed that they were quite sacred and imposed by adults. Piaget pointed out that these youngsters nevertheless seemed unconcerned about following the rules. Older children felt free to change rules by mutual consent but then felt bound by them. Piaget related this concept to the difference between guidelines for life that are imposed by others and those that children reason for themselves. The latter situation signals moral autonomy.

The way children deal with the rules of a game can help adults understand how children deal with societal rules and expectations (Piaget, 1965). As you watch youngsters playing games, you can see for yourself that their ideas about rules vary with their ages.

Dennis is amused at how his three-year-old students think about rules for their games. When they play hide-and-seek, they tend to yell out, "Here I am! Come find me!" If some adult sets up a race, the children don't wait for "ready, set, go." After the race, if someone asks who won, they all say with conviction, "I won! I won!" It is clear that young children respond according to their perceptions of what is important, not according to adult rules.

A child's view of the world and reality is different from an adult's. This often gets children into trouble.

Most preschool youngsters don't understand or can't cope with the competitive aspect of games. The first time Dennis set up a game of musical chairs with four-year-olds, he quickly learned a better way of structuring the game. He was faced with torrents of tears when youngsters were "out" after not finding a chair. Dennis immediately changed the rules so that there was a chair for everyone; the challenge was to find a seat quickly when the music stopped. The important thing was that no one was forced out of the game.

Primary-grade children become concerned about rules and about winning. The desire to win often colors the interpretation of rules. Mrs. Jensen values the arguments and discussions that are an inevitable part of board games among her first graders. She recognizes that resolving their own disputes about rules helps children learn to reason. She appreciates that young children learn about cooperation from these opportunities to consider each other's position (DeVries, Zan, Reese-Learned, & Morgan, 1991). By learning to consider the viewpoint of others, children learn about behaving in ways that are compatible with the needs of others. This lesson takes time but is an important part of the long-term goals of discipline.

It is important for adults to realize that children who break rules, whether in play or elsewhere, may not understand that they have done so. Much of what adults take for granted is unknown to children. Piaget's studies of moral development (1965) indicate that young children are not capable of understanding why certain behaviors are acceptable or unacceptable. Therefore, many behavior problems are caused by lack of understanding, and the child truly has no idea of wrongdoing.

Being Selfish

It is normal for young children to see things only from their own viewpoint. This aspect of their intellectual development affects their interactions with others. They are not necessarily being inconsiderate when they overlook a playmate's feelings; a very young child is often not even aware that someone else *has* feelings.

> Kelsey was busily engaged in painting at preschool. She had been trying out various types of brush strokes and remarking on their effects. Suddenly Matthew reached over, took the paintbrush out of Kelsey's hand, and began using it on his own paper. Kelsey's stunned silence quickly gave way to loud yelling and crying. Matthew looked startled and fearful as Kelsey screamed.
>
> The teacher, Dennis, listened to Kelsey's complaint and calmly asked her if she had told Matthew she didn't want him to take the brush she was using. Dennis's calm helped Kelsey to regain her own composure as she considered his suggestion. She was then able to turn to Matthew and try out the effect of the words her teacher had suggested. Matthew returned the brush to Kelsey, and Dennis helped him find another on the art supply shelves.

This type of situation provides opportunities for an alert teacher to help youngsters tune in to the feelings and viewpoints of their playmates. Dennis

It is normal for young children to see things only from their own viewpoint.

doesn't blame the children or make anyone feel guilty for being thoughtless of others; he understands that their behavior is normal for preschoolers. In this case, Matthew wanted a paintbrush and saw one nearby. The fact that someone else was using it was not relevant to him.

Dennis works at helping his young students grow beyond their egocentricity by encouraging them to tell one another how they feel. Often he needs to help children find the words to express themselves; they learn from his example as he walks them through the process of communicating their feelings in a constructive way. This is effective guidance, which teaches lifelong interpersonal skills. As children's intellectual abilities develop, their social development is enhanced as well.

Telling Lies

As a child, seeing things from your own viewpoint may mean that something is true because you *want* it to be true. This belief causes children to tell "lies" that they genuinely consider truths. An adult who understands how children think can help a youngster learn from this situation. When Christie tells her teacher that she is going with Kimberly to Disneyland next week, Dennis understands and is able to respond with empathy: "You really wish you could go to Disneyland." This response helps Christie separate her wishes from reality without making her feel bad about herself.

Piaget found that young children really do not understand the nature of a lie (1965). Even six-year-olds in his study could not differentiate between an honest mistake and a purposeful mistruth. Additionally, they tended to judge how bad it was to tell a mistruth in relation to how likely it was to be found out and therefore punished. Thus, with this line of reasoning, a believable lie is acceptable, while a lie that stretches the truth too far is bad. Piaget's research about children's thinking should help teachers and parents understand why explaining their adult logic to youngsters doesn't work.

Schoolwork Problems

Intellectual development stages determine what kinds of materials and activities best help children learn. If you don't match the experiences and materials to the children, you are sure to have behavior problems as well as academic problems. Piaget's work (1960) explains the importance to young children of having real experiences with real materials to construct their knowledge about the world. The term *concrete* is often used to describe the type of materials children need for productive explorations. They include the water in the water table, the hammer and nails in the woodworking center, and the blocks in the block center.

Some teachers present letters, numbers, and other symbols to children who cannot yet make sense of them. This developmentally inappropriate instruction can create discipline problems. When children are not capable of doing what they are asked to do, they are likely to behave in ways adults dislike. Certainly they are not likely to complete the work on schedule. Often youngsters who are frustrated and discouraged by school tasks that are beyond them are then punished for not doing the work. It is common to see these children sitting dejectedly at their desks during recess, staring helplessly at a worksheet. Is it any wonder that they are tempted to be less than cooperative or even to lash out in anger?

Some people get confused and think that plastic magnet letters or wooden letters that fit into puzzles are concrete. These letters can be touched and moved around, but they are still only representational symbols. Some representational materials are more easily recognized than letters or numbers are. For instance, a doll is more recognizable as a symbol for a baby than are the letters in the word *baby*. Pictures of real things are not concrete either, but they may be useful symbolic representations.

Sometimes teachers are striving for developmentally appropriate education but don't realize that their teaching materials are not concrete. Not everything that a child can touch and manipulate is concrete. Clocks and quarters are examples of apparently concrete materials that are actually representational rather than concrete. Young children can't construct knowledge through manipulation or observation of these materials. No wonder lessons in telling time and making change are such difficult activities for young children. They involve both symbolic representation and social knowledge. As such, they cannot be learned through exploration of materials.

> Mrs. Jensen thought that a play store might offer a good situation for helping her first graders learn to make change. The curriculum guide for her grade lists that skill as a goal, but her students have always had trouble with it. Mrs. Jensen decided that using real money instead of pictures in a workbook would help. It is hard to tell a nickel

Teachers who provide age-appropriate learning experiences and materials have few behavior problems.

from a quarter and a penny from a dime, even with play money. Real money seemed more concrete to Mrs. Jensen, so she thought it would help young children learn better. She donated a few dollars of her own money in coins to the cause and helped children make price tags for store items.

The children were delighted with the real money. At first, it made playing store much more fun. Real money also made the issue of correct change more important. The play store suddenly became the center of constant argument and even tears over incorrect payments or getting the wrong change. Mrs. Jensen began to observe this area closely. She saw that some children counted each coin as one dollar, and some counted each as one cent; others assigned value according to size so that the dime was worth less than a penny or a nickel. There was no way for children to prove or disprove their own hypotheses, so the disputes were not productive exchanges of viewpoint.

Finally, Mrs. Jensen came to the conclusion that even real money is not concrete but is actually representational. Each coin represents a certain amount, which is not apparent from observing or analyzing the coin. A child cannot see either twenty-five pennies or five nickels when looking at a quarter. Then the teacher reflected on the fact that our money system is only an arbitrary social convention. In fact, coins and paper money have no inherent worth but have what-ever value our society assigns to them. Mrs. Jensen decided that first grade was too early for many youngsters to learn about making change.

Teachers who understand how young children learn have fewer behavior problems because they provide age-appropriate learning activities and materials for children. They provide many real-life experiences and choices. A classroom that provides choices for children allows them to decide for themselves what type of materials and activities make sense. Mrs. Jensen's first grade has a wide assort-ment of concrete and representational materials accessible on open shelves for children to make selections. Miss Wheeler next door keeps everything but the worksheets in closed cupboards and rarely brings out anything else. She doesn't realize that the worksheets are entirely representational and meaningless to many of the children in her classroom.

> Desmond was in Mrs. Jensen's room, and his identical twin brother, Devon, was in Miss Wheeler's class. Devon tried to pretend he was Desmond so he could get into the room with all the interesting things, but he was sent back. Desmond was having a happy and productive year while Devon was in trouble constantly. One day Devon took mat-ters into his own hands and got out an armload of special things from the teacher's cupboard, placing them enticingly on the tables as he had seen them in Mrs. Jensen's room. Now his room was a nice place to be, just like his brother's. But Miss Wheeler didn't appreciate his efforts. She was enraged that he would dare to get into the cup-board without permission. How sad that she missed the important message Devon was sending about his learning needs.

SOCIAL DEVELOPMENT

We discuss social development last because we see it as an outgrowth of the pre-viously discussed aspects of development. Physical abilities, feelings about one-self, and levels of understanding all combine to determine current levels of social skill and understanding.

The early years are crucial for social development. Youngsters who do not develop social competence in the preschool years typically continue throughout the school years to experience difficulty with peer acceptance (Parker & Asher, 1987). Not surprisingly, these children are at risk as adults for social and emo-tional problems (Putallaz & Gottman, 1981).

How Children Develop Social Competence

Children construct knowledge as a result of reflecting on their experiences. As they experiment with blocks, for instance, they observe the results of trying to stack, balance, and bridge structures. Thinking about the results helps children revise erroneous ideas. This process helps them construct understanding about

The ability to understand another person's viewpoint is essential for getting along together.

such concepts as gravity, balance, and measurement. Children construct their theories of how the social world works in the same way.

As youngsters experiment with different ways of interacting with others, they observe the results of various approaches. Reflecting on the results of their social overtures can help children figure out how to play with others successfully and how to make friends. We have remarked previously on the value of peer conflicts as teaching situations. Conflicts tend to challenge children's assumptions and encourage an exchange of viewpoints. Thus, conflicts provide the necessary experience and give the teacher an opportunity to guide children's thinking about the experience. The adult role varies, depending on the child's individual levels of emotional, intellectual, and social development.

What Children Need to Learn

The basic understanding for social competence is the ability to see things from another's perspective, commonly referred to as *perspective taking*. Without this ability, youngsters remain self-centered and unable to relate to the interests, needs, and rights of others. Until children can take into consideration the viewpoint of another person, they cannot make progress in reasoning about fairness. When they can only see their own views, their idea of justice consists of that which they desire for themselves. Obviously this perception will not endear them to playmates.

There are many specific, useful skills that children can learn once they begin to develop some perspective-taking ability. One set of useful skills includes those necessary for making contact with potential playmates. "Can I play?" almost invites rejection because it offers the power to say no. Instead, children can be helped to observe what the desired playmate is doing: in other words, to work at seeing things from the other child's viewpoint. This observation provides information that the child can use by offering a way to contribute or fit into the existing play.

Children can be helped to avoid advances that disrupt the ongoing play. Simply playing alongside a potential playmate, doing a similar activity, does not interrupt and can be encouraged as a beginning strategy (Ramsey, 1991). When the child's goal is to join a group at play, it is worth the effort to figure out what the others are doing first. The child who joins a group with a contribution to ongoing play is most likely to be accepted. It is important to help youngsters experience success in these efforts and so develop confidence that they will be accepted. A child who approaches playmates with confidence is more likely to gain entry to play. Conversely, the unsure child is more likely to experience rejection.

The ability to avoid and resolve conflicts constitutes another essential aspect of social competence. It involves the willingness to give and take, the flexibility to exchange and adjust roles in play as well as the ability to manage aggression (Ramsey, 1991). All these attributes require the child to take into consideration the viewpoint of others. These sophisticated abilities require significant practice. As mentioned in chapter 1, children do not get this practice if adults solve problems for them. Instead, adults must guide youngsters in age-appropriate ways and help them to resolve their own differences. For very young children with limited language ability, the teacher may do the talking for both parties in providing the two viewpoints. As children mature, they can gradually take a more active role in the expression of their different views. The goal is for the teacher or parent to intervene as little as possible.

How Teachers Can Help

A variety of teaching methods are useful in helping children develop social competence. The teacher who respectfully considers children's viewpoints is teaching by example. When children are involved in a dispute, the teacher's appropriate role might be more of a coach, providing encouragement and recommending strategies. Sometimes the most helpful adult role is to stand back and let children experience the social consequence of their actions. While it is important not to intervene more than necessary, it is also important to be there as needed, both for safety and support. Therefore, when Dennis sends Yaisa over to Kelsey with a suggestion for joining in Kelsey's play, he also tells her to come back and talk to him if it doesn't work.

Teachers also help children become socially competent by encouraging friendships. Friendships are important for a variety of reasons. Children are more likely to meet with success when initiating contact with friends, thus increasing their confidence (Corsaro, 1985). Children's play is more sophisticated and mature when they are playing with friends, which improves their competence (Doyle, 1982). Children respond to the emotional needs of friends more than those of other people (Costin & Jones, 1989), thereby improving their perspective-taking ability. By early elementary school, many children have established a best friend. These relationships are important because they are based on success in anticipating and meeting each other's needs, which is successful practice in perspective taking.

Helping youngsters develop socially is a prerequisite for helping them learn academics. Children with social problems do not participate effectively in academic tasks. They are busy with needs more basic than school learning; their efforts to get those needs met often end up disrupting the entire classroom. Therefore, teachers must teach social skills if they are to teach anything.

HOW TO HELP CHILDREN DEVELOP SOCIAL COMPETENCE

1. Help them explain their own viewpoints.

2. Don't intervene more than necessary, but be there when needed for support.

3. Encourage friendships among children.

ACCOMMODATING INDIVIDUAL DIFFERENCES

It is important to remember that appropriate social behavior varies from group to group. The child's culture, family background, economic status, and gender generate different views of social competence. The teacher who holds all children to one standard of behavior is actually being unfair to some.

Cultural Differences

The culture of school reflects the dominant culture of the setting. Those children whose homes and family expectations are most similar to school have the least adjustment to make. Cultural differences include views about when and how speech is used, what body language means, and even acceptable ways of sitting.

For instance, white middle-class preschoolers tend to exhibit very different interaction styles from African-American and Hispanic children observed in Head Start (Rizzo & Corsaro, 1991). The Head Start youngsters teased each other and used competitive and oppositional talk without being upset by it. On the contrary, this interaction style seemed to cement friendships within the group. In contrast, the white middle-class preschoolers were very concerned about hurt feelings and were easily upset by negative comments. Rizzo and Corsaro concluded from their research that interaction perceived as friendly among one group would be perceived as aggressive and intimidating by the other. Many white middle-class teachers would misunderstand and squelch the social interactions of a child who used teasing as a friendly overture.

Underlying these behaviors are differences in social values and in learning styles. Teachers who hold all youngsters to one standard inadvertently cause some to fail socially and academically.

Socioeconomic Differences

Class differences based on family income, jobs, and educational background also result in different behavioral goals and patterns. Like cultural differences, these style differences are neither good nor bad. However, they may cause children from different backgrounds to be less comfortable with each other (Ramsey, 1991). Like other people, teachers are often less comfortable with those from different backgrounds.

Teachers of low-income children tend to rate their students as less socially competent than do teachers of middle-income children (Ramsey, 1991). This rating reflects the research suggesting that low-income children do not measure up to their more affluent counterparts. However, it is important to remember that the researchers themselves were middle class and therefore reflected their own class bias (McLoyd, 1982). Researchers have perceived behavior of their own social class as superior to that of another.

Teachers who remember that different is neither better nor worse will help more children succeed in school. The youngsters whose background values are different from teachers' are most at risk for school failure and dropping out

Teachers who accept cultural differences help prevent school failure.

(Schorr, 1989). As Patricia Ramsey says, "We must be sure that we do not exacerbate economic disadvantage by undermining the social skills and styles that children have developed, even though they may be less compatible with the current structure of the classroom" (Ramsey, 1991, p. 61).

Gender

The fact that a child is a boy or a girl also impacts acceptable behavior. While we acknowledge that sex-role stereotyping contributes greatly to behavior differences between boys and girls, we also believe that some innate differences may be unavoidable. Buying dolls for boys and trucks for girls has had limited success. Boys generally prefer to play with boys, and girls generally prefer to play with girls. More boys tend to engage in rough-and-tumble play, while girls may congregate in the playhouse. Many researchers have studied this phenomenon and recorded efforts to redirect youngsters. However, coercing cross-gender contact has made little difference in free-choice preference (Maccoby, 1986). When boys and girls do play together, the boys tend to dominate and the girls may become tentative (Phinney & Rotheram, 1982). By the time they reach kindergarten, youngsters who engage in play activities associated with the opposite sex are likely to be ridiculed by their peers (Damon, 1983).

This separation of males and females begins during the toddler years and increases from preschool into the elementary grades. Youngsters' preference for same-sex playmates may be a result of being better able to predict their responses (Maccoby, 1986). It certainly has something to do with gender-related differences in physical development. Girls tend to acquire precise coordination at a younger age than boys do and therefore enjoy skipping and jumping rope when boys are unable to participate. Boys demonstrate higher levels of large-muscle activity and are drawn to games of physical contact. Due to these developmental differences, boys may fit less well into a quiet and controlled school environment. When you understand why children are behaving as they are, you can save yourself the trouble of trying to change what you can't. You can then work at channeling children's natural energies into productive outlets.

Young children are in the process of figuring out who they are. Their identity as a boy or a girl is an important part of this process. Little girls often demand to wear a frilly dress even on a cold and rainy day because that dress is part of their sex-role identity. Trying to take a little boy into a women's rest room for convenience's sake may result in a fierce battle from a boy who is asserting his maleness. If you understand the child's developmental task in these types of situations, you will treat the behavior differently than if you merely perceive the child as being obstinate.

Social development tends to be the primary content of discipline. Children who have trouble getting along with peers and cooperating in a group create the common discipline problems. Therefore, the topic of social development leads us into our next section, which discusses approaches to discipline.

CONCLUSION

Knowledge about children's thinking can help you distinguish between immature thinking and purposeful misbehavior. Information about the development of social competency will help you intervene in more productive ways. When teachers understand child development and match their expectations to what individual children can comfortably do, teachers are happier with their work and they have more cooperative students. Matching your expectations to child development can make the difference between dreading to go to school and looking forward to each new day.

FOR FURTHER THOUGHT

1.   Observe young children playing games. What evidence do you see of their unique perception of rules?
2.   As you interact with young children, watch for examples of their inability to think about another person's viewpoint. Try to help youngsters learn to express their views and to hear those of another child. Analyze this experience and discuss with your peers how you might improve your approach.
3.   Listen to young children. Do you hear them confusing personal fantasy with fact? What is the best adult response?

4. Do you know a youngster who has difficulty being accepted into play with other children? Practice the coaching techniques described in this chapter. What are the results? What did you learn?

5. Have you or has someone you know experienced difficulty in school because of a mismatch with the culture of the school? How did you or your friend respond? What were the long-term effects?

6. A problem to solve: Paul accidentally spilled the paint at the easel, but he denies that he did it.
    a. What is the probable cause of this "lie"?
    b. What is the best adult response to the situation?

REFERENCES AND RECOMMENDATIONS FOR READING

Books

ALMY, M. (1966). *Young children's thinking.* New York: Teachers College Press.

ASHER, S. R., & COLE, J. D. (EDS.). (1990). *Peer rejection in childhood.* New York: Cambridge University Press.

CORSARO, W. A. (1981). Friendship in the nursery school: Social organization in a peer environment. In S. R. Asher & J. M. Gottman (Eds.), *The development of children's friendships* (pp. 207–241). New York: Cambridge University Press.

CORSARO, W.A. (1985). *Friendship and peer culture in the early years.* Norwood, NJ: Ablex.

DAMON, W. (1983). *Social and personality development: Infancy through adolescence.* New York: Norton.

DAMON, W. (1988). *The moral child: Nurturing children's natural moral growth.* New York: The Free Press.

DEVRIES, R., & KOHLBERG, L. (1987). *Constructivist early education: Overview and comparison with other programs.* Washington, DC: National Association for the Education of Young Children.

DOYLE, A. (1982). Friends, acquaintances, and strangers: The influence of familiarity and ethnolinguistic background on social interaction. In K. H. Rubin & H. S. Ross (Eds.), *Peer relationships and social skills in childhood* (pp. 229–252). New York: Springer-Verlag.

FURMAN, W., & GAVIN, L. A. (1989). Peers' influence on adjustment and development. In T. J. Berndt & C. W. Ladd (Eds.), *Peer relationships in child development* (pp. 319–340). New York: Wiley.

HINCHUM, B. (1975). *Motor development in early childhood.* St. Louis: Mosby.

KAGAN, J., & LAMB, S. (EDS.). (1987). *The emergence of morality in young children.* Chicago: University of Chicago Press.

KAMII, C. (1973). A sketch of the Piaget-derived preschool program. In J. L. Frost (Ed.), *Revisiting early childhood education.* New York: Holt Rinehart & Winston.

KAMII, C. (1982). Autonomy as the aim of education: Implications of Piaget's theory. In C. Kamii, *Number* (pp. 73–87). Washington, DC: National Association for the Education of Young Children.

KAMII, C. (1986). *How children learn to think* [Videotape]. Washington, DC: National Association for the Education of Young Children.

KAMII, C., & DEVRIES, R. (1978). *Physical knowledge in preschool education: Implications of Piaget's theory.* Englewood Cliffs, NJ: Prentice-Hall.

KOHLBERG, L. (1984). *The psychology of moral development.* New York: Harper & Row.

KOHLBERG, L., DeVRIES, R., FEIN, G., HART, D., MAYER, R., NOAM, G., SNAREY, J., & WERTSCH, J. (1987). *Child psychology and childhood education.* New York: Longman.

MACCOBY, E. E. (1986). Social groupings in childhood: Their relationship to prosocial and antisocial behavior in boys and girls. In D. Olewus, J. Block, & M. Radke-Yarrow (Eds.), *Development of antisocial and prosocial behavior* (pp. 263–284). New York: Academic Press.

MIZE, J., & LADD, G. W. (1990). Toward the development of successful social skills training for preschool children. In S. R. Asher & J. D. Cole (Eds.), *Peer rejection in childhood* (pp. 338–361). New York: Cambridge University Press.

PIAGET, J. (1929/1960). *The child's conception of the world.* Totowa, NJ: Littlefield, Adams.

PIAGET, J. (1964). *Judgment and reasoning in the child.* Totowa, NJ: Littlefield, Adams.

PIAGET, J. (1965). *The moral judgment of the child.* New York: The Free Press.

PUTALLAZ, M., & GOTTMAN, J. M. (1981). Social skills and group acceptance. In S. R. Asher & J. M. Gottman (Eds.), *The development of children's friendships* (pp. 207–241). New York: Cambridge University Press.

PUTALLAZ, M., & HEFLIN, A. (1990). Parent-child interaction. In S. R. Asher & J. D. Cole (Eds.), *Peer rejection in childhood* (pp. 189–216). New York: Cambridge University Press.

RAMSEY, P. G. (1991). *Making friends in school: Promoting peer relationships in early childhood.* New York: Teachers College Press.

RIZZO, T. A. (1989). *Friendship development among children in school.* Norwood, NJ: Ablex.

SCHORR, L. (1989). *Within our reach: Breaking the cycle of disadvantage.* New York: Anchor Books/Doubleday.

SELMAN, R. L. (1989). Fostering intimacy and autonomy. In W. Damon (Ed.), *Child development today and tomorrow* (pp. 409–435). San Francisco: Jossey-Bass.

SELMAN, R. L. (1980). *The growth of interpersonal understanding.* New York: Academic Press.

SELMAN, R. L. (1981). The child as a friendship philosopher. In S. R. Asher & J. M. Gottman (Eds.), *The development of children's friendships* (pp. 242–272). New York: Cambridge University Press.

SIEGLER, R. S. (1991). *Children's thinking* (2nd ed.). Englewood Cliffs, NJ: Prentice-Hall.

Periodicals

DeVRIES, R. (1984). Developmental stages in Piagetian theory and educational practice. *Teacher Education Quarterly, 11*(4), 78–94.

DeVRIES, R., ZAN, B., REESE-LEARNED, H., & MORGAN, P. (1991). Sociomoral atmosphere and sociomoral development: A study of interpersonal understanding in three kindergarten classrooms. *Moral Education Forum, 16*(2), 5–20.

FERNIE, D. E., KANTOR, R., KLEIN, E. L., MEYER, C., & ELGAS, P. M. (1988). Becoming students and becoming ethnographers in a preschool. *Journal of Research in Childhood Education, 3*(2), 132–141.

GREENBERG, P. (1988). Ideas that work with young children: Avoiding "me against you" discipline. *Young Children, 44*(1), 24–29.

McLOYD, V. C. (1982). Social class differences in sociodramatic play: A critical review. *Developmental Review, 2,* 1–30.

PARKER, J. G., & ASHER S. R. (1987). Peer relations and later personal adjustment: Are low-accepted children at risk? *Psychological Bulletin, 102,* 357–389.

PHINNEY, J. S., & ROTHERAM, M. J. (1982). Sex differences in social overtures between same-sex and cross-sex preschool pairs. *Child Study Journal, 12,* 259–269.

Papers

COSTIN, S. E., & JONES, D. C. (1989). *Friendship and emotion-control interventions among young children.* Paper presented at the biennial meeting of the Society for Research in Child Development, Kansas City, MO.

RIZZO, W., & CORSARO, W. A. (1991). *Social support processes in early childhood friendships.* Paper presented at the biennial meeting of the Society for Research in Child Development, Seattle.

2

Discipline Approaches

C hapters 4 through 10 present an overview of approaches to discipline. We present these approaches in sequence, from most to least positive; this presentation also moves in sequence from least intrusive to most intrusive.

Chapters 4 and 5 examine ways to prevent discipline problems from occurring—the most pleasant discipline option. Chapters 6 and 7 explain how adult examples of behavior and communication teach youngsters to manage potential behavior problems for themselves. Chapter 8 presents ways to enforce limits while helping children learn why certain behaviors are more desirable than others. Chapter 9 discusses the pros and cons of behavior modification, an approach we do not recommend but that is widely used. In chapter 10 we explain why punishment is damaging to the discipline goals of most people in our society.

We do not believe that any one discipline approach holds all the answers for all children at all times. We believe that teachers and caregivers with a wide knowledge of possible discipline approaches are best prepared to respond appropriately in a given situation. However, we do not believe that all approaches are good ones. This section warns against counterproductive approaches as well as recommends productive ones.

Chapter 4

Creating Environments That Prevent Discipline Problems

Some people think of discipline as just dealing with misbehavior. It is much more productive to think about how to avoid behavior problems in the first place. You may have visited a classroom where things went so smoothly that you envied the teacher for having such a well-behaved group of students. Chances are that the children were normal but that the teacher was very skilled at creating an environment that made it easier for kids to cooperate. This skill is a much more sophisticated approach to discipline than simply reacting to problems.

THE EMOTIONAL ENVIRONMENT

The teacher's attitude can create an environment that encourages either positive or negative behavior (DeVries, Zan, Reese-Learned, & Morgan, 1991). Naturally, no teacher would deliberately encourage negative behavior, yet it is possible to send messages unconsciously that are better not sent. Nonverbal communication is especially likely to reveal your inner feelings. Body language, tone of voice, and intensity often speak louder than words.

Positive Teacher Expectations

If you are convinced that children want to work and play constructively, your whole manner of relating to them communicates that expectation. However, you may be convinced that children want to get away with whatever they can and have no interest in learning. This expectation, too, will be communicated by your tone of voice as you speak to children and by the amount of freedom you give them. You can pretty well count on children to behave according to your expectations.

> Mrs. Jensen's first-grade class has just come in from recess, and youngsters are moving purposefully around the room as they prepare for their next activity. They have the freedom to choose among the classroom centers and to decide individually whether to eat a snack now or later. The classroom is alive with the sounds of decision making as children refocus their energies. Some go first to wash up before a snack and find a comfortable spot to relax and eat. Beau and Desmond are hungry but want to finish the block structure they were working on before recess. Food isn't allowed in the block area, so they postpone their snack. Yaisa and Shantae take their snack into the playhouse, where eating is allowed, and happily incorporate snack time into their dramatic play. Now that the youngsters have learned the routines and the classroom rules, Mrs. Jensen sometimes feels she really isn't needed. She is able to use this time for observing and recording children's progress. She has trusted her children to self-direct their free-choice time, and they have lived up to her expectations.

Next door, Miss Wheeler has no time for observing. She is busy directing and controlling everyone's behavior. In her first-grade class, all the children must eat their snack as soon as they come in from recess, whether they are hungry or not. This schedule makes a long wait in line for handwashing, with lots of pushing and shoving during the wait. It isn't easy, but Miss Wheeler makes the children all sit still until everyone is finished eating before they are excused for the next activity. Then she assigns them by table to specific centers, where they must stay until she flashes the lights signaling rotation to the next center. Jimmie is a constant problem, always trying to sneak out of his assigned center to the blocks. Lydia cries a lot, saying she doesn't want to play with those "mean kids" from her table. Miss Wheeler is in constant demand to settle disputes and make children stay where they are supposed to be. She sees this situation as clear evidence that these young children aren't capable of self-direction. Actually, *her* expectations make the difference.

You probably remember those teachers you really liked and those you didn't. You probably were much more cooperative with the ones you liked. They were undoubtedly the ones who let you know they had faith in you and gave you the opportunity to prove they were right. They probably also were the ones who made the effort to get to know their students as individuals, building a relationship with each. Establishing this rapport lets the teacher tune in to what is special about each child.

Clear Guidelines

It is essential to state clearly exactly what behaviors are acceptable. Your positive outlook is not enough if children are confused about what you want them to do. Young children often do not have the experience to know what is and what is not acceptable. Social norms are not self-evident.

You might also assume that children should know better than to sit up on their knees during story time, blocking the person's view behind them. But remember that young children think about their own needs and have trouble considering someone else's position. Mrs. Jensen doesn't just constantly remind children to sit down in the front rows; she structures a learning experience to help them begin to understand consideration for others. She assigns each table of children to a specific row during the first group meeting of each day. During other group sessions, they are allowed to choose their own places, but for this one group time they take turns experiencing how it feels to be in the back rows with other children in their way. Mrs. Jensen encourages the children who can't see to remind the others politely when they are thoughtlessly blocking the view. This experience provides an important lesson in seeing things from another person's perspective and in communicating about a problem. The children soon take responsibility for reminding one another to be considerate and eventually remember most of the time not to kneel up in front of someone.

Mutual Respect

Children are more likely to go along with what you want if you are also willing to go along with what they want sometimes. In other words, you encourage children to respect your wishes by showing respect for theirs (Miller, 1990). You teach them about mutual respect and shared power by your example and by your willingness to let them be decision makers. The importance of shared power is another reason to give children choices. In chapter 1, we discussed choice as crucial to the development of moral and intellectual autonomy as described by Piaget. In chapter 2, we discussed the role of choice in the emotional autonomy stage as described by Erikson. Choices are also essential for feeling good about life and about your position in it (Curry & Johnson, 1990).

Teachers who make all the decisions in their classrooms have more rebellious students. Teachers who involve children in deciding how best to accomplish goals have a much easier time. Children will scrupulously follow guidelines and observe rules they themselves have helped to determine. They will also actively remind other children to do the same.

Children behave more productively when teachers involve them in deciding how to accomplish goals.

Mrs. Jensen started the school year by reading a book called *Little Monster Goes to School.* Little Monster does a lot of bad things like sticking his arm out of the bus, tripping other kids, and getting into their lunches. Mrs. Jensen's first graders were properly horrified at this behavior. The story provided a good start for a discussion about why rules are important. Then the class was invited to brainstorm class rules. Mrs. Jensen helped them to combine their ideas into a few main ideas and to phrase them in positive instead of negative terms. "Don't run" became "Always walk." "Don't hit, don't shove, and don't spit" became "Be kind and talk things over." Mrs. Jensen wrote these rules as the children watched. They were displayed on a bulletin board that the children decorated with monster pictures they created at the paint easel. Most of the children learned to read the rules and referred to them when a classmate broke a rule.

Occasionally even the most enlightened teachers find themselves in a power struggle. Power struggles occur when you give an ultimatum and a child decides not to go along with it.

Dennis learned a lesson on the day he said, "No one eats lunch until your mess is cleaned up." Amy flatly refused to pick up the dress-up clothes she had been trying on. Now what? Dennis didn't really intend to deprive anyone of lunch; his remark had just been thoughtless. But the other children had picked up on it and were telling Amy she wasn't going to get any lunch. Amy was wailing over the thought of missing lunch, but she was not picking up any dress-up clothes.

Would the children ever believe him again if he let Amy have lunch without picking up? He couldn't in good conscience actually deny her food. What could he do?

He decided that he could teach a really valuable lesson to his young students. He could demonstrate how to admit an error graciously and to remedy it. This social skill is pertinent to the lives of preschoolers as they work at getting along. Dennis congratulated himself on modeling something much better than the "might makes right" concept, which his threat of missing lunch had perpetuated. So he went over to Amy and gently touched her shoulder to get her attention. He sat down on the floor beside her and explained that he had spoken without thinking. He assured Amy that she would not miss lunch.

Feeling calmer, Amy was able to listen as Dennis clarified his intent: to get the playthings out of the way so there would be space for eating lunch. With the ultimatum removed, Amy was able to problem-solve and reason. She proposed to move her dress-up clothes out of the way for now and finish putting them away after lunch when she wasn't so terribly hungry. Dennis was pleased to accept the compromise, realizing that it was not only logical but also a mutually face-saving solution.

Later, as he thought about the incident, Dennis examined the issue of saving face as it relates to power struggles. He acknowledged that his own pride was involved and thought about children's pride. He decided that if he got himself into a similar situation again, he would not hesitate to back off. He analyzed his reasons for going against the common assumption that adults must not lose in a battle of wills with a child. Dennis's conclusion was that losing such a battle meant damaged pride and therefore damaged self-esteem. Was his own pride and self-esteem more important than the child's? Because enhancing children's self-esteem was one of his major educational goals, Dennis was clear about the answer. He didn't want to make himself feel important at the expense of a little child.

Children's Emotional Needs

Damage to pride or self-esteem generally is expressed in some undesirable behavior. In fact, bad feelings of any kind are likely to show up as "bad" actions. Conversely, a classroom that nurtures children's good feelings will encourage "good" behavior (Curry & Johnson, 1990). Helping children in your classroom feel good about themselves and their school experience is an important part of effective classroom management and harmonious group dynamics.

It's OK to Be Different

Feeling good about yourself requires that you be accepted for who you are. In chapter 3 we discussed the danger of teachers' not understanding and accepting

Helping children feel good about themselves encourages "good" behaviors.

behavior patterns from a culture other than their own. Classrooms that accept and honor cultural differences meet the needs of minority students while teaching other children concepts of cultural pluralism (Miller, 1990). In respecting the cultural background of the child, it is also important to see the child as an individual and not just as a member of a certain group. Seeing children as individuals helps guard against stereotyping them according to their culture. The teacher's attitudes can impact the attitudes of children and may counteract prejudiced ideas (Lay-Dopyera & Dopyera, 1987).

Most teachers find that they have a lot to learn to avoid common, well-intentioned, but generally counterproductive efforts toward multiculturalism. Boutte and McCormick (1992) explain the mistaken and limited assumptions that most teachers demonstrate. They recommend significant study for learning how to achieve true cultural plurality. One of the common misconceptions is that all white children are from a common culture, a perception that overlooks different backgrounds among them.

Children with special needs who are included in regular classrooms add another dimension of diversity. Teacher example will help counteract children's fears of this and other kinds of differentness. When you focus on the child and not the handicap, you will more easily integrate a special-needs child into your group (Souweine, Crimmins, & Mazel, 1981). You can help your other students become comfortable with a wheelchair, prosthesis, or whatever special assistance a child requires. Then your students, too, can focus on the child as a person. Children with special needs often are rejected by peers because they are different (Ramsey, 1991). Sensitive teachers can help with this problem. The mother of a child with Down's syndrome spoke with tears of joy about the friends her son had found after he was included in a first-grade classroom with a helpful teacher. The little boy just couldn't stop talking about his friends.

We all have needs for friendship, success in worthwhile endeavors, and recognition for our efforts. Children spend a large part of their day in the school setting and should be able to find friends, success, and recognition at school. It is essential that a teacher understand these needs and know how to provide for them.

Friendship

You probably have seen situations where best friends have been separated in school so that they will not disturb one another's work. This well-intentioned intervention ignores the importance of friendship to the child's intellectual and emotional development. Youngsters learn a great deal as they strive to get along with a friend: They learn to think about another person's views, they learn much about compromise and problem solving, and they learn about caring and being cared for (Ramsey, 1991). These things are not learned with just any peers; they require someone who is special to the child. A child must care enough about another child to be willing to examine egocentric views and work out disagreements.

Mrs. Jensen works to ensure that children in her first-grade classroom find friends. She doesn't have a seating chart at first. Instead, she encourages youngsters to try different places for a couple of weeks. After they have had a chance to get acquainted, the children are asked to choose a place to sit for a while; Mrs. Jensen puts their names at those places for the time being. There is always opportunity to make new choices as new relationships blossom. Mrs. Jensen says, "The most important thing you can do for some kids in a school year is to make sure they have friends."

Some teachers are not tuned in to friendship as a legitimate need and over-look its educational value. Miss Wheeler is not only unaware of the importance of friendship, but she also doesn't know that children need to interact with their peers as part of learning. She spends much of her energy each day in futile efforts to keep children from socializing. Her attempts to enforce an unnatural quiet in her classroom are counterproductive to academic and emotional development.

INSTEAD OF CONTROLLING, YOU COULD BE TEACHING

❑ Encourage choices

❑ Allow talking

❑ Provide for movement

❑ Accept more than one right way

Mrs. Jensen, on the other hand, enjoys the busy hum of children sharing ideas and discussing experiences. In this environment, the several children who came to her class speaking a language other than English are fast becoming fluent in English. The interactive learning style of this classroom is perfect for their language-learning needs. Sometimes individual children need to be reminded to talk more softly, but they are not told to be silent in Mrs. Jensen's classroom. She notices that adults talk while they work and wonders why so many try to impose silence on children.

Classrooms and child-care centers where friendship and socializing are encouraged tend to be happy and harmonious places. Important social studies lessons occur daily as the teacher assists youngsters in their efforts to work cooperatively. Disagreements are viewed as teaching opportunities instead of reasons to keep kids apart. These classrooms are places where the teacher isn't continually telling children to be quiet. The teacher's energy is directed into more useful ways of helping children use their time productively. Similarly, the children's energy isn't wasted by trying not to say anything about the funny story in a library book or about the blue jay that just flew by the window. Teachers who understand the need for friendship and peer interaction don't go around being mad at kids for doing what comes naturally. And kids don't end up feeling bad about doing it. Happier teachers and children create an atmosphere more conducive to learning.

Success

Feelings of success do not result from easy schoolwork. Some children will easily succeed at almost any task the teacher comes up with, but they may not be sufficiently challenged to feel good about succeeding. Other youngsters are more vulnerable to failure. In both cases, open-ended activities can help all children experience feelings of success. Open-ended activities are those with no one right outcome and therefore no possibility of failure. In addition, open-ended activities do not have set limits, and they allow for extension beyond the expected levels. In this case, youngsters can make a project as challenging as they wish. Open-ended activities are also an important aspect of inclusion. Often children with special needs require open-ended activities in order to participate with the other children.

> The writing center in Mrs. Jensen's class provides for many levels of abilities and adapts to a variety of interests. It has a selection of paper in many sizes and colors, both with and without lines. There are also pencils and markers, staplers and hole punches. Children are free to use these materials as they wish in their work and play. Nicole's "pretend" writing is as acceptable as Eric's invented spelling, and both children are able to use writing for their own purposes. Nicole uses writing for social purposes, putting a combination of pictures and symbols on a scrap of paper and giving it to a friend to establish contact. Eric shows an impressive literary background in the stories he creates and makes into books. Yaisa uses the writing center resources to enhance her dramatic play, making menus for her play restaurant, tickets to her puppet show, or shopping lists for the play store.

Certainly, there is also a need for activities with just one correct response. You need to provide a balance of open and closed activities in your classroom to provide for the needs of all youngsters at all times. Sometimes Kelsey seeks the challenge of closed tasks in preschool, such as putting a puzzle together or learn-

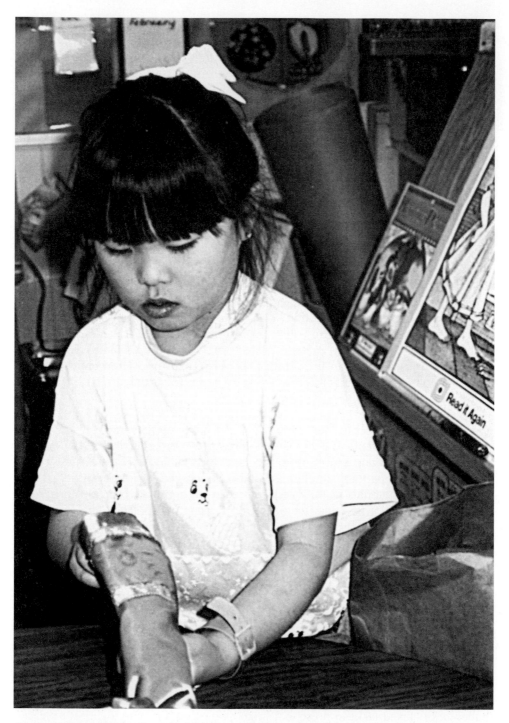

Open-ended activities allow all children to challenge themselves appropriately and to experience success.

ing how to weave paper mats at the arts and crafts table. As she challenges herself with the specific task and succeeds, she builds her feelings of competence. At other times she seeks the freedom to test what she can build with various manipulatives or to explore freely with art materials.

How can the teacher possibly provide just the right activity and material for each child all the time? You can't. What you can do is to allow children freedom of choice among a wide variety of interesting activities. You can count on each child almost always choosing the appropriate level of challenge and the right type of activity for the moment. Here is another value of child choice: Not only does it enhance the development of autonomy, but it also is invaluable for matching the curriculum to the child. Obviously, providing choice for your students is an important strategy.

Allowing children to match their level of personal challenge to a variety of open-ended activities is a good classroom management strategy (Bredekamp, 1987). Self-selection of an academic challenge also provides an alternative to ability grouping, which is a less effective effort to match the task to the child's ability. Research has demonstrated the negative impact of ability grouping on self-esteem and classroom dynamics (Ramsey, 1991). It doesn't take much time in a classroom to notice that children in the "low" group are most likely to act out or quit trying academically. If you follow youngsters onto the playground, you also see that children in the low group are frequently rejected as playmates by children from the other groups. This rejection creates a segregation effect among youngsters of different academic achievement levels. It is especially disconcerting in light of the fact that a disproportionate number of minority children tend to be placed in the low group (Murphy, 1986). Teachers need to take special care that being a child from a certain ethnic group doesn't disadvantage the child academically (Spencer & Markstrom-Adams, 1990). Teachers also need to take care that children are not socially disadvantaged because of academic labels.

Recognition

Traditional ways of interacting with students as a group causes many children to feel lost or invisible. When the teacher interacts with children as individuals, they know that they have the teacher's attention. Communicating on an individual basis also makes it easier for the teacher to interact appropriately with children of various cultures. Mrs. Jensen makes sure to notice and comment to each child about his or her activity during free-choice time. Her comments and questions help each child feel important and valued. Her students don't need to engage in inappropriate attention-getting behaviors to get her to notice them. Because each has her undivided attention at some time, they more easily share her attention during group times or when she is working with another child.

Getting to know students' families greatly enhances a teacher's ability to treat children as individuals. Home visits have been routine for Head Start teachers for years. Other preschool teachers and even elementary teachers have begun to adopt this valuable approach for getting to know their students. A home visit is a good chance to learn from parents. You can find out what the parents want

Children are less likely to act up for attention if they occasionally have the teacher's undivided attention.

from their child's educational experiences, and you can learn special information about the child. For instance, knowing the child's pet name at home and something about favorite family activities will help you relate more personally to the child.

Conferences between teacher and child provide for both individual attention and focus on individual progress. Mrs. Jensen usually manages to meet with each of her students once a week for five or ten minutes. She is convinced that the weekly one-on-one time is much more valuable than meeting with all children daily in a group. Interacting with children individually in this way also assists in building the relationships with them that are crucial to the teaching-learning process.

> Mrs. Jensen found time to meet with Blake after making the rounds of the room during quiet reading time. Everyone seemed engrossed in a book, so she hoped that she and Blake wouldn't be interrupted too much. During their conference, Blake told Mrs. Jensen about the books he had read recently and showed her how long his list of books completed had become. Then he read a particularly funny part from a book about King Bidgood in the bathtub. He also showed his teacher the letter he was writing to his pen pal in the third grade. They discussed whether or not Blake's letter explained clearly about the way the classroom snake shed its skin. A copy of the final polished version of the letter would go into Blake's writing portfolio. Mrs. Jensen suggested some books about snakes that Blake might be interested in. Blake went back to his work with confidence and a renewed sense of purpose.

Conferences like Mrs. Jensen and Blake's are increasingly being used as an alternative to tests for assessment and diagnostic purposes (Morrow & Smith, 1990). Traditional competitive ways of assessing children's progress make only the best students feel proud and accomplished. All but the top few feel just the opposite. Evaluation systems that compare children to one another have a much different impact from systems that compare children's current work with their own work a few months earlier. When a child competes with a past personal record instead of with classmates, each child can feel a sense of accomplishment. Each can feel motivated to keep trying. For instance, children who look at a folder containing their writing and drawing for the year can see for themselves how much progress they have made. New approaches to evaluation help youngsters to set personal goals for themselves and take pride in their progress toward those goals (Wortham, 1990). The ways in which you assess children's educational progress can help each child feel individually important and can help each feel successful.

THE PHYSICAL ENVIRONMENT

Did you realize that the arrangement of a classroom affects child behavior? Have you thought about whether or not a classroom invites children to do what you want them to do? Have you considered the effect on behavior when a child is either physically or emotionally uncomfortable in a school setting?

Analyzing the Setting

First-grade teacher Miss Wheeler doesn't realize that her arrangement of desks in small groups facing each other is not consistent with her expectations for children. She knows that it is more modern to have desks arranged this way than in rows, but she doesn't understand why. These groupings are designed to encourage peer interaction and cooperative learning. The problem is that Miss Wheeler doesn't want children to talk in school. Her room arrangement is not consistent with the behavior she desires. Mrs. Jensen has the same desk arrangement, but it works for her because it is completely consistent with her expectations for behavior. To avoid confusion and conflict, it is important to create an environment that sends clear, nonconflicting messages.

> As she called the children to story time with the xylophone, Joanne dreaded the inevitable power struggle that was sure to follow. Morning story time at preschool just wasn't working for her. The only floor space big enough for story time was surrounded by shelves of toys, and the children just couldn't keep their hands off them. It was impossible to keep their attention. Because the shelves were on wheels, she tried pushing them as far back as she could. But the children just inched their circle back to get to them. She repeatedly reminded them that it was time for a story, not for toys. Still, it was like trying to keep bees from flowers! Frustrated, Joanne asked the afternoon storyteller, Nancy, how she dealt with the problem. "Oh, I gave up long ago expecting them to ignore the shelves," Nancy explained. "When story time is coming, I ask for volunteers to help turn those shelves around to face the wall. They love the powerful feeling of moving furniture. Other children see the change in the room happening and know it's time for a story. And it goes without saying that it's not time to play with shelf toys—they can't even see them! "

Joanne's story-time arrangement gave a mixed message to the children. The toys surrounding them had been purchased and arranged particularly to attract people their age. These materials invited play. Conflicting with this invitation was the person with the book, also requesting their attention. Chances were high that some children weren't interested in that book just then but were fascinated with one of the toys, which were so enticingly near. Placing children in this situation and then asking them to obey you with undivided attention creates needless conflict. Nancy's solution provides a clear message about what time it is and what is expected during this time. If some children are not interested in the book she is currently reading, she tells them they may go to another area in the room, where shelf choices are still available, and play with the toys quietly at a table. She has clearly defined her floor reading space with the turned shelves. The messages from the environment and the teacher are not contradictory. It is easy for the children to recognize what they are to do.

Studying Traffic Patterns

The locations of learning centers can either make things run smoothly or can be a source of trouble. If the block-building center is not protected from people walking by, you can bet on frequent yelling and even hitting over ruined block creations. If the woodworking area is right next to the reading center, you can predict that quiet reading will be disrupted by noisy carpentering. You have already heard about Joanne's problem with the group gathering area surrounded by the toys.

Teachers work hard at planning their room arrangement. Even then, they are constantly monitoring how well it works and making adjustments as indicated. Mrs. Jensen originally had the blocks in a high activity part of the room, near the paint easels and the water table. The dramatic play area was in a quiet part of the room near the writing center to encourage writing as part of play. This arrangement seemed to make sense except that her students tended to use the dramatic play materials as an integral part of their block creations. Children working at areas between the two centers were disturbed by others moving equipment back and forth. Mrs. Jensen valued the sophisticated play that was going on and didn't want to curtail the mix of materials. Instead, she decided to rearrange the room so that the blocks were adjacent to the dramatic play area. Naturally, she involved the children in planning and implementing the changes.

Providing for Mobility

If youngsters are kept still and quiet most of the day, many will experience real discomfort. Have you ever found yourself simply unable to sit for another moment during a long meeting or a long airplane flight? You probably know what kind of physical discomfort young children feel when they are asked to sit longer than they are able. The natural reaction to this discomfort is to get up and move around. In classrooms where moving is allowed and provided for, there is no problem. However, there are classrooms where children are supposed to stay in their seats until the scheduled recess provides relief. Sometimes a child can use a trip to the bathroom as an excuse to walk around, but this often leads to lots of playing around in the bathroom.

> Mrs. Jensen not only allows children to move around quite freely between activities in her classroom, but she also makes an attempt to provide high mobility activity choices when youngsters need them. Desmond, the lucky twin, is in her room. When he has a special need for activity, he can build with the big heavy blocks and exercise his arms and upper body. He can challenge himself with the balance beam or pound nails in the carpentry area. His twin brother, Devon, does not have these opportunities in Miss Wheeler's room.

Room arrangement affects behavior: Putting the noisy woodworking center next to the quiet reading area is one sure way to cause problems.

Devon squirmed in agony after sitting at his place endlessly doing worksheets. He was not allowed to get up for a book until he was finished, and he was always the last one done. Finally, unable to take it any longer, Devon stretched his leg and tripped another child passing by. Instantly, he was in big trouble and was sent to the principal's office. At least he got to walk on the way there.

Providing for Privacy

Have you ever experienced strong antisocial feelings after extended periods of interacting with other people? Spending a full day in school, especially in the long child-care day, can be extremely wearing psychologically. You will notice youngsters getting crabby as the day wears on. They are more than just tired; they are also tired of people. Some children make hiding places for themselves if given the chance. Abby built herself a little house in the block area, got inside, and covered the top with a doll blanket. She insisted that others keep out. Sometimes you will see a child simply taking refuge under a desk or a table. One little boy even got into a wastebasket to get away from it all.

Teachers are becoming more aware of children's need for a retreat from hubbub (Bredekamp, 1987). Many classrooms now feature special places for being alone or visiting with a friend by yourself. Mrs. Jensen created a small space between two file cabinets and furnished it with cushions, books, and a reading lamp. Dennis found a spot under a stairway in the preschool that was perfect for one or two small children. It, too, has been cozily fitted with pillows and decorated with pictures. When the demand for the seclusive spots becomes too great, children can either sign up on a waiting list or create their own spots. There is no reason why children can't do the same work in private that they can do in the middle of the room. In fact, sometimes children need a bit of privacy before they feel up to constructive work.

CONCLUSION

Teachers who understand and provide for privacy and mobility save themselves a lot of trouble and also save children from being "naughty." Teachers who plan the environment so that it doesn't create problems have smoother days. Adults who expect the best from children and communicate their expectations clearly find that children behave more positively. Adults who provide choices and otherwise share power with children find them more eager and helpful. Teachers who help youngsters find friendship, success, and recognition help them to learn more effectively. When you meet children's needs in the physical and emotional classroom environment, many common discipline problems never arise.

FOR FURTHER THOUGHT

1. What are the behavior guidelines in an early childhood education program where you have spent time? How were these guidelines determined? Why do you think the youngsters either do or do not follow the guidelines?
2. In what ways have you seen teachers demonstrate respect for young children? In what ways have you seen teachers show lack of respect for young-

sters? Which examples most closely match your own interaction with children?

3. How are friendships encouraged or discouraged in an early childhood program with which you are familiar? Would you recommend any changes to help children develop meaningful friendships?
4. Analyze an early childhood program for open-ended and closed activities. Is there a balance or does one type dominate? How do children's responses to the two types differ?
5. Observe teacher-child interaction, watching for the amount of individual attention provided. How do youngsters respond differently to individual interaction with the teacher than they do to interacting as part of a group?
6. Analyze the physical setting of a classroom. In what ways does the room arrangement prevent or create discipline problems? How are mobility needs met? How are privacy needs met?

REFERENCES AND RECOMMENDATIONS FOR READING

Books

ALLEN, K. E. (1992). *The exceptional child: Mainstreaming in early childhood education* (2nd ed.). Albany: Delmar.

BERGER, E. H. (1991). *Parents as partners in education: Schools and parents working together* (3rd ed.). New York: Macmillan.

BREDEKAMP, S. (ED.). ((1987). *Developmentally appropriate practice in early childhood programs serving children from birth through age 8, expanded edition.* Washington, DC: National Association for the Education of Young Children.

CURRY, N. E., & JOHNSON, C. N. (1990). *Beyond self-esteem: Developing a genuine sense of human value.* Washington, DC: National Association for the Education of Young Children.

CURWIN, R. L., & MENDLER, A. N. (1988). *Discipline with dignity.* Alexandria, VA: Association for Supervision and Curriculum Development.

ENGSTROM, G.(ED.). (1971). *The significance of the young child's motor development.* Washington, DC: National Association for the Education of Young Children.

GROSSMAN, H. (1990). *Trouble-free teaching: Solutions to behavior problems in the classroom.* Mountain View, CA: Mayfield.

JERVIS, K. (1989). *Separation.* Washington, DC: National Association for the Education of Young Children.

KAMII, C. (ED.). (1990). *Achievement testing in the early years.* Washington, DC: National Association for the Education of Young Children.

KATZ, L. G., & McCLELLAN, D. E. (1991). *The teacher's role in the social development of young children.* Urbana, IL: ERIC Clearinghouse Document, ED313168.

KRITCHEVSKY, S., & PRESCOTT, E. (1977). *Planning environments for young children: Physical space.* Washington, DC: National Association for the Education of Young Children.

LAY-DOPYERA, M., & DOPYERA, J. (1987). *Becoming a teacher of young children* (3rd ed.). New York: Random House.

MILLER, D. F. (1990). *Positive child guidance.* Albany: Delmar.

MORROW, L. M., & SMITH, J. K. (1990). *Assessment for instruction in early literacy.* Englewood Cliffs, NJ: Prentice-Hall.

RAMSEY, P. G. (1991). *Making friends in school: Promoting peer relationships in early childhood.* New York: Teachers College Press.

ROGERS, C. S., & SAWYERS, J. K. (1988). *Play in the lives of children.* Washington, DC: National Association for the Education of Young Children.

SOUWEINE, J., CRIMMINS, S., & MAZEL, C. (1981). *Mainstreaming: Ideas for teaching young children.* Washington, DC: National Association for the Education of Young Children.

VERGERONT, J. (1989). *Places and spaces for preschool and primary (indoors).* Washington, DC: National Association for the Education of Young Children.

WADE, B. (1990). *Little monster goes to school.* New York: Lothrop, Lee, & Shepard.

WILCOX, K. (1988). Differential socialization in the classroom: Implications for equal opportunity. In G. Spindler (Ed.), *Doing the ethnography of schooling* (pp. 268–309). Prospect Heights, IL: Waveland.

WOOD, A. (1985). *King Bidgood's in the bathtub.* San Diego: Harcourt Brace Jovanovich.

WORTHAM, S. C. (1990). *Tests and measurement in early childhood education.* New York: Merrill/Macmillan.

Periodicals

CLARK, L., DEWOLF, S., & CLARK, C. (1992). Teaching teachers to avoid having culturally assaultive classrooms. *Young Children, 47*(5), 4–9.

CROSSER, S. (1992). Managing the early childhood classroom. *Young Children, 47*(2), 23–29.

DEVRIES, R., ZAN, B., REESE-LEARNED, H., & MORGAN, P. (1991). Sociomoral atmosphere and sociomoral development: A study of interpersonal understanding in three kindergarten classrooms. *Moral Education Forum, 16*(2), 5–20.

GOFFIN, S. G. (1989). How well do we respect the children in our care? *Childhood Education, 66*(2), 68–74.

HARRISON, A. O., WILSON, M. N., PINE, C. J., CHAN, S. Q., & BURIEL, R. (1990). Family ecologies of ethnic minority children. *Child Development, 61*, 347–362.

HONIG, A. S. (1985). Research in review. Compliance, control, and discipline (continued). *Young Children, 40*(3), 47–52.

KLAUKE, A. (1988). The developmental approach to kindergarten: Profile of an expert teacher. *Oregon School Study Council Bulletin, 32*(8).

LITTLE SOLDIER, L. (1992). Building optimum learning environments for Navajo students. *Childhood Education, 68*(3), 145–148.

MURPHY, D. (1986). Educational disadvantagement: Associated factors, current interventions, and implications. *Journal of Negro Education, 55*, 495–507.

SPENCER, M. B., & MARKSTROM-ADAMS, C. (1990). Identity processes among racial and ethnic minority children in America. *Child Development, 61*, 290–310.

WARDLE, F. (1991). Guest editorial: Are we shortchanging boys? *Child Care Information Exchange, 79*, 48–51.

Papers

GARTRELL, D. (1988). *Developmentally appropriate guidance of young children.* St. Paul: Minnesota Association for the Education of Young Children.

HONIG, A. S., & WITTMER, D. S. (1987). *Socialization and discipline for infants and toddlers.* Presented at the annual meeting of the National Association for the Education of Young Children, Chicago. Urbana, IL: ERIC Clearinghouse Document, ED291484.

Chapter 5

Planning Programs That Prevent Discipline Problems

Jon

Young children are better able to cooperate in school when educational approaches match their developmental stages. Therefore, teacher expectations must be geared to the maturation level of the students, and curriculum must be appropriate to the children involved. When practices and materials created for older students are used for younger ones, many problems arise. Developmentally inappropriate teaching by adults results in inappropriate behavior from children.

MAKING LEARNING MEANINGFUL

It has been said that the best discipline is a well-planned curriculum (Greenberg, 1987). Prevention of problems is the idea behind that statement. How do children act when they are bored or disinterested? Probably you remember from your own childhood how you acted under those circumstances. Most youngsters will create some action when the teacher doesn't offer any. Often, however, these creative efforts do not conform to acceptable group behavior, and we label them discipline problems.

The National Association for the Education of Young Children (Bredekamp & Rosegrant, 1992) provides us with guidelines for appropriate curriculum for preschool and primary grade youngsters. These guidelines emphasize the characteristics of developmentally appropriate approaches to teaching young children. The following discussion explains how these guidelines can eliminate many potential discipline problems you might otherwise face as a teacher or caregiver.

Children's Interests

The National Association for the Education of Young Children (NAEYC) curriculum guidelines emphasize making curriculum meaningful to children. This guideline obviously relates to keeping them engaged and on task—a classroom management challenge. What does "engaged and on task" mean and how do you do it? It means that you help children discover personal value in learning. Instead of tracing and copying a different letter each day, children should be encouraged to explore print in books they enjoy and signs that have an interesting purpose. Instead of counting the number of dots on the worksheet, children should be encouraged to figure out how to divide the raisins equally for snack time.

Tapping into children's interests is also recommended in the NAEYC curriculum guidelines. Don't we all get more involved in things we are interested in?

NAEYC CURRICULUM GUIDELINE

Curriculum addresses a broad range of content that is relevant, engaging, and meaningful to children. (Bredekamp & Rosegrant, 1992)

Mrs. Jensen is alert to questions and comments from youngsters that indicate their current interests. She encourages children to pursue these ideas and incorporates many child-generated topics into class activities. She is prepared for many of the ideas with collections of books and activity ideas for topics that frequently catch on in her classes. Mrs. Jensen knows from experience that kids are generally interested in dinosaurs, space, animals, and insects.

Ideas from individual youngsters often become major curriculum themes in Mrs. Jensen's first grade. She knows that it doesn't really matter whether the theme is spaceships or turtles; children can practice the basic skills, broaden their knowledge base, and increase their feelings of competence with any theme. She uses the various topics to provide a purpose for learning. For instance, reading to find out why turtles pull their heads inside their shells is a good way for children to practice reading and to learn to value reading skill. When children care about the work they are doing, they are less likely to be disruptive.

Mrs. Jensen also knows how to help children become interested in subjects she is directed to cover. For instance, the topic of nutrition may sound pretty boring. But it isn't when you take a trip to the supermarket to buy items from each food group and use them for class cooking projects. Interest is sustained in the subject when a play store is set up next to the playhouse. Much thought and energy goes into writing grocery lists that reflect nutritious meal planning. When you channel children's energy constructively, they don't have so much excess to burn off inappropriately.

Dennis uses the same curriculum guidelines for preschoolers as Mrs. Jensen does for first graders The principles are the same, although the expectations for children differ according to their developmental stage. He, too, ensures that the curriculum makes sense to kids. Instead of mindlessly reciting the alphabet, his students have frequent opportunity to see their names and the names of their friends used for labeling artwork and for keeping their place on a waiting list. Many children can recognize their own names and those of their closest friends. Some discuss how confusing it is when names start with the same letter, like the names Aaron and Amy or Kelsey and Kenji. The thinking that goes on during these discussions results in true learning and genuine involvement.

Integrated Curriculum

Both Dennis and Mrs. Jensen use the theme approach for organizing their curriculum. A *theme* is a topic of interest to youngsters that provides a focus for exploring many different subject areas. Studying one topic through various curriculum areas is known as an integrated curriculum (Krogh, 1990). It allows children to practice reading, writing, and math skills to find out about a topic. The topic itself usually involves social studies or science information. Art, music, and drama are incorporated as children express ideas about their learning. As we previously explained, children can learn in most subject areas using almost any theme. Dennis knows that using arithmetic to explore a subject is more useful than merely practicing arithmetic skills, so he helps children find the mathematics potential in the topics they are interested in.

Making curriculum meaningful to children helps keep them engaged and on task.

NAEYC CURRICULUM GUIDELINE

Curriculum allows for focus on a particular topic or content, while allowing for integration across traditional subject-matter divisions, by planning around themes and/or learning experiences that provide opportunities for rich conceptual development. (Bredekamp & Rosegrant, 1992)

When the resident preschool expert on dinosaurs reported that a certain type of dinosaur had two hundred teeth, Dennis challenged the child and others who were interested to discover just how many two hundred is. They got out Unifix cubes and worked together as a group to identify two hundred; then they arranged them like top and bottom teeth to visualize the dinosaur's mouth. Danny commented, "I'll bet dinosaurs can eat faster than we can!"

That remark led Dennis to suggest the idea of getting a partner and counting each other's teeth. Megan decided that they should count out the number of teeth in their mouths and make a display of them using the smallest Cuisenaire rods. Counting dinosaur teeth and their own teeth turned into quite a project, attracting different children over a period of several days. It led to further reading and further science information as a result.

Kimberly was motivated to make pictures representing herself with her teeth and the dinosaur with its teeth. Several other children followed her example. Thus, artistic representation was added to mathematics, science, and reading as the curriculum was integrated around a dinosaur-teeth theme.

The play store in Mrs. Jensen's classroom is another example of a theme for an integrated curriculum. Children thought about foods for good nutrition while playing store. They practiced writing when they made their grocery lists, and they practiced reading both the lists and the labels on the food packages. They extended their thinking about counting and money as they made price tags and tried to figure out proper payment for each item. The children learned more about their community during their field trip to the supermarket. Thus, the trip came under the heading *social studies*. The class book in which each child contributed a drawing and a dictated message about the trip also helped children learn to read and write.

Real Experiences and Real Materials

Both Dennis and Mrs. Jensen know that children will benefit more and the school day will be smoother if teaching is compatible with how children learn naturally. Integrating the curriculum is one way to match your teaching with children's learning. Children certainly don't separate the world into the categories *science, math,* and *social studies*. They just want to make sense of their world, with all its interrelationships, as they experience it. Therefore, school also needs to reflect the real world and children's own experiences in order for youngsters to perceive school as important. Teachers need to build on the experiences and knowledge that children bring to school with them.

Eric brought a bird's nest for sharing time, and other children began talking about birds' nests they had seen. Mrs. Jensen encouraged the discussion by asking what they knew about birds and birds' nests.

Children will learn more and the school day will be smoother if teaching is compatible with how children learn.

Most of the children in this suburban area had some sort of experience to share. Raymond told a story about when his mom had cut his hair outside on the patio; he had seen birds come and take the hair for their nests. Other children told about being careful of nests with eggs in them. The teacher decided to follow up on the children's experiences and build on the knowledge they already had.

Mrs. Jensen got out her own collection of birds' nests from past years for the children to examine. She had protected the nests by keeping them in clear plastic bags, which allowed children to see them from all sides but kept the nests from falling apart. A discussion about the kinds of things birds use to make nests was preparation for a field trip around the schoolyard to collect materials for making birds' nests. Each child had the opportunity to make a bird's nest model with the materials collected. Mrs. Jensen provided the "mud" to hold the material together; she had previously discovered that glue mixed with dirt and water allows for a successful nest-building experience.

As we explained in chapter 3, children's way of learning starts with real experiences and real objects from which to make sense. Mrs. Jensen's students would not have made much sense out of a lesson on birds' nests without both their personal experience and the concrete activity the teacher provided. Some teachers don't understand this; they waste precious energy lecturing children about topics totally outside their realm of experience, never giving them any real experiences related to the topic. Of course, this approach leads to discipline problems because children don't pay much attention to a discussion they cannot understand.

Some teachers cover the same topics year after year without responding to the enthusiasms and questions of the children in *this* class *this* year. Then they follow up the meaningless lessons with developmentally inappropriate worksheets. Many youngsters will dutifully go along with the teacher and complete these purposeless tasks, but many others will cause classroom problems by trying to find something interesting to do.

RESULTS OF DEVELOPMENTALLY INAPPROPRIATE TEACHING

Developmentally inappropriate teaching by adults results in inappropriate behavior from children.

Mrs. Jensen not only started with a topic of personal importance to her students when they studied birds, but she also knew how to provide concrete experiences to further their knowledge. Examining real nests, collecting real material to make nests, and going through the process of creating their own models are the kinds of concrete experiences that match the way young children learn. They have the opportunity to construct their own understanding of birds' nests from the experience of creating replicas. The children engaged in these educational experiences are involved in the business of learning and therefore aren't likely to disrupt anyone else's work. They are also building the base for thinking further about birds and will be better able to make sense of reading material on that subject.

Too often teachers forget young children's need to focus on the real world of the here and now. Well-meaning teachers frequently lead youngsters into the totally unintelligible world of long ago or far away. Thanksgiving time is particularly likely to motivate teachers to explain the history of the original feast. Young children have notoriously inaccurate ideas about time and space. They may not understand the difference between something happening three hundred years ago and something happening last week. Ask a young child who has heard the story of Thanksgiving to tell you about it, and you will hear truly amazing misconceptions. Instead of wasting children's time with a presentation of incomprehensible historical facts, you would be wise to help them think about what they are thankful for in their own lives.

Efforts to offer multicultural education can also lead to developmentally inappropriate presentations (Clark, DeWolf, & Clark, 1992). Youngsters carry away distorted pictures of native Americans as scary people in war paint who live in tepees. Some youngsters come to believe that African-American people are currently slaves. Even efforts to build an appreciation for different cultures with displays of ethnic food and dress can backfire by emphasizing the differences rather than the commonalities among people. Instead, teachers can enhance acceptance of cultural diversity in the children's own environment. The pictures on the bulletin board, the books in the library corner, and the dolls in the playhouse can all reflect cultural and racial plurality. These messages that permeate their daily lives will have a positive impact on children's lifelong attitudes (Derman-Sparks & the A.B.C. Task Force, 1989).

Using Time Wisely

NAEYC CURRICULUM GUIDELINE

The content of the curriculum is worth knowing; curriculum respects children's intelligence and does not waste their time. (Bredekamp & Rosegrant, 1992)

Perhaps the most critical curriculum guideline has to do with making sure that what children are asked to learn is worth knowing (Katz & Chard, 1989). Respect

Perhaps the most critical curriculum guideline has to do with making sure that what children are asked to learn is worth knowing.

for children should guide us away from the trivial and cute school activities that are all too common. Instead of wasting children's time having them all make identical red flowers for the bulletin board, let's think about what is truly important in their lives. Stephanie Feeney puts things into perspective by reminding us that one of the most important things any of us can learn might be "how to find a friend when you're sad." (Feeney, Christensen, & Moravcik, 1991) She makes this statement in the context of a broad view of what is worth knowing; it includes understanding the physical and social environment and yourself in order to better respect and care for the world and its people. She helps us evaluate the importance of colors and shapes in comparison to goals of becoming more human and helping our world survive. Respecting children involves respecting their time and using it wisely.

> When the children finished making their birds' nests, Mrs. Jensen called them together for a group discussion. "What did you learn when you made the birds' nests?" she asked. Expecting answers about the way the mud felt and what ingredients worked best, the teacher was astounded to hear a whole different level of response: "Birds' nests are *really* hard to make!" "I'll never knock one down out of a tree," and "I won't ever shoot a bird" were the type of ideas generated. Making birds' nest models encouraged these youngsters to think about the bird's viewpoint, and it helped them develop an appreciation for birds and their struggle for survival. Certainly, these children will be better able to respect and care for the world they live in.

Additionally, you need to ask yourself whether what you are teaching is worth the effort at this time in children's lives. Many teachers have discovered the hard way that learning to tell time in kindergarten is *not* worth the effort. Others have decided that trying to teach everyone how to make change in first grade is wasted energy. Chapter 3 explained that telling time and making change are confusing to young children because they use arbitrarily designated representational symbols. Trying to teach these symbols too soon is about as productive as trying to teach a five-month-old baby to walk. Some topics are a waste of time because they are too easy and can be learned without specifically spending school time on them. Directed instruction on colors is not necessary for most children. Colors are a part of life and are generally picked up as children decide which colored crayon to use, which shirt to wear, or what color their favorite ice cream is. Talking with children about color as they engage in other activities is all the instruction most of them need.

On the other hand, some ideas are well worth the time and effort. We hope for greater emphasis on helping children learn to respect and protect the environment and to live peaceably together with respect for individual differences. These areas of study might be called science and social studies; they might also be called essentials.

ORGANIZATIONAL STRATEGIES

Experienced teachers know when behavior problems are most likely to occur. They anticipate problem situations and plan ways to keep the day running smoothly. They use combinations of routines and novelty to avoid turmoil during transitions, waiting periods, and group times.

Routines

Routines help children know what to expect and assist them in being cooperative members of the group. Routines provide guidelines for what to do next and how to do it. Because the children know the routine, it doesn't take any time at all for Mrs. Jensen's first graders to assemble for group time. They have a system for moving smoothly from their seats to the group area, and each child knows just what to do. Routines save the teacher from having to tell children constantly what to do next; they know what comes next and what they are to do. It is important, however, that routines make sense (Gareau & Kennedy, 1991). Washing hands before snack time or hanging up coats after recess are routines that make sense. Sponging your lunch spot even though it isn't sticky may not make sense. Just like adults, children more readily go along with regulations that make sense to them.

Having a routine does not mean being ruled by the clock. It doesn't mean that you stop whatever else is going on at exactly 11:15 each day and have story time. But it is important that children have an idea of the sequence of events and what their role should be. Children in Dennis's preschool class know that they will get to work and play at their choice of activity when they first arrive at school and that there will be a time to gather together about mid-morning. They know where they can fix and eat their snack when they are ready for it. They know where to put their coats and belongings when they arrive, and they know where to find the materials they might need for a project.

Dennis observes the children in his preschool program to determine when it is time to gather for group. He tries to be sensitive to children's needs for extended periods of uninterrupted concentration. He knows that they have long attention spans when they are doing something important to them. The myth of short attention spans is the result of giving children trivial activities that are not engrossing and not their choice. Unfortunately, many teachers do not know this fact, and they unwittingly reduce children's ability to concentrate by making them constantly change activities (Nash, 1979).

When it appears that most of the youngsters may be winding down on their activities and reaching closure, Dennis moves around the room telling each child that it will be group time in five minutes. This advance warning allows children to finish what they are doing and mentally prepare to move on. Occasionally a child will be too engrossed to quit and will ask to be excused from group or to join in a few minutes. Dennis's respect for children and their work comes through as he honors these requests.

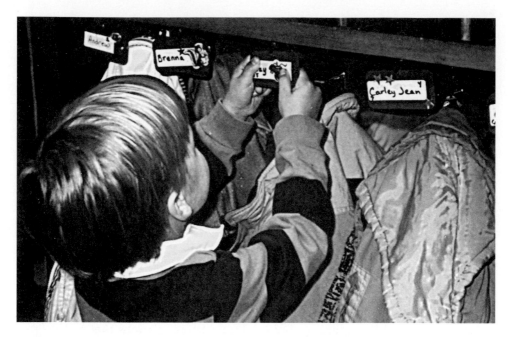

Routines help children know what to expect and assist them in being cooperative members of a group.

Making Transitions

Many discipline problems occur during transition times, when children are moving from one activity or one place to another. Many of these problems happen because teachers unrealistically expect children to wait patiently for too long while other children get ready to join them. Adults who respect children do not waste their time with prolonged periods of waiting. If they do, you can almost guarantee that children will be clever enough to find some way to alleviate their boredom. Unfortunately, this activity usually takes the form of poking or pushing the person in front of them. Few teachers appreciate these creative outlets.

> Mrs. Jensen dislikes having to line up her students and make them walk all together in a row. She knows that waiting in line is terribly boring for them and staying in line is unnatural. When they go out for recess, she lets them leave individually or in small groups as they get ready. At the beginning of the school year, she spent time with her class discussing and practicing good manners when walking through the elementary-school hallways. Her children generally remember to walk instead of run and to keep their voices down. When they forget, their classmates remind them. Not having lines is less trouble for Mrs. Jensen and her students and causes many fewer discipline problems.
>
> The librarian, Mrs. Goldman, insists on lines, so Mrs. Jensen's class gets practice in lining up when they go to the library. Instead of

making the students who get ready quickly stand and be bored while she gives her attention to the procrastinators, Mrs. Goldman creates some action of her own in the line. She leads the group in favorite songs and finger plays to head off inappropriate kinds of activity. This approach also hurries the stragglers faster than nagging does; they are eager to join in the fun.

Mrs. Jensen uses a similar approach when she is gathering children together for group time. If it takes a while for everyone to arrive, she engages in a discussion with those who are there. She often uses this time to help children evaluate their activities, with questions such as "What did you do special today at choosing time?" At other times the children want to do their favorite finger play about the five little monkeys.

Getting to and from the mid-morning gathering are the only significant transitions children must make in the morning preschool component of the Midway Children's Center day. Dennis's use of advance warning helps most children get prepared for a change of activity. When they are not interrupted in the middle of a project, they are much more agreeable. Keeping transitions to a minimum also keeps disruptions to a minimum. For most of the morning, youngsters are free to change learning activities as they are individually ready to do so.

When group time is over, Dennis avoids a stampede to the snack table by making a game out of sending a few children at a time. Sometimes he says, "Everyone wearing stripes today may go to the snack table." Next it might be those with plaid or print designs on their clothing. On other days, Dennis focuses on hair or eye color. Sometimes he holds up name cards to excuse the children one at a time; the youngsters practice reading their own and their friends' names to determine whose turn it is. These games keep children involved and learning during their short wait. Those who arrive at the snack table first must also have something to do besides waiting. They either need to be allowed to begin eating immediately, or else another adult must be there to engage them in a song or activity.

Those children who remain at the center for the full-day program are faced with a number of transitions: lunch time, nap time, getting up from nap, and parent arrival time. Each of these changes requires that children change gears and move from one mode of activity to another. Each change also involves movement of groups from one place to another. Both aspects of transition are frequently upsetting to youngsters.

Tuning in to children as individuals will help remind you not to herd them into the next activity. One key to making smooth transitions lies in not unduly rushing children. As soon as you start to hurry kids, they immediately start to rebel. Respecting individual differences in youngsters is another important guideline for smooth transitions. Joshua is always hungry at lunchtime and eagerly gets going on his meal. Andrea makes slower transitions and has trouble tearing herself away from the dramatic play she is usually involved in. These two children require different treatment. Forcing Andrea into Josh's schedule won't work for her.

Similarly, Amy, Jimmie, and Ahmed are ready for sleep at nap time, while Megan, Tory, and Kimberly rarely nap. The staff at the children's center solved their nap-time problems by separating sleepers from nonsleepers; the teachers allowed nonsleepers to play quietly after lying down with a book for fifteen minutes. It makes no more sense to attempt to force all children to sleep than to force them all to stay awake. There are real differences in the needs of children. A pro-

Rushing children into changing activities causes problems.

gram with the flexibility to accommodate these differences greatly reduces its discipline problems.

Group Time

Bringing young children together for a story or discussion time often creates trouble. Teachers complain about feeling like police officers as they continually remind children to sit down or pay attention at group time. Young children talk when they aren't supposed to; they wriggle and squirm and poke one another, and they even just walk away. Teachers with child-development knowledge realize that these behaviors are related to children's maturational stage. They understand that young children are not good at sitting still or being quiet, that they have trouble dealing with large groups, and that they aren't good at pretending interest when they are bored (Bredekamp, 1987). Many of these teachers seriously question the appropriateness of a group time at the preschool level; some question it in kindergarten as well. Yet these same teachers usually feel compelled to have at least a brief period of togetherness.

Many will argue that youngsters need to learn the social skills involved in a group gathering because the next teacher will expect it. Others reject that argument on the grounds that children will more easily gain those skills when they are a little older. They believe there is no point in putting everyone through the misery of pushing the skills before youngsters are ready. This argument is similar to the prevailing view of toilet training: Wait until the child is ready, and it will happen quickly and painlessly.

Some programs compromise on group time by having several small groups instead of one large group. Instead of two adults with twenty youngsters in a circle, each adult takes ten children for circle time. This method is a little closer to the guidelines for group size that James Hymes discusses in his book *Teaching the Child Under Six* (1990). Hymes recommends the following guide for group size: The right number of children for a child to interact with is no more than the number of birthdays that child has had.

Another approach allows choice about participation in group activities. Dennis is able to allow choice with his preschool group because there are other adults available to supervise children who do not choose to join. Dennis tries to make his circle time so attractive that youngsters will want to join in and stay involved. If he doesn't get much enthusiasm, he treats that response as useful feedback regarding the appropriateness or relevance of what he is offering at group time. For instance, if several children leave during the story he is reading, he might think twice about sharing that story again. Dennis allows for a partly involved presence at group time as another way of meeting individual needs. Some youngsters can't seem to sit and listen without having something to occupy their hands. Therefore, children in his program are allowed to look at books or work on puzzles at the back of the group area. Only activities that are quiet and do not disturb the group discussion are allowed. Allowing quiet activities lets children benefit from the discussions and stories who might not otherwise be able to cope with the enforced passivity. Through this flexibility, Dennis provides a transition into group time for children who need it.

In other programs teachers insist on full participation but try hard to make group time more compatible with the needs of young children. They keep the time short and respond to signals from youngsters that they have reached their limit. Frequent opportunities to move and actively participate extend the amount of time children can cope with group times. Songs and rhymes that involve full-body movement provide useful breaks. Nevertheless, fifteen minutes may be long enough for most preschoolers to be involved in group time. This time period will gradually increase as children get older, but teachers need to take their cues from the children.

Waiting Time

This chapter previously addressed the issues of waiting in line and waiting for groups to start. They are a serious waste of children's time as well as invitations to discipline problems. However, there is another kind of waiting that causes just as many problems: when children must wait their turn.

Waiting for a turn is incredibly hard on young children for several reasons. One reason is that they don't have a sense of time. Because time is an abstraction, telling a child to wait five minutes for a turn with the tricycle is meaningless. Another problem is that young children don't understand why they must wait. They can't see things from another person's viewpoint, so they don't relate to another child's claim. Colin wants the tricycle. That desire is the only reality for him. The fact that Alex also wants it is irrelevant to Colin. With help from adults, youngsters gradually learn about the needs and feelings of others. With experience and maturation, they also learn to approximate time spans. While youngsters are in the process of learning, understanding teachers help them cope.

Kenji ran into the large-muscle room. He was eager to get onto the climbing tower, his favorite place to play. Suddenly a teacher came to tell him that he must get off and wait his turn. There were already four other children on the climbing tower. Four is the limit; that's the rule.

Kenji looked confused and sad but climbed down. He gazed longingly at the children climbing and shouting. He kept asking Sheri, the adult in charge, when it would be his turn. Gradually, tears welled up in his eyes. Sheri realized that Kenji was in distress. She tried to explain to him that the other children were in the room first. Seeing that her explanations were getting nowhere, Sheri thought about other alternatives. Center rules allow youngsters to use equipment until they decide they are finished, so she couldn't even promise Kenji a certain time for his turn. She tried to distract him with suggestions about the block-building or woodworking centers. But Kenji was determined to be there to stake his claim as soon as someone got off the climbing tower.

Then Sheri remembered the sign-up sheet that helped children wait their turn to hold the new pet rabbit last week. She asked Kenji if he would like to start a sign-up sheet to use the climbing tower. He agreed to this plan and helped Sheri locate paper, tape, and a marker. Kenji wrote his name four-year-old style on the page and taped it to the wall near the climber. He seemed to feel better now that his claim to a turn was officially in writing. He said he would wait in the block center nearby. Sheri assured him she would call as soon as someone got off the climber. Without someone hovering nearby waiting for a turn, the pressure to stay on the climber eased. Soon there was a vacancy, and Sheri notified Kenji. He had been helped to cope with a hard situation. His feelings were respected even though he didn't immediately get his way. The experience helped him build understanding and trust in the waiting process.

Many teachers use sign-up sheets to ease turn taking and waiting. This approach fosters literacy development as well as social development. Of course, it works better if there aren't so many children in the group that it takes days for everyone to get a turn. When children are limited to a set amount of time for a turn, the sign-up sheet can be combined with an egg timer. Watching the timer ticking away or seeing the salt pour from one side to the other help youngsters to experience the passage of time, making it a little less abstract. Of course, these timed waits must be short in order to be humane.

Much of children's waiting involves waiting for help from an adult. Children have to wait less if there are more adults available to them. Public school classrooms generally not only have larger groups than recommended, but also have too few adults for the numbers of children. The maximum group size in kindergarten and the primary grades should be no more than fifteen to eighteen children with one teacher. If the group size is up to twenty-five, there should be two adults. Two adults are always necessary for preschool age groups, with two adults responsible for no more than twenty youngsters (Bredekamp, 1987). We see much higher levels of social development and involvement in preschools where there is an adult for every five children and the group size is limited to twenty.

Parent Helpers

Parent volunteers can make a major contribution to a smoothly running classroom. They can improve the ratio of adults to children, cutting down on the length of time children wait for adult assistance and being there to intervene when problems arise. When you involve parents in helping children learn, however, you accomplish more than a shorter waiting time for youngsters. A child whose parent spends time helping at school gets a clear message that the parent thinks school is important; therefore, the child believes school is important. Additionally, when parents spend time helping, they tend to gain a better appreciation for the school program. Their increased understanding of the teacher's

A sign-up sheet can ease the difficulty of waiting your turn.

goals and methods makes parents more supportive of the teacher's efforts. Parental attitudes of support for school programs are also communicated to children, and those attitudes about school influence child attitudes and behavior.

Kindergarten and primary-grade teachers generally ask for parent volunteers at the beginning of the school year. Many find that posting a list of specific jobs and asking parents to sign up is a good strategy. Parents whose work doesn't allow them to spend time at school may volunteer for something that can be done at home in the evening. Some preschools follow the same pattern, but cooperative preschools exhibit the ultimate in parent involvement. Cooperative preschools are run by parents who administer the budget, collect tuition, and hire the teacher. Parents take turns as teacher assistants to create appropriate adult-child ratios for their programs. Child-care programs generally exist because parents are not available during the day. However, with encouragement, parents may find it rewarding to visit during their lunchtime and even to take occasional time off to be part of their youngster's child-care day.

CONCLUSION

Prevention of discipline problems has much to do with respecting children. When you respect youngsters, you make it easier for them to meet school expectations; you involve their parents in their education; you accept their emotional needs as valid; you plan programs carefully to fit their level of development; and you use their time and energy wisely. When you do these things, you will find that children are more cooperative, hardworking, and committed to learning.

FOR FURTHER THOUGHT

1. Analyze materials in an early childhood education setting, categorizing them as concrete or representational. Some materials are more difficult to categorize than others. Discuss your classifications with peers.
2. Think about curriculum topics you are familiar with. Identify those that are inappropriate for children too young to know the difference between a day and a week, let alone between one year and one hundred years. Identify those that are inappropriate for youngsters who have no idea of the difference between a town and a country.
3. Observe early childhood teachers' use of transition activities. Practice using some games for guiding children's movement in small groups from one place to another. Learn some finger plays and rhymes and practice using them to assist children during waiting time.
4. Try some techniques described in this chapter to help youngsters wait for a turn. Analyze the successes and the failures to learn from them.
5. A problem to solve: The kindergartners were lining up to go to the library. Tony got into line and immediately began pushing Tim, who was in front of him. Next, Tony grabbed Tim's arm and then began playing with his hair.

a.   What is the probable cause of this problem?
b.   How can you best deal with it now?
c.   How can you prevent similar situations in the future?

REFERENCES AND RECOMMENDATIONS FOR READING

Books

BERGEN, D. (1988). Designing play environments for elementary-age children. In D. Bergen (Ed.), *Play as a medium for learning and development.* Portsmouth, NH: Heinemann.

BREDEKAMP, S. (1987). *Developmentally appropriate practice in early childhood programs serving children from birth through age 8, expanded edition.* Washington, DC: National Association for the Education of Young Children.

BREDEKAMP, S., & ROSEGRANT, T. (EDS.). (1992). *Reaching potentials: Appropriate curriculum and assessment for young children* (Vol. 1). Washington, DC: National Association for the Education of Young Children.

BROWN, J. F. (ED.). (1982). *Curriculum planning for young children.* Washington, DC: National Association for the Education of Young Children.

CHAILLE, C., & BRITAIN, L. (1991). *The young child as scientist: A constructivist approach to early childhood science education.* New York: HarperCollins.

DERMAN-SPARKS, L., & THE A.B.C. TASK FORCE. (1989). *Anti-bias curriculum: Tools for empowering young children.* Washington, DC: National Association for the Education of Young Children.

DEVRIES, R., & KOHLBERG, L. (1990). *Constructivist early education: Overview and comparison with other programs.* Washington, DC: National Association for the Education of Young Children.

FEENEY, S., CHRISTENSEN, D., & MORAVCIK, E. (1991). *Who am I in the lives of children?* (4th ed.). New York: Merrill/Macmillan.

FORMAN, E. G., & KUSCHNER, D. S. (1983). *The child's construction of knowledge: Piaget for teaching children.* Washington, DC: National Association for the Education of Young Children.

GOFFIN, S. G., & STEGELIN, D. A. (EDS.). (1992). *Changing kindergartens: Four success stories.* Washington, DC: National Association for the Education of Young Children.

HILL, D. M. (1977). *Mud, sand, and water.* Washington, DC: National Association for the Education of Young Children.

HYMES, J. (1990). *Teaching the child under six* (3rd ed.). West Greenwich, RI: Consortium Publishing.

JACOBS, H. H. (ED.). (1989). *Interdisciplinary curriculum: Design and implementation.* Washington, DC: Association for Supervision and Curriculum Development.

KAMII, C. (1985). *Young children reinvent arithmetic: Implications of Piaget's theory.* New York: Teacher's College Press.

KATZ, L. G., & MCCLELLAN, D. E. (1991). *The teacher's role in the social development of young children.* Urbana, IL: ERIC Clearinghouse Document, ED313168.

KATZ, L. G., & CHARD, S. C. (1989). *Engaging children's minds: The project approach.* Norwood, NJ: Ablex.

KROGH, S. (1990). *The integrated early childhood curriculum.* New York: McGraw-Hill.

NASH, C. (1979). *A principal's or administrator's guide to kindergarten.* Toronto: Ontario Institute for Studies in Education.

NEUGEBAUER, B. (ED.). (1993). *Alike and different: Exploring our humanity with young children* (Rev. ed.). Washington, DC: National Association for the Education of Young Children.

PUGMIRE-STOY, M. C. (1992). *Spontaneous play in early childhood.* Albany: Delmar.

SAWYERS, J. K., & ROGERS, C. S. (1988). *Helping young children develop through play: A practical guide for parents, caregivers, and teachers.* Washington, DC: National Association for the Education of Young Children.

SCHWARTZ, S., & ROBINSON, H. F. (1982). *Designing curriculum for early childhood.* Boston: Allyn & Bacon.

WOOD, J., & HERMAN, C. (1978). *Planning and communicating the emergent curriculum.* In E. Jones (Ed.), *Joys and risks in teaching young children* (pp. 57–106). Pasadena: Pacific Oaks College.

Periodicals

ALGER, H. A. (1984). Transitions: Alternatives to manipulative management techniques. *Young Children, 39*(6), 16–26.

BILLMAN, J. (1992). The native American curriculum: Attempting alternatives to tepees and headbands. *Young Children, 47*(6), 22–25.

BOUTTE, G. S., & McCORMICK, C. B. (1992). Authentic multicultural activities: Avoiding pseudomulticulturalism. *Childhood Education, 68*(3), 140–144.

BRADY, P. (1992). Columbus and the quincentennial myths: Another side of the story. *Young Children, 47*(6), 4–14.

CARTWRIGHT, S. (1991). Interview at a small Maine school. *Young Children, 46*(3), 7–11.

CLARK, L., DEWOLF, S., & CLARK, C. (1992). Teaching teachers to avoid having culturally assaultive classrooms. *Young Children, 47*(5), 4–9.

DAVIDSON, J. (1980). Wasted time: The ignored dilemma. *Young Children, 35*(1), 13–21.

GAREAU, M., & KENNEDY, C. (1991). Structure time and space to promote pursuit of learning in the primary grades. *Young Children, 46*(4), 46–51.

GREENBERG, P. (1987). Ideas that work with young children: Child choice—another way to individualize—another form of preventive discipline. *Young Children, 43*(1), 48–54.

GREENBERG, P. (1992a). Teaching about native Americans? Or teaching about people, including native Americans? *Young Children, 47*(6), 27–81.

GREENBERG, P. (1992b). Why not academic preschool? (Part 2) Autocracy or democracy in the classroom? *Young Children, 47*(3), 54–64.

HOFSCHIELD, K. A. (1991). The gift of a butterfly. *Young Children, 46*(3), 3–6.

KEMPLE, K. M. (1991). Research in review. Preschool children's peer acceptance and social interaction. *Young Children, 46*(5), 47–54.

KESTING, P. D. (1981). Transitions: Ways to smooth (or soothe) your busy days. *Day Care and Early Education*, Winter 1981, 15–17.

KOSTELNIK, M. J. (1986). Living with He-Man: Managing superhero fantasy play. *Young Children, 42*(4), 3–9.

KOSTELNIK, M. J. (1992). Myths associated with developmentally appropriate programs. *Young Children, 47*(4), 17–23.

WERNER, P. H., & STROTHER, J. (1987). Early readers: Important emotional considerations. *Reading Teacher, 40*(6) 538–543.

Papers

HILLS, T. W. (1987). *Hothousing young children: Implications for early childhood policy and practice.* Urbana, IL: ERIC Clearinghouse Document, ED294653.

KATZ, L. (1987). What should young children be learning? *ERIC Digest.* Urbana, IL: ERIC Clearinghouse Document, ED290554.

Developmentally Appropriate Curriculum Resources

Animal Defenses: Teacher's Guide. (1986). Great Explorations in Math and Science (GEMS). Berkeley: University of California Press.

Bookshelf, Stage 1: Teacher's Resource Book. (1986). Multimedia International (U.K.) Ltd. New York: Scholastic (distributor).

Buzzing a Hive: Teacher's Guide. (1987). Great Explorations in Math and Science (GEMS). Berkeley: University of California Press.

The Story Box, Level 1: Teacher's Guide. (1990). Bothell, WA: The Wright Group.

Chapter 6

Teaching Desirable Behavior through Example

Discipline is a teaching activity, and teaching by example is a powerfully effective method (Katz & McClellan, 1991). Teacher and parent examples are productive methods of guidance and discipline. If you doubt that children pick up the example of adults, watch them during dramatic play. Parents and teachers are often embarrassed as they see children copying parts of adult behavior they'd rather not have repeated. Let's look at how your positive examples can help children learn desirable and useful ways of behaving.

BE A ROLE MODEL

- ❏ Be kind to others
- ❏ Be honest with your feelings
- ❏ Be willing to try new things

INTERACTION STYLE

The way in which teachers and parents treat children greatly influences how children treat each other. A teacher who consistently speaks kindly and respectfully to students tends to have a classroom where children speak more kindly and respectfully to one another. On the other hand, a teacher who uses sarcasm and put-downs to keep kids under control will certainly generate more of that type of interaction among students.

Some classrooms and centers have a warm and friendly feeling as you walk into them, while others exude tension. The teacher usually sets the tone for the classroom, with children taking on the interaction style of the adult (DeVries, Zan, Reese-Learned, & Morgan, 1991). Children notice when teachers respectfully consider children's ideas and feelings. From this example they gain both attitudes and skills for getting along with other children and peacefully negotiating solutions to disagreements. Teachers who exhibit very controlling behavior are setting an example of demanding their own way without regard for others. If that attitude is the adult example, then youngsters will learn to behave in the same way.

EXPRESSING FEELINGS

How do you deal with your emotions? Do you hold them in and try to hide the fact that you are upset? Or do you find yourself "flying off the handle," yelling when things go wrong? The holding-in approach might sound like a more desirable model for kids, but it is actually worse for them—and you—in the long run. Counselors help clients learn to express their feelings because suppressed emo-

A teacher who consistently treats children kindly and respectfully will tend to encourage youngsters to treat each other the same way.

tions will surface in some form and can cause physical problems as well as further emotional problems.

Of course, throwing a tantrum to express your feelings isn't productive either. Adults who have learned to accept and work with their emotions achieve a happy medium between the extremes of too little emotional outlet and too much. They also know it is important to let off steam as it arises instead of allowing it to accumulate into a blowup. Teachers with this kind of self-knowledge can provide a beneficial model for youngsters.

> Kenji and Danny were full of spunk today at Midway Children's Center. First they poured sand into the paint cups. Sheri, the aide, helped them clean out the cups and mix new paint. But then "by accident" (full of giggles), they knocked over a block tower that Kimberly had carefully built. Sheri encouraged them to help Kimberly rebuild her structure. But as their goofiness escalated, Sheri felt like she was chasing a tornado around the center. The boys could tell they were starting to bother her and seemed to delight in seeing how far they could go.
>
> Then they went too far. It was time for Sheri to get the dramatic-play room clear for circle time. Kenji and Danny refused to leave. As they ran by the shelves, they knocked off a big basket of pretend foods. Sheri watched the plastic grapes and eggs scatter. She was supposed to have this room ready in two minutes. She could feel herself coming to the end of her rope with the boys. Then Kenji taunted Sheri to catch him if she could, and Danny said, "She's too fat to catch you!"
>
> That remark was the last straw. Sheri was very sensitive about her weight. She drew a deep breath and said, "Danny, I feel sad when you make fun of my weight." The sincerity of her voice made an impression on the boy. Kenji, too, stopped racing and looked at the aide. Her face really did look sad. Sheri realized that she was too upset about the scene to be positive with the boys, so she simply said to them, "I can't work with you anymore about clearing this room. And I am upset enough that I need to take a calming-down time for myself. I need to go outside for a few minutes. When I feel better, I will come back. This room does need to get ready for circle time. You could pick up the food you spilled while I work at feeling better."
>
> As she left, she briefly explained to her supervisor that she needed a brief calming break and asked her to keep an eye on the playroom. Understanding how important it is to know and communicate your limits, the supervisor gave Sheri a hug and covered for her for a few minutes. She overheard Danny say to Kenji as they were picking up the grapes, "Sheri is really sad."

A personal time-out like Sheri's is possible where there are several adults in charge of a group of children. Unfortunately, the option of leaving the scene is seldom available for public school teachers. If you are the only adult with a group of children, you can still stop and take a deep breath when things begin to feel overwhelming. You do not need to respond instantly to the problem. Children benefit in two ways when teachers briefly remove themselves either physically or emotionally when they become overstressed: The cooling-off period helps the teacher to deal more rationally with child behavior, and the example set by the teacher shows children a useful way of handling their own stress.

ACCEPTING FEELINGS

Many adults tend to deny children's feelings. They apparently think that little people have little feelings that can be easily erased. You have no doubt heard someone tell a child, "You don't hate your sister, so don't talk like that." A common response to children's unhappiness is "Have a cookie and don't cry." Although well-intentioned, these responses don't help children learn to deal with their feelings effectively. Instead, they may learn that their feelings are wrong and end up feeling guilty. This guilt, added to repressed feelings, is likely to result in negative behavior.

When Christie says, "I hate you!" she is expressing anger. The anger may or may not be justified from your perspective, but she does have that feeling and it needs to come out. Young children usually lack the language skills to express their feelings adequately. Your role as the teacher can be to help the child clarify feelings by modeling more appropriate words. In this case, your response might be "It sounds like you are angry with me." If you can find out what made Christie angry, you can help her find the words to say specifically what she is upset about. Perhaps she wanted to be the line leader, and you chose someone else. You can accept her feelings while helping her express them more suitably. This approach involves demonstrating expressive language for her, perhaps by saying, "I can tell you are very *disappointed* that you weren't chosen." Then you can let Christie know that it is more productive to tell you that she wanted to be the line leader than to say she hates you.

Sometimes adults try to deny children's feelings just because they so desperately want youngsters to be happy. It's not that they undervalue children's emotions, but that they worry too much about a child's sadness, loneliness, or jealousy. Therefore, they try to make those bad feelings go away as quickly as possible by submerging them in treats or diverting activities. These parents and teachers feel that they have failed a child who is experiencing an unpleasant emotion (Klein, 1975). They don't understand that important learning can result from facing those negative feelings. For instance, a child who has never faced the loneliness of being left out is less able to feel compassion for someone who is being excluded from a group.

Instead of trying to make children's bad feelings disappear, you can help children learn to accept and express their feelings by the example you set in accepting and expressing your own feelings. Male role models are especially important for little boys. The cultural stereotypes tend to make it harder for males to deal with emotions. The old idea that big boys don't cry hasn't disappeared from our society (Edwards, 1986). Many men not only feel uncomfortable expressing sadness or fear, but they also have trouble expressing positive feelings of affection and caring. For some men, the only emotion that feels masculine is anger. Therefore, these males camouflage sensations such as grief, loneliness, and jealousy, expressing them instead through anger. Conversely, some women have difficulty expressing anger, having learned to consider anger unfeminine. The inability to express honest emotions creates obvious difficulties with interpersonal relationships.

Dennis does his part to wipe out the macho stereotypes regarding feelings in his preschool. He freely expresses affection for his young students with hugs, smiles, and verbal feedback, such as "I like being with you." He demonstrates his joy in small things: a sunny day, a delicious snack, or a child's artistic creation. He

Teachers can help children learn to express their feelings appropriately through the example the teachers set.

also shows feelings of sadness when the guinea pig dies. Although Dennis doesn't cover up his feelings of frustration when something goes wrong, he is careful to show negative feelings in ways he wants children to imitate. He knows the children are likely to follow his example, whether it is positive or negative.

CARING FOR OTHERS

You may have noticed that some youngsters have sharp tongues and say cruel things to other children, while others show concern for anyone having a hard time. Much of that behavior is learned through example. Because adults are powerful role models for young children, your example has great impact. When this model is coupled with reminders about people's feelings, children quickly learn to think about the impact of their words (Edwards, 1986). In a classroom where students are being unkind to one another, the teacher needs to examine what type of role model is being presented.

Sometimes you will have students who have characteristics that make them the target of cruelty from other children. Maybe a youngster with a bed-wetting problem comes to school smelling of urine, while another wears ragged and ill-fitting clothes. Sometimes the child is like Pat, who has such damaged self-esteem that he actually seems to invite abuse from other youngsters. These children have many needs, but one of them is the teacher's example to encourage their classmates' kindness to them. These children are often hard to like and unappealing to be around; however, they are the ones who most need your acceptance and caring.

Learning to care about each other and to get along together in our diverse world are central issues in the curriculum area called social studies. Some teachers' guides seem to suggest that social studies only covers the food and music of other lands, so youngsters spend time learning trivial facts rather than developing attitudes and understandings that might promote the welfare of humanity (Clark, DeWolf, & Clark, 1992). If educators recognize that compassion and learning how to establish kindness and relationships are among the most important things anyone can learn, they will spend time in the classroom assisting the development of such social skills.

Children first need to learn these ideas at the concrete level: in their own environment and through their own experience. People and problems far away are too abstract for young children's thinking. Concepts such as compassion become understandable to children when they apply the principles in their own homes, classrooms, and communities. Starting with their families and friends, children can begin to understand and accept differences and similarities (Edwards, 1986). Later they will be able to expand this awareness to the greater world family.

Mrs. Jensen extended the study of homes to the topic of the homeless. After the children had discussed the different types of homes they live in and made a class book with a picture and a description of each child's home, Mrs. Jensen asked them to think about what it would be like to have no home. She explained to them that some children right in their own town didn't have a place to live. Nicole offered to let them live with her, and several others thought they might share their rooms at home. Mrs. Jensen was touched by their naive generosity and complimented them on their thoughtfulness. She had to explain that the homeless children had families they needed to stay with and that the families wanted their own places to live. But Mrs. Jensen had expected and prepared for a compassionate response from her students. She had contacted a local shelter for homeless families and found out what type of donations would be helpful. The first graders were then able to channel their generous impulses into useful activity. They decided to make a food donation box for their school, and it became a continuing project.

Mrs. Jensen showed her concern for the plight of the homeless as she brought up the topic for discussion, and her students were able to learn from her example. However, most of the examples she sets are more spontaneous. They are her responses to the situations that constantly arise during the course of the day, as twenty-five people attempt to live and work harmoniously together. Because Mrs. Jensen considers that learning to live harmoniously is an important issue, she doesn't hesitate to take time out from math or reading to help children learn to settle a group problem. She calls it social studies and considers it time well spent. By making time for interpersonal relations skills, she shows that she considers such skills important.

During morning gathering time, the children sat at their table spots throughout the room. Mrs. Jensen briefly reviewed the general plan for the day, and the children shared current events from life outside of school. Last night there had been a wild storm, and they were excitedly telling of the powerful things the wind had done in their neighborhoods. Having predicted that the storm would be a topic of interest today, Mrs. Jensen had brought in some books on storms. She showed them to the class and said that she would put them in the library corner. The children begged to hear one that had a fascinating cover. So she sat down and began to read, showing the pictures as she turned the pages.

    Then the trouble began. Raymond squirmed and scooted in his chair, trying to see. Abby nagged at Mina to move: "You're in my way." No matter what Mina did, Abby didn't seem to be satisfied. Jimmie kept trying to sit on his feet to see over Alan, which made Blake mad behind him. Blake reached across the table and pushed Jimmie down. Mrs. Jensen noticed the children's rising irritation. She stopped reading and said, "Some people are having trouble seeing the illustrations. What can we do?" First Blake sputtered, "Jimmie needs to get down!" Then some more constructive suggestions began to surface. Mina said, "If you stood up, we could all see." Mrs. Jensen seriously considered this option but decided, "You're right, it would help if the book were higher. But this book is pretty big, and it's hard for me to hold it up. Can anyone think of another solution?" Raymond said, "Why don't we move to the story rug and you sit up in the chair like we usually do?" "What do you think, class?" Mrs. Jensen checked. They agreed it would work for everybody and rearranged themselves on the rug. Before she began reading again, she showed the next picture, asking, "Now can everyone see?" To their affirmative she acknowledged, "You solved that problem really well!" Then she returned to the book, having demonstrated her respect for the negotiation process.

TAKING RISKS

Teachers can also be role models for risk taking. Why would a teacher want to encourage risk taking? Rest assured, we don't mean dangerous physical risks, but rather intellectual risks. Intellectual risks involve following up on an idea or hypothesis to see if it works. Intellectual risks may be related to science, math, art, music, or other areas. When people are talking about intellectual risk in the field

Intellectual risk taking is an essential part of learning and can be encouraged through adult example.

of science, they refer to it as generating and testing hypotheses. When they are talking about the arts, they refer to intellectual risk as creativity.

Risk taking is an essential part of the learning process and therefore a highly desirable behavior. Unless people are willing to think about concepts and test out their ideas, they are only able to memorize what other people say is true. Such rote learning is a very limited and limiting aspect of education. People who only learn this way will never add to the knowledge of the world. Throughout history, the great scientists, mathematicians, composers, artists, and others who have made major contributions to civilization have been those who questioned the status quo.

Some people might argue that children who don't think for themselves are easier to manage. They might even suggest that encouraging risk taking will increase discipline problems. After all, a child who debates the fairness of adult-imposed rules and consequences can be a real pain. But you can also consider such debates a challenge with valuable teaching potential. How you feel about this idea relates back to chapter 1 and decisions about your goals for children. Because we, the authors of this book, are committed to the goals of intellectual and moral autonomy, we definitely want to encourage children to think for themselves.

We believe you will find that teaching for autonomy rather than conformity makes guidance and discipline easier, not harder. As you help children learn to make their own responsible decisions, you are released from having to make and enforce all the rules. Additionally, children who are challenged intellectually to think for themselves tend to get excited about learning. As they explore their hypotheses, they become self-directed and self-motivated learners, which also makes the job of classroom management easier. The teacher is released from the job of police officer and freed for the role of guide and facilitator of learning.

How does the teacher demonstrate risk taking? The first step is to work on fear of failure or mistakes. This fear is a serious block to trying new ideas of any type. Mrs. Jensen starts by calling attention to all the mistakes she makes herself. She freely shares her failures, such as a fall on her new mountain bike. She doesn't belittle herself for natural human failings, but rather demonstrates acceptance of them. If she misplaces a book or some needed supplies, she might say, "I got so interested in Brianna's block creation that I didn't pay attention to where I put the book for story time today. Can you help me look for it?" Then she might use the situation to encourage children to disclose times when they, too, forgot where they put something. Her acceptance of their forgetfulness as well as her own provides an example for them to learn similar acceptance. It is also important for teachers to model taking risks as part of their own learning experience.

Russian visitors were coming to Lincoln Elementary School. One of the school aides spoke some Russian, so Mrs. Jensen invited him to her classroom to teach some basic greetings. Never having heard the language before, Mrs. Jensen was right with the children at a beginner's level. First the aide told them how to say, "My name is. . . ." "Menya zavoot," he said. Mrs. Jensen tried, "Menizoot." He repeated, "Menya zavoot." She struggled, smiling, "Menyesavoot?" The children giggled with her as she tried again. She admitted, "This is a little hard for me," and she invited the children to try with her: "Can you help?" Their keen young ears quickly picked up the nuances of sound, and within a few minutes everyone was saying, "Menya zavoot Abby. Menya zavoot Jimmie." Eventually even Mrs. Jensen mastered it!

Mrs. Jensen believes that risk taking is especially related to children's progress in writing. Emergent literacy research indicates that children learn about letters and their sounds best when they work on their own hypotheses about writing and spelling (Kamii, Manning, & Manning, 1991). Therefore, Mrs. Jensen encourages children to try out their ideas through "kid writing" or invented spelling. This approach involves risk taking. Some children charge into kid writing with gusto, while others are too afraid of making a letter wrong or spelling a word wrong. Some are risk takers and some are not.

The fearless ones produce pages and pages of scribbles; they also include some words they have memorized, such as their own name and *Mom, Dad*, and *I love you*. They proudly tell everyone about what they have written. Soon these youngsters are making good progress on their sound-symbol hypotheses, trying out different ideas about which letter makes which sound (Fields, Spangler, & Lee, 1991). Those children who are afraid of failure are hampered in their learning.

Ideas about perfection in one area, such as writing, can carry over to other topics and get in the way of other learning, too. Some children feel incapable of artistic creativity, always wanting someone to show them the "right" way to approach an open-ended project. Others will read the same book over and over, not just because they enjoy the book, but because they know all the words and it is safe. These children desperately need the teacher to model acceptance of imperfection and the courage to venture into the unknown. They need help becoming more comfortable with learning through their mistakes. They need such help in order to become effective learners and self-directed students.

TAKING RESPONSIBILITY

Adults tend to lecture a lot about being responsible. Picking up after yourself, taking care of materials, finishing what you start, and doing work on time are common themes. A much better way to teach children these important ideas is by modeling them yourself.

Cleanup time is a good place to start. You read about Dennis's power struggle over this issue, and you may know that cleaning up frequently causes conflict. It is often a problem at home as well as at school. Many young children are simply overwhelmed by the mess; they don't know where to start and think it will never end. Adults who tell kids to clean up are assuming that the children know how to do it. That is not a logical assumption. Young children need to be taught how to pick up a mess; the best way for them to learn is for you to show them what you mean by cleaning up. In other words, you work with them. Seeing you help with cleanup also gives children a clear message that the teacher thinks cleaning up is worth doing. You are an effective model.

The best way to help children learn how to clean up a mess is by helping them and showing them how.

The block area was strewn with a jumble of blocks and littered with the small cars and trucks that had been driving on the block roads. Nancy, Dennis's assistant teacher, saw Kelsey and Danny standing in the midst of this mess looking hopeless. Nancy went over to the children and offered to help. She started picking up blocks, handing the long rectangular ones to Kelsey to put on the shelf and giving the small square ones to Danny to put away. Nancy made sure the youngsters were able to match the blocks with the outlines painted on the shelves showing what kind of block goes where. She called their attention to the different sizes and shapes as they worked together. Soon she positioned herself by the shelf and asked the youngsters to hand her all the triangle-shaped blocks. Next the children got to choose which shape to work on, and before long the job was complete. Kelsey and Danny felt good about their hard work, and they gained skill in organizing the cleanup of the block area. Eventually they will be able to do it themselves with only a few verbal clues. Having Nancy work with them helped them to value the work they were doing.

Meanwhile, Dennis was working with children washing out paintbrushes. As they worked, he talked about the importance of using cold water so as not to loosen the glue holding the brush in the handle. He also encouraged his fellow brush cleaners to experiment with ways that most quickly get the paint out. While Dennis and Nancy helped with blocks and paint cleanup, Sheri, the aide, circulated among other cleanup tasks. She stopped to help get the doll babies comfortable in their bed instead of on the floor in the playhouse. Then she complimented Shantae and Andrea on how orderly the kitchen cupboard looked before moving on to help Megan and Alex at the manipulatives table.

Following through with a plan or a promise is another important area of responsibility. Like cleanup, it, too, contributes to a smoothly running classroom. Mrs. Jensen teaches this behavior effectively through modeling. She starts each day with a discussion of the day's schedule, written on the board while the children watch and learn about writing as well as planning. They get practice in reading as they refer back to the schedule during the day. Mrs. Jensen treats the daily plan like a contract, or promise of what the day will bring. If weather causes the cancellation of a nature walk that the children are looking forward to, she discusses the change and plans with them to do it another day soon. She makes sure to follow through with this plan, never deciding that the children will soon forget. She models consistent follow-through.

Children in Mrs. Jensen's class can count on this same follow-through on an individual level as well. If their teacher is too busy when they want to talk to her, they know she will soon get back to them.

Mrs. Jensen was deep in discussion with Ling Ling about the story she was reading when Raymond came up and tapped his teacher on the shoulder. A tap on the shoulder is an approved signal for a child to communicate the need for teacher attention when she is in conference with another student. Mrs. Jensen smiled at Raymond and made a signal with her fingers indicating she would be with him in a short while. To make sure that she didn't forget, Mrs. Jensen wrote Raymond's name on a note to herself. Raymond went back to his seat, secure in the knowledge that his teacher would soon be with him. As soon as she was finished with Ling Ling, Mrs. Jensen went over to see what Raymond wanted. Raymond and his classmates have begun writing reminder notes to themselves in imitation of their teacher.

Sometimes Mrs. Jensen's list of requests for attention gets too long, and she knows she can't reach so many children in a timely manner. Rather than keeping them waiting, she makes appointments with them for later on. They can still count on her, even if not immediately. Of course, if children have an urgent need, they communicate it; and Mrs. Jensen helps them find whatever assistance is required. As part of encouraging their autonomy, Mrs. Jensen has shown her students how to use a variety of resources effectively rather than always relying on the teacher. Therefore, these children are quite capable of helping each other when their teacher is working with an individual child.

Things go smoothly without the teacher's constant attention due, in part, to the time Mrs. Jensen has spent in helping children learn how to use materials in a responsible way. Her students have learned these lessons well because their teacher doesn't just lecture about proper use. You guessed it: She shows them how instead.

Mrs. Jensen spends time working with children in each learning center as a way of helping them learn independent use of materials. Independent use is much different from single use. It is not a way to limit how children use things, but rather to provide guidelines for their creative expression. Mrs. Jensen finds that her students soon take over the modeling job and begin to show one another important points. Desmond learned well that a tile is needed under the plastic clay to protect table tops. He then took the responsibility of reminding Eric when Eric forgot. Mrs. Jensen also follows the class guidelines when she uses any material. She knows that to do otherwise would undermine her efforts.

SHOW, DON'T TELL

Instead of *telling* kids to do something, show them how to:

❏ Clean up

❏ Keep promises

❏ Be safe

KEEPING SAFE

"Do as I say and not as I do" won't work in teaching safety behavior, either. All the teachers at Midway Children's Center remind each other to carry scissors with points down to keep their example consistent with their words to children. They are also careful not to walk too close to a child on a swing, and they model safe street crossing when taking walks with children. When using a car or van for a field trip, teachers as well as children wear seat belts.

Mrs. Jensen makes sure she always pushes in her desk chair when she's not using it. Pushing in chairs is an important safety rule in her school. This rule is primarily to keep passageways clear for fire drills, but it also saves a lot of tripping over chairs on a daily basis. Mrs. Jensen helps her students internalize this safety rule by her example.

> Maureen, an aide, became convinced of the impact of adult models while watching preschoolers in dramatic play one day. Several youngsters were engrossed in a make-believe trip on the boat in the play yard. Megan ran to get some life jackets that had been donated as props. She offered them to Jimmie and Tory, who scorned them, saying, "We're the dads! We don't wear those." These children had obviously noticed during family boat outings that the children had to wear life jackets but that their fathers did not wear them.

EFFECTIVE ROLE MODELS

Role models are most effective when they are people whom children look up to. Young children look up to their teachers and their parents. In fact, they tend to consider all adults powerful and infallible creatures. This belief puts a large responsibility on you as an adult who works with young children. Seize the opportunity! As children get older, they look less to adults for their models and turn more to peers they admire.

The ability to identify with the model is important to all ages. Children are more likely to copy people who are similar to them in some way. Older children often look to others of the same age for models, and models of the same gender are important for this reason, too. Therefore, we want to be sure there are male teachers as well as female teachers for young children. Children whose first language differs from their teacher's or whose skin is a different color are less able to benefit from the model of their teacher. This tendency is one reason why it is important to recruit teachers and aides from minority groups.

Children also look up to and identify with sports stars and television characters. They pick up whole behavior patterns by emulating these models. Imitations of various superheroes demonstrate that children will even emulate the behaviors of cartoon characters. Children may decide that pizza is their favorite food because Ninja Turtles only eat pizza. Of greater concern is the likelihood that they will copy the violent behavior they have observed. It is the responsibility of adults who work with children to help them think about and analyze the positive

Children learn safe and responsible use of materials when the teacher spends time working with them in learning centers.

and negative models they are sure to encounter both in real life and on television. Youngsters will learn negative behavior patterns from models as easily as they learn positive ones. It is the responsibility of teachers and parents to ensure that the negative doesn't overwhelm the positive.

CONCLUSION

Your positive examples will result in more positive child behaviors. Your models of respect and fairness toward children will be emulated in how children treat one another. How you deal with your own feelings and those of others will impact how children handle their feelings. Your demonstrations of caring and kindness will make lasting impressions on young people. Your willingness to take risks in learning new skills and trying out new ideas will help youngsters more bravely try out their emerging skills and ideas. When you set an example of being responsible and of following good safety habits, children are more apt to pay attention than when you lecture about those issues. As an adult you have a powerful influence on young children. You are teaching by everything you do.

FOR FURTHER THOUGHT

1.   Observe young children and the adults with whom they spend their days. Note the ways in which the children imitate the examples set by adults.
2.   Analyze your own expression of feelings. Are you able to express fear or loneliness? Do you have a tendency to cover up other negative feelings with expressions of anger? How do you express your anger? Do you need to work on your own ability to express your feelings effectively in order to set an example for children?
3.   Notice how adults respond when children get hurt or are upset. Do they deny children's negative feelings or accept them? Do they try to distract children from physical or emotional pain? What is your own common response? Do you need to work at learning new ways to respond to a child's pain?
4.   Observe ways in which teachers encourage or discourage children in thinking for themselves. Do you see any relationship between a teacher's own intellectual autonomy and that teacher's encouragement of children's intellectual autonomy? How would you rate yourself for intellectual autonomy?
5.   Observe the difference in classrooms where teachers merely tell children to clean up and those where teachers work with youngsters, showing them useful cleanup approaches.

REFERENCES AND RECOMMENDATIONS FOR READING
Books

BANDURA, A. (1969). *Social learning theory*. Englewood Cliffs, NJ: Prentice-Hall.
CURWIN, R. L., & MENDLER, A. N. (1990). *Am I in trouble? Using discipline to teach young children responsibility*. Santa Cruz, CA: Network Publications.

DeVries, R., & Kohlberg, L. (1987). *Constructivist early education: Overview and comparison with other programs.* Washington, DC: National Association for the Education of Young Children.

Edwards, C. P. (1986). *Promoting social and moral development in young children: Creative approaches for the classroom.* New York: Teacher's College Press.

Fields, M., Spangler, K. L., & Lee, D. M. (1991). *Let's begin reading right: Developmentally appropriate beginning literacy.* New York: Merrill/Macmillan.

Ginott, H. G. (1965). *Between parent and child.* New York: Avon.

Kamii, C., Manning, M., & Manning, G. (Eds.). (1991). *Early literacy: A constructivist foundation for whole language.* Washington, DC: National Education Association of the United States.

Katz, L. G., & McClellan, D. E. (1991). *The teacher's role in the social development of young children.* Urbana, IL: ERIC Clearinghouse Document, ED313168.

Klein, C. (1975). *The myth of the happy child.* New York: Harper & Row.

Maccoby, E. E., & Martin, J. A. (1983). Socialization in the context of the family: Parent-child interaction. In P. Mussen (Ed.), *Handbook of child psychology* (Vol. 4). New York: Wiley.

Riley, S. S. (1984). *How to generate values in young children.* Washington, DC: National Association for the Education of Young Children.

Rubin, Z. (1983). The skills of friendship. In M. Donaldson, R. Grieve, & C. Pratt (Eds.), *Early childhood development and education.* New York: Guilford Press.

Stone, J. G. (1978). *A guide to discipline.* Washington, DC: National Association for the Education of Young Children.

Periodicals

Caldwell, B. M., & Crary, D. (1981, February). Why are kids so darned aggressive? *Parents*, pp. 52–56.

Clark, L., DeWolf, S., & Clark, C. (1992). Teaching teachers to avoid having culturally assaultive classrooms. *Young Children, 47*(5), 4–9.

DeVries, R., Zan, B., Reese-Learned, H., & Morgan, P. (1991). Sociomoral atmosphere and sociomoral development: A study of interpersonal understanding in three kindergarten classrooms. *Moral Education Forum, 16*(2) 5–20.

Dodge, K. A. (1983). Behavioral antecedents of peer social status. *Child Development, 54*, 1386–1399.

Fakouri, M. E. (1984). Television and the young viewer. *Contemporary Education, 55*(4), 216–219.

Hart, C. H., Ladd, G. W., & Burleson, B. R. (1990). Children's expectations of the outcomes of social strategies: Relations with sociometric status and maternal disciplinary styles. *Child Development, 61*, 127–137.

Ladd, G. W. (1983). Social networks of popular, average, and rejected children in school settings. *Merrill-Palmer Quarterly, 29*, 283–308.

Pellegrini, A. D., & Glickman, C. D. (1990). Measuring kindergartners' social competence. *Young Children, 45*(4), 40–44.

Rabiner, D., & Cole, J. (1989). Effect of expectancy inductions on rejected children's acceptance by unfamiliar peers. *Developmental Psychology, 25*(3) 450–457.

Papers

Gartrell, D. (1988). *Developmentally appropriate guidance of young children.* St. Paul: Minnesota Association for the Education of Young Children.

Chapter 7

Effective Discipline through Effective Communication

"Get to work, young man."
"Stop acting like a baby."
"You're such a good little girl."
"No recess unless that paper is finished."
"You are being rude."
"Everything will be fine; just wait and see."
"Your picture is beautiful."
"You're okay. There's no reason to cry."
"You need to improve your attitude."

Do any of these statements sound familiar? Perhaps you heard them from your parents and teachers as you grew up. Perhaps you have said them to children yourself. You may be surprised to hear that these statements have a negative impact on behavior (Gordon, 1989). The last chapter discussed these types of responses in terms of negating children's feelings. Now let's look at how they build barriers to communication in addition to teaching children that their feelings aren't okay. Thomas Gordon, in his discipline classic *Parent Effectiveness Training*, calls them "roadblocks to communication" (1970).

Many parents and teachers grew up with these counterproductive ways of communicating, which are second nature to them. These adults automatically resort to the ways of talking to children that they have heard in the past. Knowledge about effective communication can drastically alter relationships between people of all ages. Some people use the information to improve marriages, friendships, or working relationships (Gordon, 1989). Parents and teachers can apply the information to effective communication with children. Effective communication is an essential part of effective discipline.

WHY CHILDREN DON'T LISTEN

Adults frequently complain that children don't listen to them, and they often have no idea why. Few adults ever consider that it might be their own fault. Think about the following situations:

> You have just warned Kenji to be careful of that puddle, and now he's splashing right into the middle of it.
> You have given those directions three times, and still individual children are coming up to you and asking how to do it.
> You hear yourself saying, "How many times have I told you not to do that?!"

These incidents may be symptoms of ineffective ways of talking to children. Of course, we can't guarantee that Kenji will stay out of the puddle no matter *what* you say, but you can improve your success rate. How you talk to kids makes a big difference in how they listen to you.

Criticizing and Lecturing

It isn't too surprising that people don't listen to what is unpleasant to hear. It seems like a natural self-protective device to tune out what is unpleasant. Yet many teachers and parents express dismay when children don't listen to their persistent nagging. The adults consider frequent reminders and corrections as forms of teaching. Certainly, teaching is the intent, but the teaching approach obviously is not effective when it is so widely ignored.

No matter what their age, people rarely like to hear someone tell them how badly they have behaved. Similarly, no one wants to be called derogatory names such as *selfish* or *tattletale*. Most people also get irritated at being told how they should be acting. Well-intentioned comments about why someone thinks you are acting badly are perhaps the most infuriating of all. Remember, kids are people too; and if you want them to listen to you, you want to avoid talking to them in ways that turn off listening.

Think about how you would feel in the following situation:

> You were late for work and feeling awful about it. It was a terrible morning: Everything that could go wrong did go wrong. Your alarm didn't go off, the clothes you had washed and put into the dryer last night to wear today didn't get dry, and the bus pulled away just as you got to the bus stop.
>
> You finally arrived at work, frustrated, hungry, and disheveled. Your supervisor pointed out that you were late once last month, too, and said that you have been inconsiderate. She went on to tell you how disappointed she was in your thoughtlessness and suggested that you might have a problem dealing with authority and rules. She finished by lecturing you on the importance of being on time.

Would this supervisor's approach make you open to her instruction? Would you pay close attention to what she says and want to learn more from her? How would it affect your feelings about her in general? How would your attitude about work that day be affected? Most people would get very angry, tune out the supervisor, and have an even worse day as a result. Yet many teachers regularly talk to students in this way and expect improved behavior to result. Gordon (1970) calls this behavior "sending 'put-down' messages." It is fortunate that kids often tune such messages out because they are so harmful to self-esteem.

Giving Orders

It is fairly easy to recognize the unpleasantness of hearing about your errors. However, you may not have thought about why kids (and adults) also dislike constantly being told what to do and how to do it. These instructions communicate disrespect for the other person's ideas and abilities. When you tell people everything they need to do in a situation, you also tell them that you don't think they are capable of figuring it out for themselves. Gordon calls this communication approach "solution messages" (1970). When you communicate this kind of disrespect, you don't get much cooperation in return. You are more likely to generate resistance to your directions instead. Of greater concern are the long-term effects on the child. Such disrespect not only damages self-esteem, but it also short-circuits growth toward autonomy. When you solve problems for them, children learn not to trust their own solutions. You are creating unhealthy dependency.

> Ariel couldn't get the glue to come out. She turned the dispenser's end, chewed on it, and squeezed as hard as she could. Finally she just took off the lid and tried to pour glue onto her collage. When it didn't immediately come out, she shook the container—glop! As Ariel considered the best way to approach the puddle of glue, Miss Wheeler stepped in and ordered, "Get a sponge!" Ariel frowned. She would have scooped up most of the glue with a scrap of mat board first. Then she would have gotten a sponge to finish the job. Why didn't Miss Wheeler ever let her decide how to do things, Ariel wondered.

Both Thomas Gordon and Haim Ginott, who wrote another child-guidance classic, *Between Parent and Child* (1965), discuss how differently adults talk to children than to other adults. They point out that few teachers or parents would talk to a friend or acquaintance in the bossy, rude ways that many speak to children. It tends to sound ridiculous if you think of talking to an adult in the disrespectful terms often used toward youngsters. If Ariel had been an adult, would the teacher have spoken to her that way? More likely, Miss Wheeler would have said, "You may use my table sponge if you'd like."

Inability to Express Feelings

Speaking to children with respect, as you would with adults, can be a helpful guide. But many people don't know the best ways to express themselves to people of any age. You may be one of those people who doesn't say anything when someone offends or upsets you because you don't want to be rude or unpleasant. On the other hand, you may be bold about speaking up to defend yourself. Too often, it is hard to defend yourself without expressions of anger, which generate anger in response.

If you say nothing when someone hurts or frustrates you, your resentment builds. Your nonverbal communication will be negative, indicating your true feelings. The relationship will be damaged by the unexpressed feelings and the unresolved conflicts. This is not an honest way of relating. Children with parents and teachers who provide this model of behavior do not have productive examples to follow.

If you find yourself speaking in anger frequently, you may also be covering your true feelings. Anger is often a secondary emotion. It results from a primary emotion such as fear, hurt, or embarrassment. Expressions of anger focus on what

Few teachers or parents would talk to other adults in the disrespectful ways often used toward youngsters.

the other person did, without acknowledging your own feelings. Some teachers and parents feel that revealing their own fear or hurt is not compatible with their authority role. They may think that the expression of true feelings demonstrates weakness and that their job is to demonstrate power. Like holding in unpleasant feelings, expressing them as anger also damages relationships. It is dishonest and therefore a poor role model as well.

The idea that an adult cannot demonstrate fear, sadness, or other feelings associated with vulnerability is linked to the power-based authoritarian discipline style with its repercussions of negative behaviors and negative self-esteem. The invincible adult role is counterproductive to long-term discipline goals in other ways as well. We have already discussed in the previous chapter how children's ability to express their emotions in a healthy way are impacted by their adult role models. Additionally, the invulnerable adult model gets in the way of authentic relationships with children because the adults cannot reveal their true selves. Authentic relationships between adults and children, like those between peers, encourage cooperation and empathy. These traits are clearly linked to more desirable behavior.

TALKING TO CHILDREN RESPECTFULLY

It is important to communicate your personal needs and limits. Doing so effectively means you state your feelings without labeling the child as bad and without ordering the child to change. In this way you balance expression of self-respect with that of respect for others. Gordon (1989) calls this simple statement of your own feelings an "I message." In contrast with "you messages," "I messages" do not blame or condemn another person and they contain no put-downs. "I messages" also don't tell someone else what to do, thus avoiding a "solution message." They focus on your needs instead of on the other person's actions. Therefore, people are more willing to listen to this type of communication; it generates little argument or defensiveness.

A complete "I message" has three components according to Gordon's book *P.E.T. in Action* (1976):

1.   It is specific about what the unacceptable behavior is.

2.   It states your feeling.

3.   It explains why it makes you feel that way.

We might add another component: 4. It stops after saying those three things. Too many people start out with a good "I message" and then ruin it by telling the child what he or she should be doing differently. Then the child hears the instructions for improvement and tends to react negatively. The communication has turned into another roadblock message.

It is more effective and respectful to communicate a request for help with your problem and then to back off and allow the child to make things right. The following examples show proper use of "I messages."

While Mrs. Jensen was reading a story to the group, Abby was talking to her friend quite loudly. Mrs. Jensen looked at Abby and said, "I can't read with so much noise in the room. It gives me a sore throat to try to talk loudly enough for people to hear me." Abby had a reason for keeping her voice down and willingly complied.

Dennis was bending over to help Andrea with her boots when Sam came up behind, threw his arms tightly around Dennis's neck, and hung on his teacher's back. Dennis nearly fell over backward but understood that Sam was expressing affection and meant no harm. As calmly as possible, Dennis told the affectionate child, "I'm afraid I'm going to fall over with you on my back, Sam, and I can't help Andrea with her boots this way." Sam hopped off, and Dennis gave him some attention as soon as Andrea had her boots on.

Mica was spilling paint on the carpet as she exuberantly worked on the class mural. Mrs. Jensen walked over to where Mica was working and told her, "I am worried that this paint won't come out of our rug, especially after it dries." Mica got a sponge for cleanup and then put down papers to catch the drips.

The children in these examples were free to think about their teachers' concerns instead of defending themselves against accusations of wrongdoing. The children were also free to think about how they could make things right again. Did you notice that Mrs. Jensen didn't tell Mica what she needed to do about the problem, but instead respected the child to come up with a solution? This approach helped Mica feel good about herself and increased the likelihood of future desirable behavior. If Mrs. Jensen had tacked on a solution message, it would have taken away from the effectiveness of the communication. Instead, Mrs. Jensen indicated belief in the child's ability and desire to figure out a solution.

Sometimes people get confused about what an "I message" is. They think that it is any statement that starts with "I feel. . . . " Remember, an "I message" is the expression of your own perspective; it doesn't aim the blame at someone else. Be careful or you might actually send a "you message," fooling yourself into believing that it is an "I message" (Gordon, 1970). For example, Mrs. Jensen might have told Mica, "I feel irritated when you are being such a messy painter." Her "I feel irritated" would then have only been a preface for an insult.

The real key to "I messages" has little to do with using the word *I*. Instead of saying, "I feel hurt when you kick me," it would be much more natural to say, "Ouch, that hurts!" The message is the same: It isn't calling the youngster bad for kicking; it is just expressing your perspective about being kicked.

According to Richard Curwin and Allen Mendler (1990), "I messages" are effective for the following four reasons:

1.   They say how you feel about what a child is or isn't doing.

2.   They give a reason why the behavior is a problem.

3.   They never criticize or blame the child.

4.   They invite the child to solve the problem.

It takes practice to get good at "I messages," but eventually you can retrain yourself so that it comes more naturally to express your own perspective instead of judging someone else's behavior. You will find that the results are worth the effort. People of all ages will respond much more positively to what you say.

DEVELOPING POSITIVE "I MESSAGES"

Can you think of positive "I message" alternatives instead of the "you messages" used in the following examples?

1. A child forgets for the fourth day in a row to return a library book you checked out to him. You are being pressured by the librarian to get the books back on time. You say to the child, "You are very forgetful!"

2. A co-teacher is clearing a counter for a project and doesn't notice that five children behind her have their hands raised. You are overwhelmed by trying to meet their demands for attention alone and say to the co-teacher, "You should be more attentive to the children!"

3. A parent brings in a child late, as is her habit. It disrupts your morning gathering time. Besides, this boy really needs help with the daily separation from his mother. You wish she would bring him either earlier or later so that you could be available for him. You say to the mother, "You really need to be on time."

BEING A GOOD LISTENER

Maybe one of the reasons children don't listen to adults is that adults often don't really listen to children. Too often teachers and parents respond to children's problems by brushing them off. The reasons for this attitude, as discussed in the previous chapter, may be varied. Sometimes adults believe that children's concerns are trivial, or they worry too much about children's being upset. Sometimes an adult is unable to deal with real feelings. It is also possible to be so busy that you don't realize you are not truly listening. You may even think you are paying attention to a child and still be saying something that proves otherwise.

Not Listening

Many common, well-intentioned ways of responding to what a child says amount to quick brush-offs. Trying to distract a youngster from feeling sad is one way of not really listening. Diversions may be something like the old cookie rou-

Maybe one of the reasons children don't listen to adults is that adults often don't really listen to children.

tine or the words that say, "Let's think about something nice instead." Quick reassurances that everything will be fine also communicate that you are not interested in hearing the child's concerns. Even trying to solve the child's stated problem with advice is a way of not listening. Think about how you feel when someone does those things to you.

> Maureen has a friend, Jane, who is quick to give out advice. Maureen really hates it when she is upset about something, then confides to Jane, and gets an instant solution. The advice is always shallow and nonproductive anyway, because Jane hasn't had time to think through the problem. Naturally, Maureen has thought of all those obvious and easy solutions and already come to the conclusion that they won't work; otherwise, she wouldn't still have the problem. Because Jane doesn't know all the complexities of the situation, her thoughts are mostly irrelevant. What Maureen really wants is someone who hears and understands how upset she is. Instead, Jane's response shows that she isn't hearing the seriousness of the problem; her offer of an easy answer says clearly to Maureen, "Your problem isn't any big deal. If I were in your place, I could solve it in a minute. You aren't handling things very well."

Talking Instead of Listening

Sometimes adults are so busy telling kids what *they* think that they don't hear what a child is saying. When children bring up a problem, many teachers and parents think it is their job to tell youngsters what to do. Some talk to kids about what they "should" do from a moral standpoint, while others tend to dish out facts, trying to influence young people with logic. Still others just give orders and expect compliance. None of these approaches hears out the child or respects the child's ability to figure out answers to problems. You can surely remember how you felt when you got these kinds of lectures yourself. They didn't make you feel like listening!

Passing judgment on a person confiding in you is another sure way to stop further communication. You have heard responses like "It's your own fault" or "You're not making any sense." You may have even heard worse. One of the worst things anyone can say to a young child striving hard to be grown up is "You're being a baby." Such name-calling is just one way of shaming children and making them feel worthless. Some teachers unfortunately use ridicule and other forms of humiliation to keep youngsters from challenging authority.

Have you ever thought about praise as another way of passing judgment? In this case, you have judged that things are good, but the implication is clear that you will continue to judge and next time may come up with negative findings. This message is also counterproductive to the communication process. Gordon (1970) includes praise along with reassuring, diverting, and probing in his list of roadblocks to communication. These methods are attempts to help the child feel better; but like the rest of Gordon's "twelve roadblocks to communication," they are nonlistening responses.

Adults can teach good listening by being good listeners. Adults can also learn a lot by listening to kids and finding out what they are thinking. In addition, you can build productive relationships with children by showing that you care enough about them to genuinely listen. When you have a good relationship with children, they try harder to cooperate with you. Good listening can reap many rewards.

Passive Listening

One way to show you are listening is to stop talking yourself. Some people just can't seem to be quiet long enough to hear what anyone else is saying. Quiet attention to a child's words with only minimal comments, such as "Is that so?" or "How interesting," can be very effective. Sometimes more is required, such as "What do you think about that?" or "Would you like to talk about it?" These responses indicate acceptance and respect for the child's opinion. They are basically passive listening approaches.

Reflective Listening

Thomas Gordon (1989) suggests that active listening is even more productive than passive listening. He uses the term *active listening* to describe an approach common among counselors and therapists. It is designed to ensure the accuracy of communication by reflecting back to the speaker what the listener has heard. We prefer the term *reflective listening* as being more descriptive of the process. When you practice reflective listening, you will discover how often misunderstandings occur. The different experiences and perspectives of the people involved can give totally different meanings to the same set of words. Reflective listening involves the speaker and the listener in a mutual effort to ensure accurate communication. When you give this kind of effort to understanding a child, you show the child you care.

> Most of the children finished up their projects and eagerly went down the hall to music class. They were learning a medley from the movie *The Little Mermaid* to sing at an all-school assembly. Mrs. Jensen noticed Shelley dawdling in the manipulatives area. Shelley was a great singer and usually couldn't wait for music time. The teacher was surprised when Shelley announced, "I'm not going to music today." Mrs. Jensen responded, "You don't want to go to music class." Shelley continued, "They're singing those dumb *Little Mermaid* songs." This was a second surprise! Shelley had a mermaid doll and mermaid stickers; and if the teacher's memory served her, Mrs. Jensen swore she'd heard her humming tunes from that soundtrack. She recovered from her shock and replied, "You don't like singing

Reflective listening assists understanding and shows caring.

those songs." Shelley threw out another piece of the puzzle, "We're acting them out at that stupid assembly." Mrs. Jensen then said, "You think that acting the songs out is silly." Finally the real problem surfaced: "She wants me to be the mermaid for the 'kiss the girl' song, and everybody laughs at me when Alan blows kisses at me!" The teacher said empathetically, "That embarrasses you." "Yeah," sighed Shelley. Mrs. Jensen pondered, wondering if she should offer to talk to the music teacher with Shelley to help her get out of the uncomfortable scene. But Shelley was thinking, too, and she came up with another solution: "In the movie it's not a boy who sings that song; it's a shrimp! Alan needs a shrimp costume." That idea sounded like a very possible solution. They decided to talk to Alan after music class about what kind of costume he'd like. Shelley asked how much time was left in music class. When the teacher replied, "Ten minutes," Shelley said, "Bye!" and scooted down the hall to sing.

There are other important benefits to reflective listening. By encouraging children to talk about a problem or concern, you also encourage them to think about it. Because you are just listening and not giving solutions or advice, the children are free to figure out their own solutions. Chances are good that their solutions are similar to yours, but they are more likely to implement them because they are their own. Chances are also good that their solutions are more in tune with the children's perspective.

Cautions about Reflective Listening

When you practice reflective listening, watch yourself for some common pitfalls. Most people find it very hard to avoid trying to solve the problem. Sometimes this tendency is shown by inappropriate probing questions, such as "Why do you think that happened?" or "When do you feel this way?" At other times, the urge to solve the problem is less subtle, and you end up giving suggestions for making things better.

Reflective listening is appropriate when the problem belongs to the child; you use "I messages" for your own problems. When the problem belongs to the child, the best solution is the child's own. If you decide how the problem should be solved, then you communicate lack of respect for the child's problem-solving ability. You get in the way of children's learning when you try to solve their problems for them. The experience of personally resolving a problem teaches children how to do it and empowers them in the future. Besides, kids generally don't use adult solutions. If they do use an adult's solution, it only creates dependency.

You may initially feel awkward when trying to find the right words for reflective listening. This type of listening involves telling the speaker what you heard him or her say, but it should be your own interpretation rather than mere parroting of the same words. When you provide your interpretation, you are asking for confirmation that you did understand the speaker's intent. The process of clarifying the message encourages the speaker to continue and to delve more deeply into the subject. By clarifying the idea for the listener, the speaker tends to clarify his or her own thinking. An additional caution: You also need to be careful about how you word your reflected message. If your response is worded in such a way that it requires a yes or no answer, you may inadvertently short-circuit the conversation. The intent is to encourage a sharing of ideas through an in-depth conversation.

The reflective-listening process may sound contrived to you at first, and you may feel like a phony paraphrasing back to someone what he or she just said to you. If you are honestly trying to understand what the other person is saying, however, your sincerity will come through. Keep focused on the other person's feelings and on accurate communication; then you will not only feel more comfortable with reflective listening, but you will also be a more effective listener.

Very young children can't easily tell us what is bothering them. Their vocabulary generally doesn't have precise words for feelings. In addition, they often lack a clear idea of what is bothering them. Reflective listening with very young children requires you to tune in to the children carefully and pay close attention to their nonverbal communication. With children you know, you can usually get clues from their behavior about what is bothering them. You can follow up these clues by checking out your impressions with the child: Respond to the message that the child's behavior or appearance sends to you. The process is the same as reflecting back what you hear being said with words. Just as with oral communication, you may not receive the message accurately. When you verbalize your hypothesis about her feelings, the child may shake her head, "No." That reaction means you need to try other ideas until you get an affirmative response.

> Corrie grabbed the handlebar of Joshua's tricycle, yanking him sideways. Joshua tried to shove him away and screamed for the teacher. When Nancy arrived, 2 1/2-year-old Corrie was saying, "Off! Off!" The teacher assumed he wanted to use a tricycle. There were other free trikes she could help him get, and she almost offered. But she thought she'd better check to see if that was really his problem. "You want to ride a trike?" she asked. He shook his head vehemently no, still clinging to Joshua's handlebar. He had planted himself firmly in front of the trike. She thought again, looking around for other clues. Then she saw the chalk dust smeared all over Corrie's hands and clothes. Nancy looked ahead on the sidewalk and saw a big colored section. "It looks like you are worried Joshua will drive over your picture," she guessed. "Yeah!" Corrie cried. Nancy then modeled some words Corrie could use to ask Joshua to please go around his drawing. They communicated, the conflict was resolved, and both boys returned to their play.

HELPING CHILDREN RESOLVE CONFLICTS

Both reflective listening and "I messages" come in handy when conflicts arise. When your needs and the needs of a child conflict, sophisticated communication

Reflective listening with very young children requires you to pay close attention to their nonverbal communications.

skills can help you to negotiate a solution. You can protect your own personal limits and still respect the needs of children. Your classroom can become a laboratory for learning the fine art of conflict resolution. This skill may be one of the most important subjects you can teach.

Many people think that conflict is bad and should be avoided; however, avoiding conflict usually means repressing feelings. Rarely can people live and work together in total harmony with no one's needs impinging on those of another. Conflict in the classroom and on the playground can be viewed as a learning opportunity. It is a chance for children to learn about the needs and wants of others, and it is also a chance for them to learn lifelong skills for mutual problem solving.

Schools have traditionally used a power model rather than a negotiation model (Gordon, 1989). Because children have so often seen threats and intimidation used as ways of resolving differences, it may take some effort to teach them a peaceful, respectful alternative. But it is worth the effort both to enhance the social skills of your students and to increase peace in your classroom.

Negotiating mutually acceptable solutions allows both sides to have power and respect. No one says, "You do it my way or else." No one ends up angry and resentful; therefore, general attitudes and relationships are more pleasant. Because everyone is involved in selecting the solutions, each person is more likely to follow through on them. In addition, the solutions tend to be higher quality, reflecting the needs and ideas of all involved. The process helps children to consider the views of other people. Consideration of others and the thinking process involved in problem solving both contribute to the long-term goals of intellectual and moral autonomy.

Mutual problem solving not only assists children toward long-term goals, but it also makes life more pleasant in the here and now. It relieves youngsters from the anger and the fear of punishment that accompany teacher power approaches. It relieves the teacher from constantly having to nag, enforce, and police instead of teach. It makes school a much more enjoyable and productive place for teachers and children to be. Thomas Gordon (1989) presents the following model for peaceful negotiation and problem solving.

STEPS FOR NEGOTIATING SOLUTIONS TO PROBLEMS

1. Identify the problem

2. Generate solutions

3. Evaluate solutions

4. Make a decision

5. Implement the plan

6. Evaluate the plan

Identifying the Problem

How does the problem-solving process work? First you need a clear statement of a problem. This step is where "I messages" come in to help you express how your needs or expectations are not being met. You need to explain that you would like to work together with those involved to figure out a solution to the problem. Reflective listening is useful for hearing the other side, and often it's necessary for discovering the actual cause of the problem. You may even find out that the problem is a different one from what you thought.

> "Don't run on those stairs!" Mrs. Jensen called out *again*. As usual, the youngsters zipped up one side of the small classroom stage and down the other without hearing her. What a nuisance that stage was: nothing but an invitation to run up and over it. Too bad it was bolted to the floor, or she would throw it out. Children saw it and instantly forgot the class safety rule about no running. The problem didn't just involve her own twenty-five students, but also the neighboring class that had to pass through her room on their way to the library or gym. Each youngster passed through the room via the stage. The noise of children's feet pounding on the hollow wood made Mrs. Jensen's head ache. She felt frustrated and powerless.
>
> But she thought, "There *must* be a solution." She decided to talk to the class about the problem. "I am upset about all the running up and down the stage stairs. I am afraid that someone will get hurt, and the noise makes it hard to concentrate in here," she explained. She timed her gathering and discussion so that the neighboring class was about to pass through the room. She asked her youngsters to watch the problem with the stage as Miss Wheeler's class came through. Mrs. Jensen's class was suitably impressed by the noise and the running. They agreed that it needed to stop.

Generating Solutions

Next, everyone needs to be involved in thinking up possible solutions. No idea is too wild, and no ideas are rejected at this point. In fact, no ideas should even be evaluated yet. You might want to start with kid ideas as a way of showing that you are serious about giving them a say. Be sure to continue getting ideas until everyone has run out of possibilities. Writing down all the ideas where everyone can see them is helpful, even if the children are too young to read yet. You can refer to the list as you review, and they will recognize their ideas.

> Mrs. Jensen invited her students to brainstorm solutions to the problem. She had certainly exhausted her ideas. She wrote each of their ideas on the board.
>
> "We could tell kids not to run on the stage," suggested Brianna.
>
> "Let's put a sign up!" said Jeffrey.
>
> "How about making a barricade with the chairs in front of the stage," was Eric's idea.
>
> "I think we should put the teacher's desk in front of the stage," replied Allison.

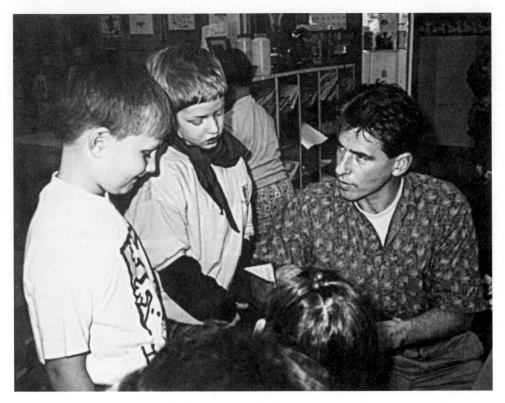

Negotiating mutually acceptable solutions to conflict allows both sides to have power and respect.

> "I know! We need to put those new pillows we just got on top of the stage," exclaimed Raymond.

Evaluating Solutions and Making a Decision

Now you are ready to evaluate the suggestions. Which ones are just impossible or totally unacceptable to someone? Cross those out immediately. Now what is left? Do any of them stand out as great ideas? Continue the discussion until everyone agrees to try one or a combination of solutions. Make sure the children understand that choosing a solution means a commitment to carrying it out. Voting is not a part of the process. This is a consensus model: Everyone agrees to try a solution, and no one is forced into it by a "someone loses" or "minorities lose" method, such as a vote.

> "I've certainly tried telling you and reminding you," commented Mrs. Jensen. "I don't think that one will work."
> "If we pile our chairs in front of the stage, we won't have any chairs to sit on," Blake reminded everyone.

"And I won't be able to sit at my desk if it is up against the stage," added Mrs. Jensen.

"Well, I don't think Miss Wheeler's kids would read the sign," Joel declared.

"I don't understand how the cushions on the stage would help," said Mrs. Jensen doubtfully about the only remaining suggestion.

"They are *so* pretty. No one would want to step on them," explained Raymond. The other children agreed. They were delighted with the colorful print pillow covers that Mrs. Jensen had made just last week. Their teacher was skeptical but agreed to try out the suggestion.

Implementing the Plan

You aren't finished yet. A plan isn't worth much unless you figure out how to implement it. Who will do what? When and how often? Where and how? To what standards? Who checks? When children make these kinds of decisions and plan to implement them, they tend to follow through with little teacher direction.

Raymond immediately went to get the cushions from the reading corner and carefully positioned them on top of the small stage. But what should the class do when they needed to use the stage for sharing time or for putting on plays? It was decided that moving and replacing the pillows would be added to the class jobs chart. A different child would have that responsibility each week. Everyone agreed that no one else would move those cushions.

Evaluating the Plan

But what if the solution doesn't work? There are many reasons why it might not. Perhaps it was too difficult to implement or perhaps there were conditions you and the children neglected to consider. Evaluating the solution after you have tried it for a while is an essential final step. If you find that things aren't working, that situation isn't a signal for you to take over. It just means that the group needs to try again to generate workable solutions.

What a surprise! It worked! Mrs. Jensen was amazed at the change. No one ever ran up the stage again. Even Miss Wheeler's class, which hadn't been in on the discussion, no longer took detours over the stage on their way through the room. Those beautiful cushions did indeed keep kids off the stage. Mrs. Jensen would never have thought of that solution herself and still had trouble believing it could be that easy.

Saving Time

Does conflict resolution sound like it takes a lot of time? This is a common concern. Sometimes problem solving can be accomplished in just a few minutes; at other times it does take quite a lot of time. However, if you have a recurring problem, that takes a lot of time, too. Teachers and parents who use this problem-solving approach report that it saves a lot of time in the long run. Instead of ineffectively dealing with the same problem over and over, time is set aside to deal effectively with the problem until it is resolved.

> Mrs. Jensen had been fighting the battle of the stage for three years without success. She had reminded and nagged and pleaded with youngsters in her classes each year. They had simply been unable to resist the temptation to run. The time spent on this problem-solving session was certainly time well spent for her.

Independent Problem Solvers

Obviously, conflicts don't occur just between adults and children. Children frequently find themselves engaged in a battle over a toy, a turn, or a space in the classroom. You can save yourself time and trouble by teaching youngsters to negotiate their own problems. The model you provide in group problem solving is an important part of this teaching, but you will probably need to talk children through the process individually while they are learning.

> Raymond and Sam were trying to play together at the sand table again, but as always, they had very different game plans. Raymond was trying to make carefully groomed patterns in the sand. Sam was chugging around with a bulldozer, trying to get all of the sand up against the edges, exposing the bottom.
>
> Raymond complained as the dozer kept undermining his space, making the patterns sluff away. Mrs. Jensen observed the conflict and suggested that the boys try to figure out a way to play together at the sand table. Raymond frowned, wishing she'd just tell Sam to stop ruining his work. Then Mrs. Jensen reminded him, "You did so well at solving the stage problem. I bet you could come up with a way to fix this one!" He brightened up. She then asked, "Do you remember the first thing we did to problem-solve?" Sam recalled, "Brainstorming!" He had liked that part; anything you thought of was OK, so you could be silly or serious. Sam was silly: "Measure every grain of sand and divide it *exactly*!" Raymond offered, "We could take turns at the sand table." "We could build the Great Wall of China, and neither one could cross it!" Sam said excitedly, remembering a picture he had seen of the wall. Raymond thought again and came up with one last idea: "Sam could play with the funnels instead of the bulldozer."
>
> Mrs. Jensen reminded them that in the next stage of problem solving—evaluating—they had to both agree on a solution to try. Measuring sounded like a challenge, but both boys thought it would be too hard. Taking turns was rejected because neither wanted to be

second, and Sam wasn't interested in playing with the funnels. But the "Great Wall" idea intrigued both of the boys. They asked if they could use some blocks in the sand table to make a barrier wall. Mrs. Jensen thought to herself that the idea might not work but told them to go ahead anyway. They were eager to try out their solution. It didn't perfectly hold back sand, but it was completely effective at resolving the conflict between the boys. Whenever it collapsed, they ignored their patterns and bulldozing to rebuild their barrier cooperatively, the new major focus!

If you teach children how to negotiate their own solutions, soon they will be teaching each other and won't constantly be coming to you with their arguments. Even preschool-age children are capable of problem solving. In the process of learning to problem-solve, your young students will learn about peaceful negotiation of differences. Perhaps they will even put this skill to work as adults, possibly helping the peoples of the world struggle to resolve their differences.

CONCLUSION

When we communicate with children respectfully, we can prevent many discipline problems and solve many others. When we state our own needs respectfully, children are more apt to behave considerately in the first place and are generally more willing to change their behavior if it has become inappropriate. When we listen to children respectfully, we can help them to resolve their problems, either before their behavior is adversely affected or in time to remedy the situation. When we teach problem solving skills, children learn to use them to avoid a dispute as well as to solve one.

FOR FURTHER THOUGHT

1. Listen to adults talking to children. Think about those same words used with another adult. Do they sound ridiculous or reasonable? Analyze your own ways of talking to children. Do you show less respect to children than to your adult acquaintances?
2. Practice using "I messages" when someone upsets you. What are the results? Were you careful not to send a disguised "you message"? Were you able to stop yourself from also telling the other person what to do or not to do? Keep on trying. It takes time to break old habits.
3. Practice reflective listening with friends who confide in you about a problem. Be careful not to give advice or reassurance, but only to clarify your understanding of the other person's feelings. How does this attitude affect the communication? Is it difficult to do?
4. A problem to solve: Angie comes to you complaining because another child is using the swing and she wants to swing.
    a. Describe a common ineffective response.

b. Describe a reflective-listening response.

5. A problem to solve: Matt and Jason are experimenting with magnets together at preschool. Jason goes off to play elsewhere, and Matt starts crying.
    a. What might a teacher say who is skilled in reflective listening?
    b. What might a teacher say who doesn't understand about roadblocks to communication?

6. Try out the steps to negotiating conflicts as described in this chapter. Analyze the results to learn how to be more effective in the future.

REFERENCES AND RECOMMENDATIONS FOR READING

Books

BRIGGS, D. C. (1970). *Your child's self-esteem.* New York: Doubleday.

CURWIN, R. L., & MENDLER, A. N. (1990). *Am I in trouble? Using discipline to teach young children responsibility.* Santa Cruz, CA: Network Publications.

GINOTT. H. (1965). *Between parent and child: New solutions to old problems.* New York: Macmillan.

GINOTT, H. (1972). *Teacher and child.* New York: Macmillan.

GORDON, T. (1970). *Parent effectiveness training.* New York: Wyden.

GORDON, T. (1974). *T.E.T.: Teacher effectiveness training.* New York: Wyden.

GORDON, T. (1989). *Teaching children self-discipline: At home and at school.* New York: Random House.

GORDON, T., & SANDS, J. S. (1976). *P.E.T. in action.* New York: Bantam.

KATZ, L. G., & MCCLELLAN, D. E. (1991). *The teacher's role in the social development of young children.* Urbana, IL: ERIC Clearinghouse Document, ED313168.

ROGERS, C. (1951). *Client-centered therapy.* Boston: Houghton Mifflin.

ROGERS, C. (1961). *On becoming a person.* Boston: Houghton Mifflin.

RUBIN, Z. (1983). The skills of friendship. In M. Donaldson, R. Grieve, & C. Pratt (Eds.), *Early childhood development and education.* New York: Guilford Press.

Periodicals

CARLSSON-PAIGE, N., & LEVIN, D.E. (1992). Making peace in violent times: A constructivist approach to conflict resolution. *Young Children, 48*(1), 4–12.

GOFFIN, S. (1989, Winter). How well do we respect the children in our care? *Childhood Education,* pp. 68–74.

HENDRICK, J. (1992). Where does it begin? Teaching the principles of democracy in the early years. *Young Children, 47*(3), 51–53.

PELLEGRINI, A. D., & GLICKMAN, C. D. (1990). Measuring kindergartners' social competence. *Young Children, 45*(4), 40–44.

Videocassette

The Little Mermaid. (1990). Buena Vista, CA: Walt Disney Home Video.

Chapter 8

Helping Children Understand Rules and Limits

What if you need to change a behavior immediately? What do you do when it's too late to prevent a problem because it is already happening? What do you do if prevention, modeling, listening, and problem solving don't work? Now do you turn to punishment?

Related consequences, not punishment, provide the answer for effective immediate results that are compatible with long-term positive outcomes. Punishment merely impacts the immediate response and generally produces negative side effects. With related consequences, you can teach toward long-term discipline goals while still stopping unwanted behavior.

Related consequences help children reason why certain behavior is undesirable, giving them personal reasons to change. At the same time, they respect the child's right and ability to choose more appropriate action. Instead of forcing children to do what adults know is best, related consequences help youngsters figure out for themselves the best ways of acting. In the process, this form of discipline helps develop the personal responsibility necessary for self-discipline and moral autonomy.

The concept of related consequences has been described in different terms by various authors. Publications by Jean Piaget (1932/65) and Rudolf Dreikurs (1964) laid the foundation for the idea; subsequently, others have continued to explore why and how this discipline approach works (Curwin & Mendler, 1988; Kamii, 1982, 1984; Miller, 1990; Grossman, 1990).

The 1965 English translation of Piaget's 1932 book *The Moral Judgment of the Child* uses the terms *expiatory punishment* versus *punishments by reciprocity*. Piaget says that expiatory punishment is pain inflicted for the purpose of making sure a person who broke a rule is made to feel appropriately guilty. With this approach, the suffering inflicted by the punishment is supposed to match the severity of the misdeed. Piaget points out the arbitrary nature of the punishment and its lack of relation to the misbehavior as reasons for not using this approach.

In contrast with expiatory punishment, he describes several types of alternative discipline strategies. Because they are designed to help the child learn rather than to inflict pain and guilt, the term *punishment by reciprocity* seems an inappropriate translation. In explaining Piaget's ideas, Constance Kamii has used the term *sanctions by reciprocity* to show more clearly the distinction between this approach and punishment (Kamii, 1982).

Regardless of the label, Piaget (1965) recommends five responses to misbehavior that help children move toward moral autonomy. They may or may not be imposed by an adult; they may simply occur as the natural outcome of the child's actions or may happen within the child's peer group in response to antisocial behavior.

1.   Exclusion: The child may no longer play with the other children. Piaget says this situation may be temporary or permanent.

2.   Natural consequences: The child experiences the direct results of his or her own behavior. Piaget uses the example of a child who has a cold room as a result of breaking his or her own bedroom window.

3.   Deprivation: The child may no longer have access to that which has been abused or misused.

4.   Reciprocity: What the child has done to another is done back to the child. Piaget is very clear that this response does not mean doing evil for evil, such as biting a child who has bitten another. He says that action is not only a poor model but also "absurd" (Piaget, 1965, p. 208). He refers rather to a response such as not doing a favor for a child who has not helped with assigned chores. Thus, if the child doesn't help you, you don't help the child.

5.   Restitution: The child pays for or replaces that which has been damaged or lost.

Dreikurs's concept of natural and logical consequences has much in common with Piaget's concept of sanctions by reciprocity. They were explained in his book *Children: The Challenge* (1964) and were elaborated on in his subsequent writing (Dreikurs, Greenwald, & Pepper, 1982). Natural consequences are those that automatically result from the child's behavior with no intervention from an adult. According to Dreikurs, logical consequences are those imposed by an adult but linked to the child's actions.

In this book we blend the viewpoints of Piaget and Dreikurs. We prefer the simplicity of a distinction between consequences that happen without adult intervention and those that require such intervention. Therefore, like Dreikurs, we make a distinction between natural consequences and imposed consequences. As we have already explained, we chose the term *related consequences* for imposed consequences that help a child learn. We find Piaget's several categories of consequences helpful in remembering to consider a variety of options in discipline situations. It is important to keep in mind also that some outcomes in these categories may occur naturally or within the child's social group.

It is important to remember that related consequences are designed to help children think about *why* certain behaviors are unacceptable and others are desirable. This is a teaching approach in which punishment has no place. Consequences are designed to help children view themselves as capable and willing problem solvers. Punishment tends to have the opposite effect, making children consider themselves bad and teaching them to be sneaky to avoid being caught (Kamii, 1984). Punishment will be discussed further in chapters 9 and 10.

NATURAL CONSEQUENCES

Both Piaget and Dreikurs recommend allowing children to experience the results of their actions when possible. Natural consequences are mostly a matter of getting out of the way and allowing children to learn from their experiences. Too often adults deprive children of the chance to experience the consequence of their actions because they care about the children and don't want them to have unpleasant or disappointing experiences. Unfortunately, the result is that the

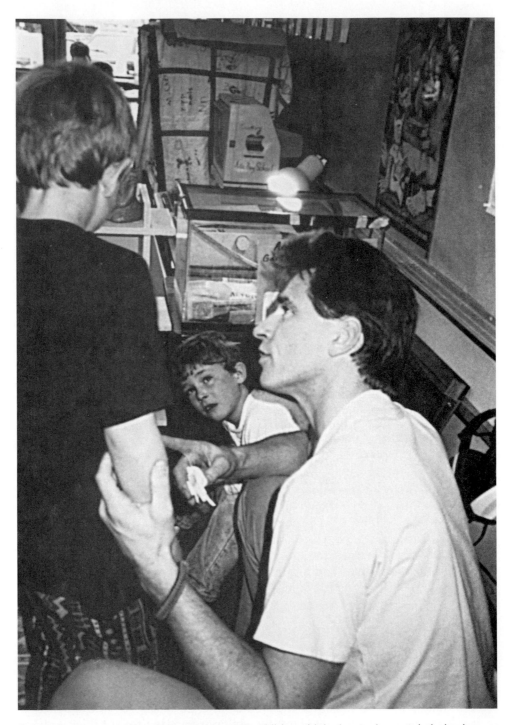

Related consequences are designed to help children think about why certain behaviors are unacceptable and others are desirable.

children don't become responsible for their own actions (Kamii, 1982). The following example is one that most teachers see frequently.

> Shantae forgot her library book again. It was library day, and the librarian would not let the children check out new books until they returned the ones checked out last week. But Shantae wasn't worried; she was confident that her mom would bring it for her. Sure enough, Shantae's mother arrived soon, harried and disgruntled at having to fit this errand into her day's schedule. She was cross with Shantae and fumed, "Why are you so irresponsible? I even reminded you this morning. You never listen."

What has Shantae learned here? She has learned to depend on her mother instead of on herself. She has become convinced that she is, indeed, irresponsible and that her mother needs to take responsibility for her. Instead of learning that she needs to return her library book if she wants to check out another, she has learned to depend on her mother. Instead of having the experience of not getting a new book, she experiences her mother's anger. Anger teaches nothing; it only brings resentment and retaliation. It focuses the child's attention on the "mean" adult instead of on her own behavior. It deprives her of the opportunity to think about and learn from the outcome of her own actions.

Mrs. Jensen does try hard not to protect children from learning through their mistakes. She reminds herself not to take over their responsibilities when they forget. She doesn't nag, coax, and remind children to do the things they are supposed to remember on their own. Mrs. Jensen thinks that youngsters learning to take responsibility for themselves is more important than making sure everyone remembers to take home the book order list or even the class newsletter. She shows her faith in her students by allowing them to figure out the cause-and-effect relationship between their actions and the results. They soon find out that they don't get to buy a book if they don't take the book order form home, get permission and money to place an order, and then return the form with the money to school. She knows that children learn through their experiences and that learning takes time.

The real world offers much more opportunity for natural consequences than school does. By its nature, school is an artificial environment that doesn't allow much opportunity for natural responses. At home Mrs. Jensen can allow her own children to learn much more freely from their mistakes than she can at school with her students. If her own children don't put away their things at home, they naturally get lost. At school, the custodian picks things up and gets cross when they are lying around. When her own children go running outside without a coat on a cool day, she lets them find out for themselves that they need to come back for a coat. At school, she worries that parents will think she is shirking her responsibility if she lets her students go out to recess without coats. Besides, school rules don't allow youngsters to run back inside for coats in the middle of recess. Mrs. Jensen has trouble allowing natural consequences at school.

While teachers and parents are often uncomfortable with allowing natural consequences, children still manage to experience them often. They will build an unstable block tower and experience its collapse. From this natural consequence they can begin to learn about balance, physical limits, and maybe the way hard blocks feel when they land in their lap. At least they will learn, that is, if some overprotective adult doesn't stop them by controlling their constructions. Social behavior and friendships are also molded a great deal by natural consequences (Rizzo, 1989). A child who repeatedly hurts others physically or hurts their feelings may reap the consequence of peer rejection, as in the following example.

> On the playground at Lincoln Elementary School, the ratio is 2 aides to 250 children. Here, free from the ever-watching eyes and ears of the classroom teacher, the children learn how to get along on their own. Allison had been particularly bossy to her table mates in class one morning. She told Rose to get out of the book corner and ordered Ling Ling to clean up her mess. When Allison came out for recess, they all avoided her, leaving her out of their games. She complained, "Why can't I play?" Rose answered directly, "'Cause you always have to be the boss!" Allison was experiencing a delayed natural consequence for her earlier behavior.

The teacher can help Allison by helping her to think through this experience, not by saving her from it. Some adults would insist that no child be left out and thus would ruin Allison's lesson. A much kinder teacher response is to encourage Allison to think about how she might act differently in the future in order to be accepted on the playground.

RELATED CONSEQUENCES

Related consequences are useful when natural consequences won't work. Not only do school rules make natural consequences impossible at times, but also the natural consequences in many situations are unacceptable. Adults do have the responsibility of keeping children safe from harm. Obviously, no one allows a child to experience the natural consequences of playing in the street. Instead, adults watch carefully and plan related consequences to help youngsters learn to stay away from traffic.

Different teachers have varying views on the safety issue as it relates to consequences. Some let children use paring knives to prepare fruit salad, supervising the use but accepting that a small cut may be the occasional result. They feel that the minimally unpleasant experience is a natural consequence that will teach care with knives. Others might be willing to use that method with their own children but don't feel comfortable doing so with other people's children. It is a matter of personal comfort level, as are the varying amounts of risk that different parents allow their children. However, there is general agreement that children cannot be allowed to take risks that could result in serious injury.

While teachers and parents are often uncomfortable with allowing natural consequences, children still manage to experience them often and learn from them.

What if Sam hits Danny? Do you allow the natural consequence, in which Danny hits him back? Occasionally, Dennis decides that this response is the learning experience one of his preschoolers needs. Perhaps the child hasn't had enough social interaction to realize that hitting gets a negative response from peers. In that case, Dennis pretends not to notice what is happening yet keeps an eye out to be sure no one really gets hurt. Usually, however, Dennis doesn't allow hitting and uses related consequences, as in the following example.

> Sam wanted to play with Danny after nap time. Unfortunately, Danny was waking up slowly and just wanted to be left alone. Frustrated, Sam got increasingly aggressive and eventually resorted to physical contact to get Danny's attention. Action escalated from nudges to pushing and somehow to hitting. Danny wailed and Dennis intervened. Sensing that Danny was in no condition to verbalize his need for privacy at the moment, Dennis chose to impose the consequence of removing Sam, explaining that he could not let him hit Danny. "Hitting hurts," Dennis said as he calmly took Sam to the next room. He told the child, "You may go back to the sun room when you are ready to use your words instead of hitting. Danny is hurt and he needs to feel safe."

Notice that Dennis did not tell Sam how long he had to stay away from Danny. Instead of using his adult power to make all the decisions here, Dennis allowed the child to be in charge of his own change. He allowed Sam to reflect on his own actions and to decide when his feelings were under control. This approach helped Sam learn to take responsibility for himself and become more autonomous.

In a situation like the one with Sam, be sure you don't ignore the child's feelings that lead up to an incident. But this doesn't mean you interrogate the children to determine who started it. That action would put the adult back in charge of kids' behavior. Instead, think about how you can help the children deal with their feelings. Imposing consequences to stop the hitting doesn't preclude the use of other guidance techniques. For instance, after Sam and Danny have calmed down from the incident, you could work with them on the communications skills discussed in chapter 7. Each boy could be helped to tune in to his feelings and put them into words. Hitting is often a primitive form of communication; learning higher level communication skills can help a child give up hitting.

Chapter 1 introduced examples of related consequences as a way of helping children understand why certain behaviors are more desirable than others. The example of removing Kenji from the block area until he decides to stop knocking over other children's block constructions is the same type of consequence that Dennis used for Sam's hitting. Piaget (1965) classified this type of response as *exclusion*. Dreikurs (1964) introduced the idea that Kenji and Sam must be allowed to determine when they are ready to try again to get along with their friends. Telling Kenji he may not play in the block area until *he decides* he can play without knocking over other children's work is very different from simply removing him. Asking him to decide about returning gives him the message that you have faith in his ability to make the necessary adjustments in his behavior.

The example from chapter 1 in which Aaron wipes up the water he spilled is also a related consequence. Cleaning up the mess you make is a way of making restitution, a method that Piaget (1965) recommends. An example of making restitution that we particularly like involves children who hurt each other through carelessness. If Desmond is throwing rocks and one accidentally hits Beau, Desmond learns much more about the dangers of rock throwing by holding a cold cloth to Beau's head than by being banished to the principal's office. In addition, helping Beau lets Desmond see himself as a helpful person rather than a bad one. All of these examples describe ways of motivating children to build rules of conduct for themselves from within.

Consequences or Punishment?

Related consequences can easily turn into punishment if the adult is not careful (Curwin & Mendler, 1990). Because the adult administers them, they demonstrate adult power over children. For this reason, other less intrusive methods of discipline should be tried first. Prevention of problems is the least intrusive approach to discipline; and teaching by example, coaching, "I messages," and conflict negotiation all teach discipline without the use of adult power. However, there are times when judicious, respectful, and limited use of adult power is required. That is when you need to plan a related consequence.

Sometimes it's hard to remember the judicious and respectful aspects of related consequences. Imposed consequences can quickly lead to a power struggle for the unwary adult. Remember Dennis's problem with the "no lunch until you clean up your mess" ultimatum in chapter 4. Dennis had a practical rationale for that ruling: He wanted to clear the room for lunch. However, it was really Dennis and not the situation that was depriving Amy of her lunch. Amy's dress-up clothes weren't on the lunch table, and she couldn't see any reason why they had to be put away before she could eat. Dennis had only his power as an adult to enforce his hasty ultimatum, and that power led to the confrontation. Effective consequences strive for adult withdrawal from power rather than an application of power. Fortunately, Dennis's ego allowed him to back down, listen reflectively, and negotiate a solution with the child.

Related consequences take planning and forethought. The connection between the child's behavior and the results must be clear. Dreikurs (1964) reminds parents that there is no relationship between not taking out the garbage and not getting to watch television. He suggests that there may be a relationship between a parent's refusal to fix dinner and a kitchen with smelly garbage. Notice, too, that the adult must assert power over the child to enforce the no-television ruling but impacts only the adult's own behavior in refusing to fix dinner. Therefore, being deprived of television is a form of punishment, while not fixing dinner is a consequence reasonably related to the situation.

Not fixing dinner, however, can also be turned into punishment. If the adult expresses anger about the garbage, then not fixing dinner will come through as a

Related consequences can easily turn into punishment if the adult is not careful.

retaliation rather than a consequence. Instead, the parent might use an "I message" and say, "The garbage makes the kitchen smell too bad for me to be in there cooking." It is important to be calm and matter-of-fact about imposing consequences. In fact, it is important not to *be* angry, or your anger will be all that is heard. Effective consequences involve adult intervention without anger or recrimination.

   If you use the impending consequences as a threat, that treatment also turns them into punishment (Dreikurs et al., 1982). "Take that garbage out before I come home from work, or no dinner tonight" is not in the spirit of related consequences. There are times when you want to inform children in advance of consequences, but it needs to be done in a nonthreatening and calm manner.

Variations of the "I told you so" theme are another way to ruin the educational value of related consequences (Dreikurs, 1964). Perhaps, in addition to not fixing dinner, the parent might be tempted to say, "Maybe that will teach you a lesson." These words take the focus away from the actual problem and invite an angry power struggle. Often it is better to say nothing. Let the consequences speak for themselves.

Selecting Reasonable Consequences

As a result of trying to think up reasonable consequences, Mrs. Jensen sometimes finds that there really is no good reason why some actions aren't acceptable. What *was* the reason for the rule against water in the sand table? She knows that children will more easily accept limits when they can see their value. She believes children deserve an explanation of reasons why certain behaviors are unacceptable. If she can't think of such an explanation, she is inclined to allow the behavior. Sometimes her decision means not conforming to school traditions, such as walking in lines.

> Walking through school hallways in regimented lines under the stern gaze of the teacher is a time-honored tradition. Yet Mrs. Jensen can't convince herself that lines are necessary or helpful. Why shouldn't youngsters be allowed to walk in quiet groups like adults? Won't they learn more about respecting others if they are in charge of their own behavior than if the teacher is standing guard? Won't many behavior problems be solved if kids aren't walking so close together and don't all have to go at the same time? Mrs. Jensen sees many children poking the kid in front of them just from the sheer frustration of waiting until everyone is ready. She has been working to teach her students about walking through the halls without disturbing other classes or blocking the hallway for people coming in the opposite direction. She finds this approach a much more productive use of her energy than enforcing the lines.

It is much easier for Mrs. Jensen to explain to her students the importance of not bothering others than to explain why they have to stay in a line. She feels good about the time spent helping children learn to be independent in the halls. She leads class discussions about what hall behaviors would bother other classrooms. During these discussions, Mrs. Jensen sees careful thinking; the children are definitely making progress in understanding the views of others. She sees children feeling important and proud as they practice being responsible for their own behavior in the hallway. Children who continually forget about thoughtful behavior can be helped to remember by experiencing a consequence. Mrs. Jensen simply asks forgetful children to walk with her until they think they can manage on their own.

Living and working harmoniously in a group requires much mutual consideration and cooperation (DeVries, Zan, Reese-Learned, & Morgan, 1991). Related consequences can be very useful in helping children develop and remember these attitudes. Mrs. Jensen plans this part of her curriculum as carefully as the academic aspects. As she plans, she keeps in mind her goal of assisting children's growth toward autonomy. She wants to give them freedom while helping them understand that freedom implies responsibility. This responsibility includes not impinging on the freedom of others, such as the rights of other classrooms not to be disturbed. Mrs. Jensen's plans are also built around the principle of respect for each child, which she demonstrates through her belief in their ability and desire to behave responsibly. She firmly believes that all people, including children, have equal claim to dignity and respect. She likes the way Dr. Seuss puts it in *Horton Hears a Who* (1954): "A person's a person, no matter how small."

Mrs. Jensen employs a variety of strategies to help her students determine the value of mutual consideration and cooperation. In addition to imposing related consequences, she also demonstrates desirable attitudes and behaviors through personal example. She makes sure that the class environment encourages harmonious social interaction, too. The best approach to guidance and discipline is usually a combination of approaches. Related consequences serve to help youngsters judge the pros and cons of a certain behavior as they experience the ramifications.

Consequences must be selected carefully. Besides picking something related to the behavior, you need to think of a consequence that matters to kids. Telling them they have to hurry up or they'll be late may carry no clout if being late isn't important to the child. The consequence also needs to be something that you can live with and are actually willing to follow through with, unlike Joanne's threat below.

> The children kept running across the plot that had been rototilled for a garden at Midway Children's Center. They delighted in how the fluffy soil felt! The parent who had promised to build a fence to protect it kept putting off the job. Joanne tried steering the children away, telling them that the ground would get packed down too hard to plant in, but they had no concept of the problem. As yet another group raced through the garden area, she gave up. Crossly she told them, "That does it! We just won't have a garden if you step in there again!" Intimidated by her anger, the children avoided the tempting dirt for most of the afternoon.
>
> Then Kenji blew it. Right before pickup time, he got carried away with a game of tag and tromped through the forbidden zone. A few minutes later, the parent volunteer arrived with an armful of tools to work on the fence. Kimberly piped up, "We don't need a fence anymore. We can't have a garden 'cause Kenji stepped in it!" Embarrassed, Joanne looked at the confused parent. She wondered how she could get out of this one. She really wanted to have a school garden.

Selecting a consequence related to the action takes thought and understanding. Many people misunderstand and misuse the term *consequence*. They impose totally unrelated outcomes on children's behavior and call them conse-

Selecting a consequence related to the action takes thought and understanding.

COMPARING APPROACHES

You may find it helpful to compare punishment, natural consequences, and related consequences as they might be applied to a single behavior problem. Kids seem to love throwing sand, and teachers always get upset about it. They lecture endlessly about the dangers of sand in playmates' eyes. Here is how the different discipline approaches would look if Jimmie threw sand at Joshua.

Punishment

No doubt you have observed or experienced the punishment response to this behavior. There are many variations of punishment, ranging from sending Jimmie to the principal's office to having him stand in the corner.

Natural Consequences

You probably have not seen any adult deliberately use natural consequences for sand throwing, though such consequences certainly do occur. If you were going to use natural consequences in this case, you would have to ignore Jimmie's behavior until Joshua or Jimmie got sand in his eyes. Then you could discuss what happened with them and help them relate the unpleasantness to the sand throwing.

Related Consequences

Related consequences involve adult intervention without anger or recrimination.

One type of related consequence would involve reminding Jimmie about the dangers of throwing sand and remove him from the sandbox until he thinks he can play without throwing sand. If he immediately goes back and starts throwing sand again, you need to impose a longer period away—such as the rest of the play period. Although it is preferable to encourage Jimmie to decide for himself when he is able to behave acceptably, some youngsters need guidance for such reflection.

Another type of consequence would also be appropriate if sand actually got into Joshua's eyes. Jimmie would be put in charge of helping Joshua go to the nurse's office, and then he would stay with Josh while he got his eyes washed out. This experience would help Jimmie learn why throwing sand is dangerous.

quences. They don't realize that without the relationship between the action and the result, there is no learning involved; the result is merely punishment (Curwin & Mendler, 1988).

A typical public school discipline guide lists a variety of nonrelated consequences: losing a recess for chewing gum, staying after school for talking back to a teacher, doing push-ups for hitting someone. Totally unrelated to children's behavior, these punishments teach resentment, calculation of the risk of getting caught, and consideration of whether the benefits are worth the costs (Kamii, 1984). Gum chewing might have a reasonable consequence if there is a need to scrape gum off floors and desks. Discipline for talking back to a teacher or hitting someone should depend on the causes for those behaviors. No pat solution could address all the various sources of those behaviors. Discipline solutions are of questionable value if they do not take into consideration the nature of the individual child, the particular situation, and the relationship between those involved.

Applying Consequences

Mrs. Jensen frequently uses her experiences with her own children to guide her with her students. When she needs inspiration about how to apply related consequences at school, she reflects on the following successful use of them at home.

> Getting ready for school in the mornings had become an unpleasant ordeal. Mrs. Jensen not only had to get herself ready and out the door early, but she had four children who also had to get to school on time. If they missed the bus and she had to drive them, then she was late for work. It had happened once, and there were several other narrow escapes. The pressure of this situation was making her cross with the children as she hurried everyone along. It seemed that the more she tried to hurry them, the slower they moved. Her frustration was building, and her days were getting off to a bad start. Her children were leaving for school upset, too. She had to find a way out of this problem.
>
> How could she change the situation so that the children's behavior did not affect her personally? The part that was upsetting to her was the prospect of being late for work because of driving the children to their school. If only they lived close enough to walk when they missed the bus. The walk and their tardiness would be good learning experiences. But this natural consequence wasn't available because their school was ten miles away. However, the city bus route was within walking distance. Her children were experienced bus riders. Sure, it was a long, slow trip, probably involving a wait for the bus and assuring tardiness, but those were learning experiences, too. Mrs. Jensen thought the idea might work. She bought a roll of bus tokens and showed her children where they were. Then she explained that she simply couldn't be late for work and that they could take the city bus to school if they ever missed the school bus.

What a relief! Mrs. Jensen could relax and be cheerful with her children in the mornings. She could make sure she left the house on time, but it was up to the youngsters to make certain they did. Sure enough, before long it happened. The four children dragged sadly back to the house after seeing the bus pull away. Their mother calmly reminded them where the bus tokens were as she left for work. The problem was the children's, not hers. She was not at all upset because she knew they would be fine. She was careful not to say, "I told you so." She merely waved as she drove off to work. That evening she could be truly sympathetic about how awful the long bus ride had been and how they felt about being tardy. However, she also sent the clear message that getting to the bus on time was their responsibility, not hers.

This learning experience worked so well at home that it has become a model for Mrs. Jensen at school. She uses the same principles and procedures when she applies reasonable consequences with her students. She withdraws from any power struggle and turns the responsibility over to the children. This plan helps her remain calm and pleasant. She knows that any anger on her part will ruin the consequences by turning them into punishment.

She used these guidelines to solve the problem of kids' not keeping track of their own crayons and scissors. She has classroom boxes for crayons, markers, and scissors. Any of these items found lying around after cleanup go into the boxes and become community property. Children are free to borrow them and use them, but they now belong to the class. The boxes solve several problems at once. They provide a place for the things that have been left out, a source of needed supplies, and an incentive for children to keep their own things put away. With this solution in place, Mrs. Jensen is able to turn the problem over to the children.

Younger children may be somewhat less adept at linking cause and effect, but preschoolers are able to learn from related consequences. Dennis and Maureen know that related consequences will help their students to think about cause and effect as well as about how their actions affect others. Therefore, experiences with related consequences are a valuable part of their preschool curriculum. As the following example shows, both teachers are careful not to ruin the learning experiences with sermons or scoldings.

Colette and Leo were being too rough with Pinky the guinea pig. As the frightened creature squealed and tried to pull away, Colette grabbed its fur. Tufts of fur came out in her hand. Leo thought the tufts were neat and tugged off another bunch of fur. The teacher heard Pinky's cries and came to his rescue. As she examined his patchy coat, she decided he deserved a respite to recover. She moved his cage up out of the children's reach, explaining as she did so, "Pinky's hair has been pulled out, and I want him to have a chance to grow it back. He needs to be in a safe place for a while. When you feel you can play gently with him, he can come back down."

Related consequences are ways of helping children learn through experience.

Depriving the children of Pinky's company matches one of Piaget's recommended responses. Dennis finds that these young children respond to the inherent justice of such a consequence. They do not usually resent or rebel against a truly related outcome. Noting this fact, Dennis is challenged to think of the best possible consequences. Still, he keeps in mind that the behavior may be a symptom of another problem. Dennis wants to do more than merely stop the behavior; he wants to get at the cause as well. If the cause is simply that the child does not understand why an action is inappropriate, then consequences alone are sufficient. If the behavior is signaling an unmet need, as it may have when Sam hit Danny, that need must also be considered.

> When Sam was harassing and eventually hurting his friend Danny, Dennis stopped the escalating behavior by removing Sam. Recognizing that Sam's behavior was probably a symptom of his unmet need for attention, Dennis could have helped Sam get that need met. If Sam had complained that Danny wasn't his friend anymore, Dennis could have listened reflectively to find out more. Maybe Sam just wanted a playmate, so Dennis could have coached him in positive ways to get friends' attention. He could also have asked Sam to choose what he would like best to play with. Then he could have asked the boy to decide who might like to do that activity with him. And, of course, the option of trying again with Danny would always be open. Maybe inviting Danny to join him in a game in process would perk up his sleepy playmate!

CONCLUSION

Related consequences are ways of helping children construct moral rules and values by reflecting on their experience. Like teaching through example, teaching through experience is an extremely effective method. Of course, just the experiences themselves are not sufficient for learning. The child must reflect on the experiences and try to make sense out of them. It is this process of thinking about the experiences that results in learning. Children construct their own sense of right and wrong in this way. Moral rules that children construct from within are compelling to them, unlike rules that have been imposed by others. Children will respect the rules they have made for themselves. Similarly, the values they construct for themselves are more likely to guide their actions.

Thus, related consequences teach self-discipline. They not only help children take responsibility for their behavior at the time, but they also assist with the development of lifelong autonomous behavior. When you help children move toward autonomy, you work toward the ideals of a democratic society. Instead of being imposed by authority, order is maintained by each person for the benefit of all. When schools employ democratic principles and treat students according to those principles, students will rebel less and learn more.

FOR FURTHER THOUGHT

1. Observe in an early childhood education program, watching for how often children experience the results of their actions and how often an adult protects them from those results. Are adults getting in the way of child learning, or are they merely protecting them as necessary?

2. Watch for situations in which making restitution would be the most educational consequence for inappropriate behavior. Are you quick to discover these situations, or is your thinking still locked in to more punitive approaches?

3. Practice planning and implementing related consequences. Do you have trouble thinking of actual relationships to the behavior? Is it hard not to use consequences as threats? Do you find times when there may be no real reason not to allow the behavior?

4. A problem to solve (use this chapter and the previous ones to help you): Chelsea knocked over Katie's block construction. Katie is yelling at Chelsea and threatening to knock down what Chelsea has built.
   a. Describe an appropriate related consequence.
   b. Describe other guidance approaches that might also be useful.
   c. Describe how this problem might have been prevented.

REFERENCES AND RECOMMENDATIONS FOR READING

Books

ADLER, A. (1964). *Social interest.* New York: Capricorn Books.

CURWIN, R. L., & MENDLER, A. N. (1988). *Discipline with dignity.* Alexandria, VA: Association for Supervision and Curriculum Development.

CURWIN, R. L., & MENDLER, A. N. (1990). *Am I in trouble? Using discipline to teach young children responsibility.* Santa Cruz, CA: Network Publications

DREIKURS, R. (1964). *Children: The challenge.* New York: Hawthorne Books.

DREIKURS, R., GREENWALD, B., & PEPPER, F. (1982). *Maintaining sanity in the classroom: Classroom management techniques.* New York: Harper & Row.

GROSSMAN, H. (1990). *Trouble-free teaching: Solutions to behavior problems in the classroom.* Mountain View, CA: Mayfield.

KAMII, C. (1982). Autonomy as the aim of education: Implications of Piaget's theory. In C. Kamii, *Number* (pp. 73–87). Washington, DC: National Association for the Education of Young Children.

KATZ, L. G., & MCCLELLAN, D. E. (1991). *The teacher's role in the social development of young children.* Urbana, IL: ERIC Clearinghouse Document, ED313168.

MILLER, D. F. (1990). *Positive child guidance.* Albany: Delmar.

PIAGET, J. (1928/1964). *Judgment and reasoning in the child.* Totowa, NJ: Littlefield, Adams.

PIAGET, J. (1932). *The moral judgment of the child.* London: Routledge & Kegan Paul.

PIAGET, J. (1965). *The moral judgment of the child.* New York: The Free Press.

RIZZO, T. A. (1989). *Friendship development among children in school.* Norwood, NJ: Ablex.

SEUSS, DR. (1954). *Horton hears a Who.* New York: Random House.

Periodicals

DEVRIES, R. (1984). Developmental stages in Piagetian theory and educational practice. *Teacher Education Quarterly, 11*(4), 78–94.

DEVRIES, R., ZAN, B., REESE-LEARNED, H., & MORGAN, P. (1991). Sociomoral atmosphere and sociomoral development: A study of interpersonal understanding in three kindergarten classrooms. *Moral Education Forum, 16*(2), 5–20.

GREENBERG, P. (1992). Why not academic preschool? (Part 2) Autocracy or democracy in the classroom? *Young Children, 47*(3), 54–4.

HENDRICK, J. (1992). Where does it begin? Teaching the principles of democracy in the early years. *Young Children, 47*(3), 51–53.

KAMII, C. (1984). Obedience is not enough. *Young Children, 39*(4), 11–14.

Chapter 9

Controlling Behavior Externally

Behavior that gets pleasant results is likely to be repeated. Behavior that gets unpleasant results probably won't be repeated. That is the natural response of both people and animals. It is the principle used in training circus animals to perform, housebreaking a puppy, or getting laboratory rats to run a maze. It is also widely used to control children's behavior. The method is called behavior modification.

The authors of this book are opposed to behavior modification as a discipline approach in most cases. We are convinced that praise, stars, stickers, tokens, and other behavior modification reinforcement systems are counterproductive to the development of self-discipline and autonomy. Behavior modification does not teach children why certain behaviors are more desirable than others; instead, it uses rewards to coerce better behavior. Coercion replaces teaching as a means of enhancing children's behavior (Katz & McClellan, 1991). Performance based on rewards requires the presence of an authority figure who dispenses or withholds rewards; therefore, it is not consistent with the goal of autonomy.

Behavior modification is based primarily on the research of B. F. Skinner (1965, 1971), who conducted experiments with laboratory rats and pigeons. He tested theories about using reinforcement to get rats and pigeons to perform, discontinue, or persist with specific actions. Skinner's principles have been widely used in working with retarded or severely disturbed children. When used on a carefully planned, individual basis, they may be effective in controlling surface behaviors temporarily while underlying problems are gradually addressed through other means. However, schools have widely adopted and misapplied behavior modification to classrooms (Gordon, 1989).

We don't believe this method is a good way to elicit desired behavior for most children, and we will discuss our reasons later in the chapter. However, we think you need to understand how behavior modification works—because it does work. Even if you don't deliberately use the technique, it is an inevitable side effect of your interactions with others. It can work for you or against you. Your reactions are constantly impacting the behavior of others, just as their reactions are affecting your behavior. If the reactions are pleasing, chances are the person will repeat an action. In behaviorist terminology, the behavior has been reinforced. When you smile at what someone says, your action is a pleasant response. When you pay attention to what someone is doing, your interest, too, can be a rewarding response. It is easy to reinforce undesirable behavior accidentally if you don't know about reinforcement theory. Do the following examples seem familiar?

> Have you seen an adult chasing after a runaway toddler? If so, you know the glee with which toddlers play this game. It is a lot of fun to have Dad or a teacher running after them and giving them so much attention. Of course, the attention encourages running away again.
>
> What about adult laughter at a preschooler's rude or improper language? It may sound funny to hear such words come out of the mouth of an innocent child, but laughter as a response can unintentionally act as a reward and will ensure repetition of the inappropriate language.

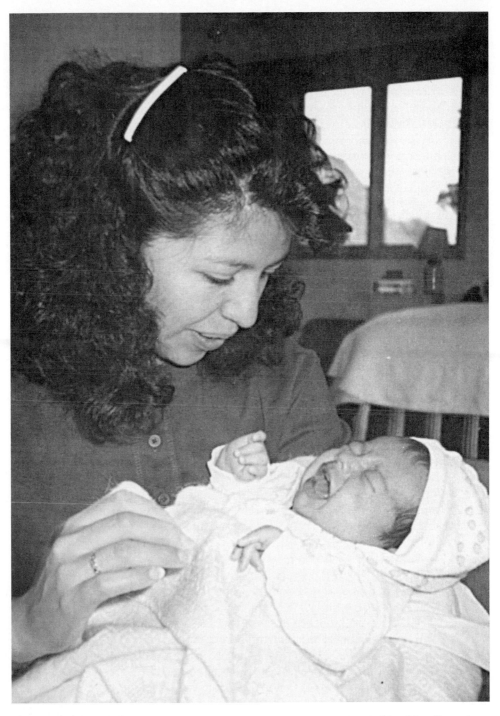

Even if you don't deliberately use behavior modification, it is an inevitable side effect of human interactions.

Who tends to get the most attention from the teacher in a classroom? Is it the child who responsibly does what is asked or the one who never does? Is the teacher unconsciously rewarding the irresponsible behavior by paying attention to it?

You can more easily avoid these pitfalls if you understand how behavior modification works. It is essential to remember the link between the action and the reward. Rewards can take many different forms, depending on the person and the circumstance. Even a spanking may actually be a reward if it is the only way a child can get attention. Close observation of children will help you discover what reactions a child finds rewarding. In the following example, Sheri and Maureen make an important discovery through observation.

James had been making life difficult at the children's center. He was throwing tantrums regularly and often chose the block area to do it. If there was a structure standing there, he knocked it over. If the blocks were on the shelves, he pulled them all off. If they were on the floor, he scattered them and threw them about. The staff had been trying hard to help him. They tried everything they could think of. Recently, they were implementing sanctions of reciprocity, but the method didn't seem to be working at all. James helped to clean up the mess he had made, but then he went and did it all over again.

Sheri was watching him as he went through his block-scattering routine; she was trying to figure out what the teachers could try next. As she watched, she caught James glancing out of the corner of his eye to see if she was looking. Then Maureen came over and stopped the destructive behavior. While Maureen talked to James about the problem, she held him on her lap and rubbed his back lightly with her hand. James sat with a little smile on his face, not appearing to listen. Sheri thought the experience seemed to be a pleasant one for him. She began to think about the possibility that James was getting what he wanted through his disruptive actions. Later, she suggested that perhaps the staff had been unintentionally reinforcing James's tantrums.

The teachers made a new plan. The next time James began his inappropriate behavior, they left the area. No one paid any attention to what he was doing. Pretty soon he stopped and went over to join a group listening to a story. He seemed quite content and under control. His teachers were amazed. Always before, his tantrums had gone on and on until an adult finally was able to calm him down. This time he had calmed himself down. It appeared that James got bored without an audience for his behavior. As the adults at the children's center continued to resist reinforcing his undesirable behavior, it disappeared.

This example demonstrates how mislearning occurs when an unproductive behavior is inadvertently reinforced. The child learns to use inappropriate behavior to get the desired response (Miller, 1990).

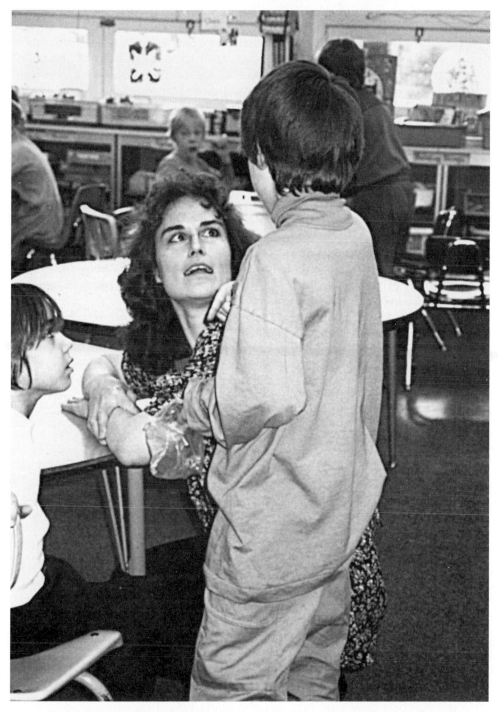

Mislearning occurs when an unproductive behavior is inadvertently reinforced.

REINFORCEMENT THEORY

The pleasant or rewarding responses that encourage behaviors are called reinforcers. Reinforcement is generally divided into two categories: social and tangible reinforcers. Smiles, laughter, and attention are social reinforcers, as are a hug, a touch, or even eye contact. Words of praise are commonly used social reinforcers as well. Food is often used as a tangible reinforcer. Raisins, Cheerios, or M&Ms are often handed out to children to reinforce certain actions. Seals prefer fish, and puppies like dog biscuits. Common tangible reinforcers used in school include stars, stickers, and smiley faces. Because older children are better able to delay gratification, behavior modification systems for them often give points or tokens, which can be accumulated and redeemed for prizes.

Social reinforcement is readily available and may occur without intent. Sometimes accidental reinforcement is fine, but at other times it isn't. Smiling at a child who has just helped a friend with her paint smock is a natural and harmless reinforcement. But the story of James's tantrums shows a situation in which accidental reinforcement causes problems, as do the examples of the runaway toddler, the rude preschooler, and the irresponsible student. It takes practice to become aware of when you are reinforcing negative behaviors. If you are attentive to the possibility, you can relax and feel free to otherwise interact naturally with children. Some teachers become overly sensitized to social reinforcement and no longer react naturally. Fear of providing accidental reinforcement can cause stiffness and lack of warmth in responding to children. Teachers who consciously use social rewards to control children's behavior also may have difficulty spontaneously showing their enjoyment of youngsters. This lack of warmth limits the teacher's ability to establish a relationship with the child. A caring relationship is essential for effective discipline (Curwin & Mendler, 1990; Katz & McClellan, 1991).

Punishment

Remember, there are two sides to behavior modification: the pleasant rewards and the unpleasant punishments. Chapter 10 focuses on punishment and explains its dangerous side effects. Most proponents of behavior modification emphasize the positive aspects and usually deny that punishment is used. However, any time a hoped-for reward is denied, it can feel like punishment.

> Miss Wheeler wanted to "motivate" Karin to finish her *Excel Math* worksheet on time. The girl always dawdled and just wouldn't stay focused. The teacher knew that Karin loved manipulatives; so she said that if Karin got her sheet done by 10:30, she could join the advanced group working with the Unifix cubes. Enticed by the possibility, Karin worked diligently for ten minutes. But the deadly worksheets soon took their toll, and she started daydreaming as usual. Her wandering gaze settled on the table with the Unifix cubes. She began wondering if you could make them into a horse. . . ? Then she

remembered the time limit, glanced at the clock, and panicked: 10:27! She scrambled to finish the page, but it was hopeless. She'd blown it again! Discouraged, she thought, "I hate math!"

Reinforcement Schedules

Behavior modification research provides guidelines for the most effective ways of using reward and punishment: Responses must be immediate, specific, and consistent (Miller, 1990). These guidelines are designed to demonstrate the relationship between the action and the result. If you want to use behavior modification, this information is essential to its effective use.

Behaviorists emphasize that the response needs to be immediate; otherwise, the child or the puppy may not realize what behavior is being rewarded or punished. For instance, the puppy may have picked up his bone since he wet on the rug. He may consider the swat with the newspaper to be a response to his chewing the bone. Likewise, Amy may have sneezed since she put away her trash. She may perceive your hug to be a response to the sneeze rather than to proper disposal of trash.

Being specific also helps make clear which behavior is being rewarded or punished. Usually, specificity guidelines refer to verbal feedback. The idea is to say exactly what you like or dislike rather than to make a vague "good girl" or "bad girl" statement. A recommended behaviorist response might be "I like the way you put your garbage in the wastebasket after snack time without even being reminded." (We prefer the more respectful and less manipulative "Thank you for remembering to put your garbage in the wastebasket.")

Consistency is also recommended to further clarify the desired behavior. Unless the response is consistent, the child or the puppy can get confused about whether the behavior is OK or not. Suppose a mother smiles and says, "Thank you," when Patricia picks a dandelion and brings it to her; then Patricia picks a petunia and her mother gets angry. What will Patricia think?

Behaviorist theory considers immediate and consistent reinforcement to be essential for initially getting the desired behaviors but does not recommend it for permanent use. Not only is it exhausting to have to watch for a desired behavior constantly and then immediately reward it, but it also works better to reduce the frequency of reinforcement gradually. If the rewards were to stop suddenly and completely, the desired behavior would be expected to stop quickly also. So a gradual reduction in rewards is suggested, with the goal of eliminating them entirely. Unfortunately, both adults and children tend to get hooked on the rewards, and the phase-out process often doesn't happen in practice.

Instead of reinforcing Amy each time she puts her trash away, an intermittent approach would reinforce it every other time and then switch to every third or fourth time. Behavior modification research indicates that unpredictable intervals between rewards have the most lasting effect (Miller, 1990). Therefore, if Amy never knows when she will be reinforced, she will tend to keep trying for a reward. That reasoning is behind the idea of the intermittent, variable reinforcement schedule: You keep the behavior going the longest with the least amount of effort in this way.

Even though we don't recommend that you formally implement behavior modification, we think you should know that intermittent and variable reinforcement has the most lasting impact. This knowledge can save you from accidentally applying the principle to behavior you *don't* want. The parent who *usually* doesn't give in to her children's nagging or whining may, in fact, be teaching them to keep trying. If their behavior works sometimes, youngsters will be motivated to keep it up. Similarly, the teacher who is trying hard not to reinforce attention-getting behavior may inadvertently be strongly encouraging it through intermittent variable reinforcement. As demonstrated in the following example, it takes practice and self-control to follow through with a strategy of "planned ignoring" (Grossman, 1990)

> Jeremy tipped back in his chair, precariously balanced on two legs. Mrs. Jensen knew that his action was attention-getting behavior. She was determined to ignore Jeremy and quit reinforcing him by expressing her concern. The danger in the behavior wasn't great because the floor was carpeted. Mrs. Jensen continued the class discussion. Oh! Jeremy started to fall! Mrs. Jensen called out his name in alarm just as he caught himself. He had won. He not only had the teacher's attention, but also that of the entire class. Mrs. Jensen knew she was going to have to work harder at ignoring his behavior.

IS THIS THE APPROACH FOR YOU?

Behavior modification obviously gets results, so why do many teachers and parents refuse to use it as their discipline approach? The answers can be found in the less obvious aspects of the system. They include the impact on autonomy as well as self-discipline and intrinsic motivation. Adults who reject reward and punishment to control children's behavior do so primarily out of concern for the child's long-term welfare.

Many adults are also personally uncomfortable with using their power to coerce someone with less power. To do so violates their value system and models a principle they reject (Greenberg, 1992). The power involved may not be physical but rather the power of access to resources that children desire. Because this use of power is effective, the system of reward and punishment is a method of forcing children into compliance.

Autonomy?

Autonomy requires that a person be skilled in thinking about issues and coming to personal conclusions (Kamii, 1982). These skills require practice. Behavior modification eliminates the opportunity for practice with decision making or self-evaluation of behavior options. The person with the rewards or punishments is in

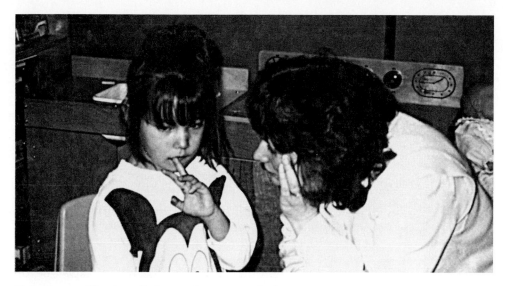

Behavior modification eliminates the opportunity for practice with decision making or self-evaluation of behavior options.

charge, not the child. With behavior modification, the child's thinking centers around how to get the reward or avoid the punishment, not about what is right under the circumstances. By taking responsibility for the child's behavior, the adult denies the child the opportunity to learn by experience and by reflection on those experiences (Piaget, 1965). When adults are constantly in charge of children's behavior, the message to the children is that they are not capable of making good decisions for themselves. Their confidence in themselves as thinkers and decision makers is damaged. Therefore, behavior modification creates both a lack of experience with making decisions and a lack of confidence to do so.

Self-discipline?

With behavior modification, the teacher decides what the children should do and enforces that decision through reward or punishment. Many adults apparently think that children become self-disciplined by being bribed and coerced in this way. Actually, the opposite is true. When adults force children to behave responsibly, they deny children the opportunity to learn self-discipline. The hope of behavior modification is to make certain behaviors a habit; however, the common result is to make reliance on external controls a habit (Kamii, 1982). Making the decisions for youngsters takes away their chance to make the decisions for themselves. They have no opportunity to develop inner controls when adults are imposing external controls. Young people who have been controlled by adults often have difficulty when they are old enough to be on their own. They don't know or maybe don't care what is right without the rewards.

Intrinsic Motivation?

Intrinsic motivation means doing something for its own sake. The value lies in the behavior itself, and the reward is in how you feel about it. The reward is internal to you. Extrinsic motivation is the opposite; it means doing something for a reward. The value lies not in the behavior, but in what you get as a result of the behavior. The reward is external to you because it comes from someone else. Obviously, behavior modification relies on extrinsic motivation.

The relationship between self-discipline and intrinsic motivation is just part of the problem. Rewards can teach people to expect them and to perform only for them. Thus, the extrinsic motivation of rewards goes against the development of self-discipline. Self-disciplined people don't behave appropriately only when a reward is offered. They have come to appreciate the value of learning appropriate behavior as a reward in itself. They recognize the natural benefits of positive interactions and making good choices. However, it is possible to destroy intrinsic motivation by rewarding behavior that a person was doing for personal satisfaction (Grossman, 1990). Such a counterproductive result is another aspect of the problem with extrinsic motivation.

> Mandy was in third grade but loved to go to her old first-grade classroom and help. She would frequently offer to stay after school and help clean chalkboards or tidy up the shelves. Helping made her feel good, and it also made her feel grown-up. Miss Wheeler decided she should reward Mandy's helpfulness and began giving the girl a prize each time she came in to help. Somehow helping wasn't as much fun anymore, and Mandy went to Miss Wheeler's room less and less often. Neither the teacher or the girl understood the relationship between the rewards and Mandy's lessened enthusiasm.

In this case, Mandy's reaction to rewards caused her to discontinue her volunteer work. Sometimes extrinsic rewards do more critical damage. It is possible to override a child's joy in learning and change the focus to getting rewards.

> Mandy was an avid reader when she started first grade. She had been an early starter and had already read a great deal for her own pleasure. She frequently borrowed books from the classroom library to read at home, and her parents took her to the community library as well.
>
> Miss Wheeler was pleased with how much Mandy read and wanted her other students to read more. She thought that it might help if she made a chart and put stars by each child's name for every book read. The children did like the stars and enjoyed seeing how many they could collect after their names. Competition developed among the better readers to see who could accumulate the most stars. Mandy wasn't the only one who began looking for the smallest

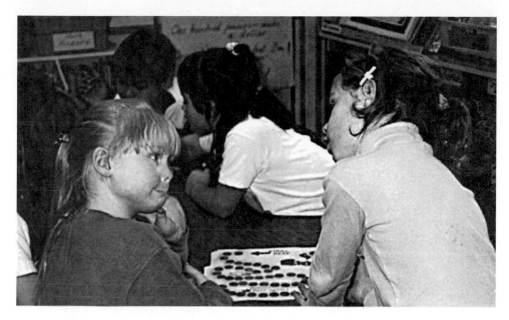

It is possible to override a child's joy in learning and change the focus to getting rewards.

and easiest books so that she could read more books faster. She also wasn't the only one who began reading too hastily to know what the book was actually about. The focus had become winning and getting stars instead of enjoying reading.

That was the outcome for the good readers. Youngsters who were less proficient readers were embarrassed by how few stars they had. Jimmie started pretending he had read books that Miss Wheeler knew he hadn't. Devon was more straightforward: One day he took a black marker and scribbled all over that chart. The chart had made him feel bad every time he saw it.

Mrs. Jensen has a theory that guides her general use of extrinsic motivation and helps her avoid the problem Miss Wheeler had with her reading chart. She won't give rewards for anything that she hopes children will do for its own sake. Therefore, she doesn't give rewards for reading because it can bring enjoyment and information. Additionally, she doesn't give rewards for being kind and caring: That behavior brings love and friendship. Instead, Mrs. Jensen helps youngsters tune in to the pleasures of reading and kindness themselves. She helps them find books they enjoy, with appropriate challenge. She also models loving interactions so that they can learn more readily. Of course, she sometimes has a special-needs child in her classroom who can temporarily benefit from extrinsic rewards. In that case, the reward system is a carefully selected part of the Individual Education Plan (IEP) for that child. Special-needs children and IEPs are discussed further in chapter 14.

Necessary Motivation

Mrs. Jensen is aware of another kind of motivation in addition to intrinsic and extrinsic: *necessary* motivation (Hymes, 1990). Many activities may not be pleasing in themselves, but they lead to goals that are. Washing dishes falls into this category for Mrs. Jensen personally. She doesn't like doing dishes, but she does appreciate a tidy kitchen. In this case, the clean kitchen provides necessary motivation. Mrs. Jensen tries to help students find such motivation for some dull tasks by focusing on a purpose for doing them.

> Storage space was tight in Mrs. Jensen's classroom. The only way all of the multishape blocks could fit on the shelves was if they were carefully arranged and neatly stacked. To help the children accomplish this task, Mrs. Jensen had traced the various shapes on the shelves so that the children could match and fit. Today Jeffrey was in a hurry and tried to cram the blocks in haphazardly. Finding himself with a pile of blocks left over and nowhere to put them, he complained to Mrs. Jensen. She helped him problem-solve. Brain–storming, he came up with three options about what to do: have fewer blocks in the classroom so they could be put more loosely away; find more shelf space or a basket to put the leftovers in; or remove the blocks and take a little more time to put them back on the outlines. He liked the idea of putting them somewhere else. But after a tour of the classroom with his teacher, Jeffrey had a new appreciation of how scarce space really was! Finding no free shelves or empty baskets, he reconsidered his other two options. While he was evaluating his solutions, several friends in the area insisted on making it a group decision. He had been leaning toward reducing the available blocks because that would be easiest. But the rest of the children adamantly resisted letting go of any fun arches or cylinders. Mrs. Jensen interjected, "Well, if you want to have all of these blocks out, the only way they fit is if they are put in place carefully. That takes a bit of work. We do have enough time for it, though. Lunch isn't for ten more minutes. Do you think you could do it in that much time?" Challenged, Abby jumped in, saying "I'll take them all back off the shelves!" Meadow offered to sort them; she liked sorting. Mrs. Jensen joined in, too. As they set the last block in place, she commented, "Isn't it amazing how much we can fit on our tiny classroom shelves with a little work?"

What about the pay you receive for a job? Is that extrinsic reward the reason you work? If you really like your job and are interested in what you do, the pay probably just makes it possible for you to follow your intrinsic motivation. It frees you from having to do something else to support yourself. If your work is boring or unpleasant, the reward of a paycheck is part of necessary motivation. You really do want to have food and shelter; therefore, you go to work.

COMMON FORMS OF BEHAVIOR MODIFICATION

Regardless of the criticism it receives, behavior modification is a tradition in the public schools. You have experienced it as a student, and you will see it as a teacher. We want you to recognize it when you see it so that you won't just go along with tradition, not realizing what you are actually doing.

You are probably most familiar with tangible rewards, such as Miss Wheeler's chart and stars. Your memories probably focus on how you felt about either getting or not getting the coveted reward; you probably remember little about the actual purpose or content of the papers. That fact is evidence of the damage done by rewards: they take attention away from what is truly valuable.

Time-out

Time-out is another pervasive school tradition. It is often used as a behavior modification technique and considered an improvement over the old stand-in-the-corner punishment. In actuality, there often is little difference (Katz & McClellan, 1991). An analysis of the various ways in which time-out can be used may help you understand the differences between some approaches to discipline.

> Joanne prides herself on her morning circle at Midway Children's Center. It is a time when her ability to be in control shines. When all the children are on their designated rug scraps in their circle spots, she begins singing, "I like the way that Christie sits; she's got her legs crossed, and her hands are in her lap. I like the way that Ling Ling sits; she's got her legs crossed, and her hands are in her lap. I like the way that Ashley sits; she's got . . . " until all the children are dutifully in position. Then she begins the "educational" presentation part of her circle program. If children get out of position, she says, "I need your whole body's attention, and you can't do it that way. Please sit up crisscross-applesauce style!" Some are not enticed by her sugary request and continue to resist the rigid posture. Her firm rule is that the second time they get out of position, they are sent to a time-out chair for the remainder of circle time. Aide Sheri usually has her hands full by the end of Joanne's "well-behaved" circle time. She wonders if this behavior modification approach to time-out is really working. The same kids are in those chairs almost every day, and the same few get the daily dose of praise. It sure doesn't seem to be teaching them anything.

Sheri uses a different approach to a similar problem:

> Sheri's story time before lunch has looser seating requirements. But even though children can sit where and how they please, there are still problems. Children get in each other's way or quarrel over who

Helping children learn to give themselves time alone as needed is very different from the usual time-out approaches.

sits by whom. If their disagreements escalate into shoving and whining, Sheri tells them, "It's too hard for me to read while you're not getting along. I can see you are upset with each other. You need to go to
the calming chairs in the other room until you can calm down enough
to talk to each other about your problem. When you are ready to
come back and listen to the story, you may." Sheri views time-out as
a related consequence of children's failure to behave appropriately in
a place or time by providing an alternative place for them to go. Her
term for the place, calming chairs, shows what she expects of their
occupants. She leaves it up to the children to decide when they are
capable of trying again.

Dennis gives children a choice of not only when to return to the group, but
when to leave, too.

Dennis knows the kids can be tired and irritable at the good-bye gathering at the end of the day. If a child is having a particularly hard time
getting along with his friends during this time, Dennis sometimes
asks, "Might you feel better in a place by yourself for a while? Where
could you go to get some alone time?" If the child does take him up
on it, Dennis is sure to add, "Come on back whenever you feel like it!"
Dennis recognizes times when children are too upset or tired to be in
a group. He helps them learn that time alone can help them get in
touch with their feelings and gain control of themselves. He thinks
that the most productive time-out is one you give yourself.

Assertive Discipline

A program called assertive discipline (Canter, 1976) is one example of how behavior modification has been interpreted in classrooms. Although it is a misinterpre-
tation that violates many basic behaviorist principles, it does come from that base.
This program recommends a series of reward and punishment systems designed
to gain student compliance.

Miss Wheeler had just completed a summer training course in
assertive discipline. She had watched the course videos and filled out
the worksheets. Now she was excited to try it out. The authors, Lee
and Marlene Canter, promised the rapid and decisive result of a well-
behaved classroom.
    On the first day of school, Miss Wheeler clearly told the children
her firm discipline guidelines. She began by telling them what she
wanted. They were to sit in their seats until they had permission to get
up. They were to follow directions the first time they were given. They
were to raise their hands and wait to be called on before they spoke.
The list went on.
    Next she told them what would happen when anyone disre-
garded the rules. For a first infraction, the student's name would be

put on the board, and he or she would stay in for the first five minutes of recess. Second failure, the name would get a check mark by it. The check mark meant the student would lose the whole recess. Anyone who received more than two check marks would have his or her parents called. (She didn't tell the children that the course had recommended that she make a point of calling the parents at work to be sure to embarrass them.)

On the bright side, Miss Wheeler said that for each hour that the whole class followed all the rules, she would write one letter of the words "popcorn party" in the blanks she had made on the opposite end of the blackboard. When the class had done so well that all of the blanks were filled in, they would have the party!

To start out on a positive note, she wrote in a "P," telling the students how much she liked the way they had listened to the class rules. She added, though, that the group would also lose a letter each time anyone got his or her name or a check mark put up. Kaila was confused. She asked, "Does just the person who was bad lose a letter?" Miss Wheeler decided to use the girl as an example, saying, "You didn't raise your hand before you asked that question. So I will put your name on the board to help you remember to do that. And you will stay in for the first five minutes of recess. But no, it isn't only you who are affected. The whole class will lose the "P" because a class member broke a rule. That will help everyone learn, too!"

The children moaned, and several frowned at Kaila. Pleased with herself for having used the opportunity to illustrate the system of consequences to everyone's advantage, Miss Wheeler went on with her classroom orientation. No one else asked any questions. But Kaila wasn't listening to the detailed descriptions of how to use the centers. She kept staring at her name on the board, flushed with embarrassment.

Most of the next hour was filled with lecturing and a story. Miss Wheeler didn't catch anyone misbehaving, so she made a show of writing in a "P" on the popcorn blanks again, trying to excite the kids by talking about the party. Next she assigned the table groups to different centers. Delighted when her table was sent to the reading center, Kaila eagerly skipped over, taking three attractive books off the shelves and nestling into the beanbag chair to decide which one to read first. She had settled on *Frog and Toad Together*, one of her home favorites, when she saw Miss Wheeler's feet next to where she had put down the other two books.

"Who took more than one book off the library shelf?" the teacher demanded. "Kaila did it!" tattled Simon. He had learned her name off the board. Miss Wheeler looked down at the girl and reprimanded, "Kaila, because you didn't follow the instruction of one book at a time, you have chosen to have a check mark by your name. We need to follow instructions after hearing them once, and I told you the library limits this morning. You will lose the rest of recess now. You can use the time to think about the rules of our classroom." Then in her clearest "teacher voice," Miss Wheeler caught the group's attention as she checked Kaila's name and erased the "P" again, saying, "I'm sorry, but we all need to work on remembering the rules. Maybe you can help Kaila learn." Kaila squirmed. She hated Miss Wheeler and her dumb rules. She hated school!

Like other forms of behavior modification, assertive discipline only deals with surface behaviors; it does not consider the child's feelings or the cause of behavior problems. Additionally, this approach doesn't consider maturation stages and the behaviors inherent in each. It uses power to gain compliance and ignores child development.

Praise or Encouragement?

Praise is another form of behavior modification. Teachers and parents are often told to praise children for desirable behavior. It is common to hear teachers make these kinds of statements: "I like how Shelley is sitting so straight and quiet." They hope to make Shelley feel good and to make other children want to be like her. Often, it just makes the others resent Shelley as they hear the unspoken message, "Why aren't the rest of you as good as Shelley?" Even young children quickly learn to see through this type of insincere and manipulative comment. "I'm proud of you" is an even more dangerous type of praise because it is more likely to become addictive.

Praise is a form of social reinforcement. It has the same uses and the same side effects as other forms of behavior modification. Certainly, it has the same effects on autonomy, self-discipline, and intrinsic motivation as any other reward system (Potter, 1985). Many psychologists and educators have expressed concern that children have become addicted to praise. (Shalaway, 1980). Both children and adults seem to perform only for the purpose of pleasing others and obtaining their praise. Without that feedback, it is hard for some people to continue to function optimally. Nevertheless, most people are reluctant to give up praise because they see that children are used to it and like it.

Praise is often recommended as a tool for guidance and discipline, and most people consider it positive and helpful. Few seem to have considered that praise is an external judgment about another person (Katz & McClellan, 1991). When you praise someone, you are setting yourself up as an authority who knows what is best. This attitude implies that you are able to evaluate others' performance better than they are. The message can make children dependent on others to tell them whether or not they are doing well. It keeps them from judging for themselves and developing autonomy.

You can learn to give positive verbal feedback that is not praise by substituting comments that help children learn to self-evaluate and self-congratulate. Instead of telling them what *you* think about their accomplishments, you can help

Have you ever thought about praise as being a way of passing judgment?

children identify their own feelings of pride or success. For example, instead of giving your opinion, saying something like "You did a nice job" or "I'm proud of you," you could substitute a comment, such as "You must feel good about that" or "Don't you feel proud of yourself?"

Notice the shift from external judgment toward internal satisfaction. Randy Hitz and Amy Driscoll refer to this type of positive feedback as encouragement rather than praise (1988). Comments that focus children's attention on their own judgment of their behavior help children feel good about what they have done without damaging their autonomy.

It might be helpful to think about praise and encouragement in relationship to the communications skills described in chapter 7. Praise is another of the "roadblocks to communication" described by Thomas Gordon (1970, 1989). In contrast, encouragement can be a form of reflective listening. Encouragement responds to the message sent by what a child says or does. If Blake calls you over to look at his block tower, you can tell by his expression that he is pleased with himself. Reflective listening and encouragement respond to that message about his own feelings. "It looks like you really liked making such a big tower" tunes in to the child's feelings rather than judges what he has done.

PRAISE VS. ENCOURAGEMENT

Praise	Encouragement
I'm proud of you.	I'll bet you feel good about that!
	You must be proud of yourself.
Good work!	It looks like you were working hard on that.
	You must have enjoyed doing that.

Positive "I messages" are a form of encouragement also. For instance, when a child does something helpful for you, a sincere "thank you" gives a more respectful message than praise for the behavior. On the surface, "thank you" may not sound like an "I message," and "I'm proud of you" may sound like it is. Analysis of the two statements, however, reveals just the opposite. "Thank you" actually tells your feelings and means "I appreciate what you have done." Remember not to think that any statement starting with *I* is an "I message." The statement "I'm proud of you" really is a judgment of the other person. If you decide you do want to give a value judgement, think about what you say to children in comparison to what you would say to an adult acquaintance. Then you might decide that "I'm impressed" is more respectful than "I'm proud of you."

CONCLUSION

Behavior modification happens whether you plan it or not. Understanding how it works can help you keep it from working against you. Recognizing that many common discipline approaches are forms of behavior modification can help you make more informed decisions about discipline approaches. Thinking about the possible effects of behavior modification can help you decide whether to implement it purposefully or not. This chapter has explained why behavior modification tends to create people who can be manipulated by reward and punishment. It has also discussed why the manipulative aspects of rewards and praise are not compatible with a relationship of mutual respect. Such respect is crucial to the type of human relationships that nurture the development of autonomy. If autonomy and self-discipline are your long-term goals, you do not want to use behavior modification approaches to discipline.

FOR FURTHER THOUGHT

1. Think about things you do only because of the payoff or reward as opposed to those things you do purely for your own purposes. Which things do you put more effort into and get more pleasure from? What are the implications for education?
2. Observe in a classroom, watching for the focus of the teacher's attention. Is inappropriate behavior or desirable behavior more apt to get attention? What are the consequences for child behavior?
3. Closely observe your own interactions with children. Do you accidentally reinforce undesirable behavior? What can you do to focus more on the desirable?
4. Talk to children about the stars and stickers they get for school performance. Do the children focus on the learning or on the prizes? How do you think getting rewards affects a child's education and attitude about learning?
5. A problem to solve: Courtney finally wrote something in her journal today instead of just drawing in it: a major breakthrough!
   a. If you were using praise to motivate her, what might you say?
   b. If you were using encouragement to keep her going, what might you say?
   c. How are the two approaches and their goals different?
6. What's wrong with a teacher's putting a marble into a jar when the class is especially cooperative and then letting the class have a party when the jar is full?
7. How does the traditional approach to time-out differ from a related consequence?

REFERENCES AND RECOMMENDATIONS FOR READING

Books

BANDURA, A. (1969). *Social learning theory.* Englewood Cliffs, NJ: Prentice-Hall.
CANTER, L. (1976) *Assertive discipline: A take charge approach for today's educators.* Los Angeles: Lee Canter and Associates.

CURWIN, R. L., & MENDLER, A. N. (1988). *Discipline with dignity.* Alexandria, VA: Association for Supervision and Curriculum Development.

CURWIN, R.L., & MENDLER, A. N. (1990). *Am I in trouble? Using discipline to teach young children responsibility.* Santa Cruz, CA: Network Publications

DWECK, C. S., & ELLIOTT, E. S. (1983). Achievement motivation. In E. Mavis Heatherington (Ed.), *Handbook of child psychology* (Vol. 3, 4th ed.). New York: Wiley.

GORDON, T. (1970). *Parent effectiveness training.* New York: Wyden.

GORDON, T. (1989). *Teaching children self-discipline: At home and at school.* New York: Random House.

GROSSMAN, H. (1990). *Trouble-free teaching: Solutions to behavior problems in the classroom.* Mountain View, CA: Mayfield.

HYMES, J. (1990) *Teaching the child under six* (3rd ed.). West Greenwich, RI: Consortium Publishing.

KAMII, C. (1982). Autonomy as the aim of education: Implications of Piaget's theory. In C. Kamii, *Number* (pp. 73-87). Washington, DC: National Association for the Education of Young Children.

KATZ, L. G., & McCLELLAN, D. E. (1991). *The teacher's role in the social development of young children.* Urbana, IL: ERIC Clearinghouse Document, ED313168.

LOBEL, A. (1972). *Frog and Toad Together.* New York: Harper & Row.

MACHT, J. (1990). *Managing classroom behavior: An ecological approach to academic and social learning.* White Plains, NY: Longman.

MARION, M. (1991). *Guidance of young children* (3rd ed.). New York: Merrill/Macmillan.

MILLER, D. F. (1990). *Positive child guidance.* Albany: Delmar.

PIAGET, J. (1965). *The moral judgment of the child.* New York: The Free Press.

SKINNER, B. F. (1965). *Science and human behavior.* New York: The Free Press.

SKINNER, B. F. (1971). *Beyond freedom and dignity.* New York: Knopf.

Periodicals

BROPHY, J. E. (1981). Teacher praise: A functional analysis. *Review of Educational Research,* 51(1), 5–32.

CANTER, L. (1988). Assertive discipline and the search for the perfect classroom. *Young Children,* 43(2), 24.

CHANDLER, T. A. (1981). What's wrong with success and praise? *Arithmetic Teacher, 29*(4), 10–12.

CLEWETT, A. S. (1988). Guidance and discipline: Teaching young children appropriate behavior. *Young Children, 43*(4), 27–31.

DEVRIES, R., ZAN, B., REESE-LEARNED, H., & MORGAN, P. (1991). Sociomoral atmosphere and sociomoral development: A study of interpersonal understanding in three kindergarten classrooms. *Moral Education Forum, 16*(2), 5–20.

GARTRELL, D. (1987a). Punishment or guidance. *Young Children, 42*(3) 55–61.

GARTRELL, D. (1987b). Assertive discipline: Unhealthy for children and other living things. *Young Children, 42*(2), 10–11.

GREENBERG, P. (1992). Ideas that work with young children. How to institute some simple democratic practices pertaining to respect, rights, responsibilities, and roots in any classroom (without losing your leadership position). *Young Children, 47*(5), 10–17.

HENDRICK, J. (1992). Where does it begin? Teaching the principles of democracy in the early years. *Young Children, 47*(3), 51–53.

HITZ, R. (1988) Assertive discipline: A response to Lee Canter. *Young Children, 43*(2), 25–26.

HITZ, R., & DRISCOLL, A. (1988). Praise or encouragement? New insights into praise: Implications for early childhood teachers. *Young Children, 43*(5), 6–13.

KAMII, C. (1984). Autonomy: The aim of education envisioned by Piaget. *Phi Delta Kappan, 65*(6) 410–415.

KLAUKE, A. (1988). The developmental approach to kindergarten: Profile of an expert teacher. *Oregon School Study Council Bulletin, 32*(8).

POTTER, E. F. (1985). "Good job!" How we evaluate children's work. *Childhood Education, 61*, 203–206.

SHALAWAY, L. (1980, October). Are your students addicted to praise? *Instructor*, pp. 61–62.

Chapter 10

Punishment vs. Discipline

Spanking or slapping children is outlawed in most schools today (Simmons, 1991). Society has come to recognize the negative effects of punishing children physically. However, many other types of punishment are still commonly used to control and direct students. Although this chapter examines various forms of punishment and their negative effects on children, our book is primarily about alternatives to punishment. Chapters 4 through 8 explain how and why other approaches work.

Punishment is intended to hurt or humiliate a person in response to undesirable behavior; its goal is to make a person pay for misconduct (Curwin & Mendler, 1988; Piaget, 1965). Emotional pain is often more intense and lasting than bodily harm. You may have personal memories of intense embarrassment about being banished to the hallway for an offense. You might still be able to feel your childhood despair and frustration at being denied an eagerly awaited outing after an infraction of the rules. Or perhaps your worst memory of school is the shame and anger you felt from a teacher's sarcastic put-down.

PUNISHMENT

In general, punishment does not appear to change behavior. Even if the action being punished does stop for the moment, worse behavior is almost sure to follow. Punishment creates seriously counterproductive feelings that are demonstrated in numerous ways.

RESULTS OF PUNISHMENT

People who use punishment believe it will improve behavior. In fact, it can appear to stop the undesirable behavior because punishment may force negative behaviors "underground" (Curwin & Mendler, 1988). This quick result convinces many people that punishment is effective. However, extensive research proves that punishment is not an effective way of correcting behavior (Sabatino, 1991). In general, punishment does not appear to change behavior. Even if the action being punished does stop for the moment, worse behavior is almost sure to follow. Punishment creates seriously counterproductive feelings that are demonstrated in numerous ways.

Anger

Anger is a common reaction to punishment (Bettleheim, 1985). Because anger tends to be expressed as aggression, kids often vent their anger by hitting and hurting others. The negative feelings inside these angry children inevitably surfaces. Having experienced punishment, they have learned from a powerful role

Punishment is not an effective way of correcting behavior.

model how to give punishment. Children who have been hit when they have displeased a big person are very likely to hit a smaller person who displeases them. Children who experience other forms of punishment may be physically hurtful, too, but they will have also learned other methods of getting even (Sabatino, 1991). These youngsters might ruin another child's work or take someone else's possessions. Such unacceptable behavior is then likely to be punished, creating further misbehavior. This negative cycle is behind the behavior of many "bad kids."

> Mrs. Jensen chose her words carefully as she shared her concerns about Raymond with his parents at their conference. "When Raymond doesn't like what someone else is doing, he often hurts them." Looking concerned, his mother said, "Oh, dear. What does he do?" Referring to her observation notes, Mrs. Jensen described an inci-

dent. "When he didn't like a classmate's singing, he told her to quit it. She did for a while but started up again. Raymond hit her and said, 'I told you not to do that!' He usually says those words right after he hurts someone." A flash of recognition came across his mother's face. She knew where he got that line! And the hitting, too! She glanced accusingly at her husband. He retorted, "That sounds like a normal kid thing."

The father questioned Mrs. Jensen, "What do you do to him when he hits?" The teacher explained how she generally handled the situations, with attention to the hurt child and modeling alternative ways for Raymond to get what he needs. Raymond's dad leaned back in his chair and said knowingly, "Yeah, well, that soft-touch stuff just doesn't work with this kid. You have to tell him not to do something and then just don't let him do it! Giving him a quick wallop works at home." The mother stared intently at the pattern on the carpet, trying to avoid both the teacher's and her husband's eyes.

Mrs. Jensen could tell she had touched a sensitive area with this couple. Still, she was glad she had brought it up. She promised to keep them updated on Raymond's progress. In the meantime, she had some new insight about why Raymond was exhibiting such physically aggressive responses; it seemed he was following his father's model.

Damaged Relationships

Punishment also creates feelings of hostility and resentment toward the person administering it (Gordon, 1989). This result is particularly serious when it damages relationships between children and their parents. Whether the negative feelings are aimed at parents, teachers, or other authority figures, those emotions get in the way of positive discipline teaching. People don't want to be around someone who hurts them or makes them feel bad. Certainly, no one is eager to listen to or learn from that person. Some children merely withdraw from contact, while others try to get even. Getting even takes many forms, depending on the experiences and the personality of the child. One child may be openly defiant and rude, while another may retaliate through helplessness and refusal to try anything. Still another may become a bully, using smaller children as substitute targets. All of these behaviors are self-defeating, and all are only made worse by punishment.

Fear

Punishment controls through fear (Curwin & Mendler, 1990). This fear keeps some children from positive activities as well as negative ones. When they are punished without warning for something they didn't know was unacceptable, many children will tend to avoid any new activity. Their strategy is caution about anything that might possibly get them into trouble. Exploration and initiative are sacrificed to the need for safety and security. Therefore, fear of punishment can hamper academic learning. Remember Kaila in the assertive discipline example in chapter 9? Scared of check marks on the board by her name and of classmates who had lost "popcorn" letters, Kaila rarely initiated conversation or joined activities.

Missed Opportunity for Learning

Punishment undermines social learning as well. It focuses on what *not* to do rather than teaching what *to* do. Young children need information about acceptable ways of behaving, and they need help in understanding why certain actions are better than others. In other words, they need *teaching* instead of punishment.

> Caroline, the children's center director, was concerned about the row of sad faces in the back of the room during morning choice time. It was Joanne's policy to remove youngsters from play if they weren't able to get along with others. Caroline decided to discuss this policy with Joanne.
>
> Caroline met with Joanne and shared her concern that the children who most needed practice with social skills were not getting that practice. When they were removed from play, they were no longer in the learning situation. She asked Joanne to problem-solve with her about ways to help these youngsters learn to get along instead of just expelling them from play.
>
> As they discussed the kinds of learning experiences these problem children needed, Joanne began to think of ways to teach instead of punish. But she realized that the changes required more than one adult in the large playroom. "I'll have to ask Sheri or Maureen to work the blue room with me during choice time," she planned. That change, however, meant having fewer options available for children. The teachers would have to alternate between opening the woodworking center and the painting area. Joanne decided that the sacrifice was worth it. With two adults to intervene, teachers could help children individually resolve disputes.
>
> Caroline was pleased with the outcome of the discussion. She and Joanne reviewed the kinds of role modeling and problem-solving assistance that would be most helpful in teaching social skills. Joanne arranged a meeting with her assistants to go over this new plan.

Damage to Self-esteem

Punishment also damages self-esteem because children get their opinion of their worth from how others treat them (Miller, 1990). Being punished can convince youngsters that they are bad children. That feeling is likely to become a self-fulfilling prophecy, resulting in further undesirable behavior. A child who is punished does not feel respected or valued. Both physical and psychological punish-

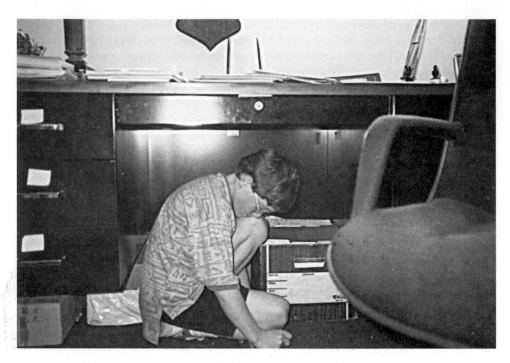

Punishment damages self-esteem because children get their opinion of their worth from how others treat them.

ment attack personal dignity by putting the child at the mercy of a more power-ful person. Additionally, many punishments are undignified, as shown in the fol-lowing example.

> "Beep! Beep! Beep! Beep!" sounded the intercom, the library light flashing. The secretary had two people on hold on the telephone and new parents at the counter needing forms. She switched on the speaker, "Yes, this is the office." The librarian sounded stressed. "Ian bit Serge and then ran out of the room. He's somewhere in the halls, and I can't leave the group to go find him." The secretary responded, "Sorry, but I'm the only person in the office, so I can't go look for him right now." Leaning by the message board, the custodian overheard the exchange. He volunteered, "I'll go get him." Relieved, she called the library back and said, "George is going to go look for Ian. I'll let you know when we find him."
>
> The custodian strode down the hall on his mission to bring in the wayward child. Not finding him on the first floor, he went upstairs. Still failing to see the boy, he checked the playground. Darn it, he needed to go set up the lunchroom soon. Where was that kid? Then he thought of the bathroom. Sure enough, there were two feet stand-ing in the back corner of a stall. "Come on out!" ordered George. The

boy froze, wondering if the custodian could see him. "Come out now!" he repeated. The other boys in the bathroom giggled as George crouched to look under the door and demanded, "Move it!" Ian slowly opened the stall door, his eyes darting around like those of a trapped animal. His mind raced as his playmates Alex and Tory teased him about being caught.

Once outside the bathroom, George scooped Ian up like a bag of potatoes. He hauled the boy past the library, while the child flailed and demanded to be put down. His classmates crowded to the door to glimpse the spectacle. Humiliated, Ian's temper flared. He pounded on the back of George's leg, but the custodian just held him more tightly and headed for the office, proud to have successfully completed his mission. Dumping Ian in the detention room, George announced, "Here's your biter!" Ian felt about one foot tall as the custodian described the bathroom scene to the secretary. And wasn't that his friend Kenji's mom at the counter listening, too? Ian wished he were invisible!

Unfortunately, this disrespectful treatment of children is not uncommon. The damage to a child's self-respect is immeasurable.

Lack of Inner Controls

For some kids, fear of punishment becomes the only reason to behave in socially acceptable ways. These youngsters are only likely to act appropriately when someone is there to catch them. Even then, the seriousness of the punishment is often weighed against the potential pleasure of the inappropriate action (Kamii, 1982). Often youngsters will choose to go ahead with the action and "face the music" later. Accepting the punishment can even become a sort of challenge to their courage. Not getting caught can become another type of challenge.

Deceitfulness

Many people whose only restraint comes from fear of punishment become incredibly sneaky (Kamii, 1982). They become skillful at lying and other forms of deceit. You have probably known people who have adopted this dishonest approach to life. They get what they want behind people's backs. Although they can act innocent, others soon catch on to them and learn to distrust them. Certainly, this behavior is not a desirable outcome of discipline.

WHY PUNISHMENT IS USED

Obviously, the results of punishment are totally incompatible with the goals of self-discipline and autonomy. Punishment undermines the development of understanding and attitudes that lead to personal responsibility. Adults who rely on punishment are looking for the quick fix referred to in chapter 1, but they may not get that result because some children are not submissive enough to give in. Their defiance leads to escalation of punishment and even greater defiance. When punishment clearly doesn't stop the behavior, many parents and teachers still persist in using it because they don't know any other methods. However, some adults also use punishment for other reasons.

Adult Stress

Even adults who really don't believe in punishment and know better than to use it sometimes resort to it (Sabatino, 1991). There are times when the stresses of life push people beyond their limits, when an adult's behavior doesn't live up to his or her personal expectations. In these cases it is best to forgive yourself and try to redeem the situation.

> Mrs. Jensen had such an experience several years ago, when she was driving across the state on a very hot summer day with her four children in a van with no air-conditioning. The children were uncomfortable and fussy from the heat and from being confined in the van. Andrew was screaming that he wanted out of his car seat, and Joe was teasing John by his hat. There was no place to pull over and deal with the problem sensibly, so Mrs. Jensen reached back and grabbed Joe's arm, yanking him into his place with a barking order: "Sit!" She just didn't know what else to do; besides, it actually made her feel better at the time. But later she felt bad and apologized to Joe, explaining her frustration. When everyone was calm and cooled off, the family was able to problem-solve about the situation.

Such instances are less likely in the controlled environment of Mrs. Jensen's classroom. Sometimes, however, a child does push her beyond her limits. In her professional role, Mrs. Jensen maintains her professional ethics. She would never hit a child or even grab a youngster in anger. She knows the importance of being in control of herself to deal with discipline problems effectively.

> Desmond was making Mrs. Jensen exasperated. He was running in the classroom *again*. How many times just today had she reminded him of the safety rule? Frustrated, she could feel the irritation rising up inside her; she knew she shouldn't try to deal with Desmond now. Instead, she privately told him, "I need you to go and be quiet someplace away from me for a while. I'm feeling too angry to talk to you right now about running. When I'm feeling calmer, we'll talk about how to help you remember."

Any time you feel angry, you run the risk of punishing behavior rather than teaching self-discipline (Curwin & Mendler, 1988). Chapter 8 described how anger can change related consequences into punishment, just by the inevitably negative tone of voice and body language. Similarly, anger destroys the tech-

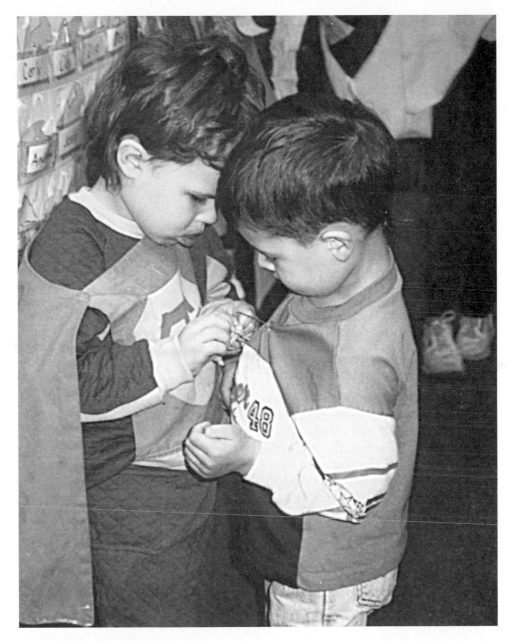

Punishment would undermine the development of understanding and attitudes that lead to this type of considerate behavior.

nique of holding a child to calm him or her. Restraining a child when you are infuriated is different from the reassuring embrace needed by an out-of-control youngster. It is important to know when you are not emotionally able to provide helpful guidance to youngsters and to call in someone with a fresh perspective. This action also models an adult's personal time-out to calm down.

Misconceptions

Some adults say they don't believe in punishment and yet routinely rely on it. Apparently, they don't perceive their actions as punishment. Some teachers humiliate children in front of classmates and call it peer pressure. Others pride themselves on their "humor" when they cut down a child with a sarcastic response. Still others call it a "consequence" when they take away privileges totally unrelated to a behavior problem. All of these responses inflict hurt, create anger, and fail to teach. They are all punishment.

> Simon was notoriously slow at cleaning up before circle time. The truth was that he didn't like going to circle time, so he dragged his feet. It distracted Joanne to have a child otherwise occupied during her circle. Today she decided to break Simon of this habit. She announced in a voice that carried across the room, "We're waiting for Simon to join our group so that we can begin our circle."
>
> Embarrassed because all of the kids were staring at him, Simon hurried. Trying to carry both the basket of trucks and the box of animals at once, he dropped everything with a clatter. With his classmates laughing, he got even more flustered and put some trucks in the animal box. Joanne noted his error and asked, "Can anyone tell Simon which container the trucks go into?" "The orange basket!" taunted several children, enjoying what seemed to be the teacher's approval to pick on Simon. By now Simon was nearly in tears, but Joanne couldn't see his face. She made another effort at using what she called peer pressure to bring his behavior into line. "Simon, we'll wait for three more minutes; then we'll have to start our circle. It's just not fair to keep your friends waiting." Thoroughly upset, he fumbled at putting away the rest of the toys. Finally the teacher pronounced, "Time's up! Sorry, but you have used up too much of our time being a slowpoke." Steaming, Simon thought, "You're not sorry at all! I hate you!"

Lack of Discipline Skills

Many people fear that children will go wild without fear of punishment; it is the only discipline approach these adults understand (Gordon, 1989). They are not informed about how other approaches to discipline set limits and communicate expectations about desirable behavior. Not understanding these other approaches, they think their choice is either punishment or a total lack of discipline, as we discussed in chapter 1. To many people, discipline *is* punishment.

Any concern about a lack of guidance and discipline is justified. Overly permissive child rearing can be as damaging as a punitive approach. Freedom without limits or responsibility is chaotic and dangerous. There are times when adults must step in to keep youngsters safe as well as to help them learn. Children must be helped to learn socially acceptable behavior and respect for the rights of others. These understandings are good for the child who learns them, as well as for

Punishment may stop kids from doing something if they think they may get caught, but it won't help them understand why it is important to avoid the behavior when no one is around to catch them.

those around that child. Youngsters who don't learn socially acceptable behaviors are not pleasant to be around. They damage property and are rude and inconsiderate. Naturally, no one wants to spend time with them, which leads to feelings of rejection and damages self-esteem. Understanding the rights and needs of others is also essential to the development of self-discipline. Self-discipline doesn't result from forced behavior, but neither does it occur by itself. It is a product of careful teaching through constructivist approaches to discipline.

Social Norms

Many truly loving and caring people are firmly convinced that punishment will have long-term positive effects. They mean well but are misinformed. Their beliefs are based on tradition rather than evidence. Education must be used as a tool to help these misinformed people learn the other, more useful approaches explained in this book.

The violent traditions of our society make it difficult for many people to give up punitive approaches to discipline. Movies and television promote violence as a legitimate way for the "good guys" to win. Many sporting events involve violence that is eagerly applauded. World leaders still rely on force to settle differences, and soldiers returning from war become heroes. The use of force is continually glorified.

Yet our society also recognizes values that should counteract the use of force to discipline children. Respect for the rights of all people is increasingly evidenced in laws and attitudes. Minority groups are speaking up and insisting on equal treatment. Perhaps the least represented group is the one with the smallest voices: the children. The U.S. Constitution guarantees equality, rights, and the protection of all. Perhaps children, too, will soon be included in this guarantee. Teachers can be effective advocates for the rights of young children. Professional organizations representing early childhood teachers, such as the National Association for the Education of Young Children (NAEYC) and the Association for Childhood Education International (ACEI), have been vocal about the subject of punishment (Simmons, 1991; Greenberg, 1992).

ACHIEVING EFFECTIVE DISCIPLINE WITHOUT COPRORAL PUNISHMENT

The Association for Childhood Education International (Cryan, 1987) recommends the following measures to promote effective discipline in schools without resorting to corporal punishment:

❏ Improve school climate with support by all school personnel.

❏ Provide inservice training to increase staff competence and help educators see the theory-practice link.

❏ Improve teacher training by focusing it on techniques for student motivation and effective handling of discipline problems.

❏ Identify children's potential problems early and follow up with counseling designed to prevent discipline problems.

CONCLUSION

We have hope that punishment will cease to be considered a reasonable means of discipline, for we believe that when parents and teachers understand the dangers of punishment and learn more effective approaches to child guidance, the world will become a better place. There will be fewer angry people who need to get even with society through violence. There will be fewer people who have come to believe they are worthless. There will be less dishonesty and less energy spent to avoid getting caught. Personal inner controls and concern for others will become the norm among morally autonomous people.

FOR FURTHER THOUGHT

1. Were you punished as a child? If so, what are your memories of the way you felt and what you thought about being punished? How do your memories of physical punishment differ from those of other types of punishment? How did each method affect your self-esteem?
2. Were you raised with no discipline? Did you wish for controls and guidance? How did this experience affect your attitudes about discipline? What was the impact on your self-esteem?
3. Were you given constructive discipline as a child? How has it affected your life, your attitudes, and your self-esteem?
4. Observe aggressive young children. Do they seem to be imitating a model of adult aggression?
5. Observe socially competent young children. Do they seem to have learned from adult models for peaceful negotiation of conflict?
6. How would you explain to someone the fundamental differences between punishment and discipline? Can you relate those differences to the differences between moral autonomy and heteronomy?

REFERENCES AND RECOMMENDATIONS FOR READING

Books

CURWIN, R. L., & MENDLER, A. N. (1988). *Discipline with dignity*. Alexandria, VA: Association for Supervision and Curriculum Development.

CURWIN, R. L., & MENDLER, A. N. (1990). *Am I in trouble? Using discipline to teach young children responsibility*. Santa Cruz, CA: Network Publications

GORDON, T. (1989). *Teaching children self-discipline: At home and at school*. New York: Random House.

KAMII, C. (1982). Autonomy as the aim of education: Implications of Piaget's theory. In C. Kamii, *Number* (pp. 73-87). Washington, DC: National Association for the Education of Young Children.

KATZ, L. (1989). Family living: Suggestions for effective parenting. Urbana, IL: ERIC Clearinghouse Document.

KATZ, L. G., & McCLELLAN, D. E. (1991). *The teacher's role in the social development of young children*. Urbana, IL: ERIC Clearinghouse Document, ED313168.

MACCOBY, E. E. (1980). *Social development*. New York: Harcourt Brace Jovanovich.

MILLER, D. F. (1990). *Positive child guidance.* Albany: Delmar.

PIAGET, J. (1965). *The moral judgment of the child.* New York: The Free Press.

SABATINO, D. (1991). *A fine line: When discipline becomes child abuse.* Summit, PA: TAB Books/McGraw-Hill.

SAVAGE, T. V. (1991). *Discipline for self-control.* Englewood Cliffs, NJ: Prentice-Hall.

Periodicals

BETTLEHEIM, B. (1985, November). Punishment versus discipline. *The Atlantic Monthly*, pp. 51–59.

DEVRIES, R., ZAN, B., REESE-LEARNED, H., & MORGAN, P. (1991). Sociomoral atmosphere and sociomoral development: A study of interpersonal understanding in three kindergarten classrooms. *Moral Education Forum, 16*(2), 5–20.

GREENBERG, P. (1992). Ideas that work with young children. How to institute some simple democratic practices pertaining to respect, rights, responsibilities, and roots in any classroom (without losing your leadership position). *Young Children, 47*(5), 10–17.

MILLER, C. S. (1984). Building self-control: Discipline for young children. *Young Children, 40*(1), 15–19.

PARPAL, M., & MACCOBY, E. E. (1985). Maternal responsiveness and subsequent child compliance. *Child Development, 56*, 1326–1334.

SIMMONS, B. J. (1991). Ban the hickory stick. *Childhood Education, 68*(2), 69.

Papers

CRYAN, J. R. (1987). The banning of corporal punishment: In child care, school and other educative settings in the United States. A position paper of the Association for Childhood Education International. Wheaton, MD: Association for Childhood Education International.

EDUCATIONAL RESOURCES INFORMATION CENTER. (1990). Positive discipline. *ERIC Digest.* Urbana, IL: ERIC Clearinghouse Document, ED327271.

3

Matching Discipline Causes to Discipline Approaches

art 2 explained the different approaches to discipline. While this information is essential, its organization is not in the format most useful in real life. In working with youngsters, we are first confronted with the behavior, not the discipline approach. Part 3 looks at discipline from the real-world perspective: We start with the behavior and move backward to discover the cause, select the approach, and then implement that approach.

Discipline is effective only if it addresses the cause of the problem. In chapter 1 we explained this idea by comparing the guidance of children to gardening: Getting rid of unwanted behavior is like weeding the garden, while the cause of the behavior is similar to the roots of the weeds. Because it is necessary to get at the roots of a problem, parents, caregivers, and teachers are constantly challenged to determine what is causing unwanted behavior.

In the following chapters we look at some common behaviors that disrupt school and child-care settings. We hope the examples provide useful practice in matching behaviors to probable causes. We also hope that the process of matching discipline approaches to the cause of the problem becomes more clear as you read this section.

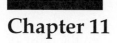

Chapter 11

Immaturity

Being young means being immature, and just being young is often the cause of problems. Early-childhood teachers face this issue daily as their students demonstrate lack of skills for success in daily living. Young children are prone to spilling, falling, spitting, biting, hitting, crying, and screaming. These behavior problems can be directly traced to immature coordination, undeveloped communication ability, childish social skills, and other perfectly normal aspects of early childhood. Knowledgeable adults are able to distinguish between misbehavior and childlike behavior. This distinction is essential for helpful guidance (Curry & Johnson, 1990).

SOME NORMAL BEHAVIORS OF YOUNG CHILDREN

Physical immaturity can cause:

- ❑ Spilling
- ❑ Bumping
- ❑ Wetting
- ❑ Moving

Social immaturity can cause:

- ❑ Hitting
- ❑ Kicking
- ❑ Biting
- ❑ Grabbing

Cognitive immaturity can cause:

- ❑ Being selfish
- ❑ Telling "lies"
- ❑ Taking things
- ❑ Misunderstanding

IMMATURE COORDINATION

Spilled juice at snack time is an everyday occurrence in preschool. It is a result of the immature coordination that is normal for young children. Providing child-sized pitchers and furniture increases children's successful independence, but it doesn't eliminate all spills. Adults with realistic expectations prepare for this inevitable outcome with handy cleanup sponges. Piaget (1965) calls it "making restitution" when children clean up their mistakes. We call it helping children take responsibility for themselves without making them feel bad. This approach to accidents is an example of using related consequences, as described in chapter 8. Teachers also prevent spills from becoming a problem by locating snack tables on a washable floor surface. These preparations help teachers remain calm and allow for productive responses to mistakes. This attitude is a description of the approach to discipline we call *creating environments that prevent discipline problems* (see chapter 4).

Unfortunately, not all adults realize that spilling is a natural part of learning to pour. Some act as if they think that yelling abuse at a child will improve pouring ability. Common responses are "Not again!" or "That's the third time today! Can't you be careful?" Other adults simply eliminate spills by denying children the chance to practice. Both responses are counterproductive to the child's skill development. Both approaches also damage the child's self-esteem and hinder development of autonomy. Being yelled at makes youngsters feel ashamed and afraid to try, while having things done for them makes kids feel inept and unable to succeed. Both responses create helplessness. In contrast, related consequences help children feel capable and proud (Curwin & Mendler, 1988).

Young children frequently experience negative feedback for the clumsiness natural to their age. As a teacher, you may see lack of sensitivity not only from other adults but also from children's own peers. The following example demonstrates how opportunity for making restitution can make everyone involved feel better about an accident. It is another example of a related consequence.

Young children frequently experience negative feedback for the lack of controls natural to their age.

Christie and Ashley were at the inventions table. They were busily cutting out pictures from catalogs and picking bits of ribbon, shells, and Styrofoam to glue onto larger pieces of paper. Ashley accidentally spilled some of the gooey white glue on Christie's paper. Christie started yelling in frustration and anger about her spoiled project. Ashley kept saying over and over how sorry she was, but Christie kept on screaming.

Maureen quickly came to the rescue. Ashley looked frightened and fearful of punishment as the teacher came near. Maureen reassured her that accidents do happen and then turned her attention to the screaming Christie. "I know you are angry about your paper, but such loud screaming hurts everyone's ears. Let's see what we can do to fix your paper. Ashley feels bad about spilling on it, and I'm sure she will help you clean it up. What would be a good thing to wipe up glue with?"

Ashley did indeed want to help. She suggested that Kleenex might work to wipe up the glue and ran to get some. Together, the girls carefully wiped away the excess glue, leaving Christie's paper almost as good as new. Then they were able to continue working cooperatively together.

OTHER PHYSICAL LIMITATIONS

"Someone wet on the floor!" Physical immaturity sometimes means a youngster doesn't make it to the toilet on time. The accident can be a serious blow to a child's pride and must be handled with care to preserve self-esteem. Mrs. Jensen remembers how her own kindergarten teacher publicly humiliated children who had accidents. They had to wash out their underpants, and then the teacher would hang them up to dry in the classroom for all to see. Mrs. Jensen is sure she can improve on that technique. She doesn't consider the incident to be a discipline issue; her only approach in the following example is to treat Meadow with respect. Mrs. Jensen knows it is not a discipline problem, but rather a maturation issue.

Meadow was working on a puzzle during choice time when she suddenly realized she had to go to the bathroom. She was very uncomfortable, but it wasn't time for the bathroom break yet. She knew she could ask permission to go any time she wanted, but it was just too embarrassing. Everyone would know where she was going. She decided to wait until the scheduled time. Oh, oh! She couldn't hold it any longer. Meadow was mortified but hopeful that no one would notice the puddle on the floor around the chair. She quickly got up and moved away from the evidence. Her skirt didn't seem too wet and maybe no one would see that her underpants were soaked. Meadow just didn't think she could stand it if anyone knew what she had done.

"Mrs. Jensen! Someone wet on the floor!" shouted Jimmie indignantly. The teacher replied calmly, "I guess it will have to be wiped up. Just don't walk there for now." Mrs. Jensen noticed Meadow's damp skirt and furtive looks. She quickly put the pieces together and realized how distressed the shy girl must be. The teacher's challenge was to get the floor cleaned, help Meadow get dry, and still preserve the child's privacy and dignity. Mrs. Jensen noticed that recess was in just ten minutes and decided to wait until then for the custodian to come and clean up. It would make much less fuss that way. Recess would also be a good time to get Meadow aside and quietly give her some dry undies as well as a plastic bag for her wet ones.

INABILITY TO SIT STILL

Children often get into trouble for moving around when they aren't supposed to. The inability to sit still for very long is another example of the physical limitations of being young (Bredekamp, 1987). Forcing young children to sit still or controlling their bodies for long periods of time can cause problems. Unable to satisfy

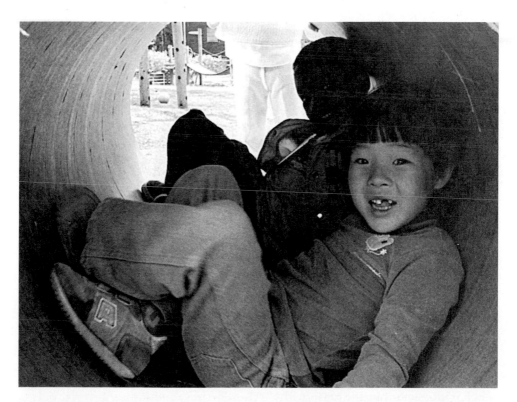

Young children have difficulty sitting still for long and need frequent opportunities to move around.

this unreasonable expectation, the young child *will* move. Chapter 3 described this aspect of early childhood development, and chapter 4 explained the importance of allowing children to move around as a way to prevent discipline problems.

Allowing them to move freely about the classroom and to find comfortable body positions lets children meet their need to move. Teachers who are aware of children's physical development provide meaningful reasons for them to move around. These teachers are also sensitive to the group's energy level. They recognize squirming and children's frequent requests to move—to go get a drink, to go to the bathroom, to *go!*—as symptoms of their need for movement. These teachers know that sometimes the only reasonable thing to do is to have everyone push the tables back and play an energetic game or action song! The following example shows how even a normally sedentary activity like reading can accommodate the movement needs of young children.

> Mrs. Jensen asked Beth, the aide, to take a group to the library corner to read *The Three Little Pigs* together. Most of the children settled right in and found their place in their individual books. But Allison, Jeffrey, and Randy couldn't get settled. They pushed and jostled for seats. They juggled their books into every conceivable position, flipping pages and occasionally dropping the books. Beth was having a hard time keeping them still and focused on reading. How could she get them through the story with all of this activity and fighting? Deciding to ask for help, she excused herself from the group for a minute and described her difficulty to Mrs. Jensen.
>
> Aware of the high energy level that morning, Mrs. Jensen suggested they try acting out the story. Beth checked with the children to see if they'd like to do a play. Affirmative! She assigned the three little pigs to—you guessed it—Allison, Jeffrey, and Randy. They went to the adjacent block area to build their houses. She sent Brianna, a strong reader, along with them in the narrator/cuing role. Brianna brought the book to each construction site as the part came up in the story. Beth read the wolf to help pull the play together. The piglets frantically built while the narrator read. They read their pig parts with intensity. Then they squealed in delight and scrambled to the next house as Beth huffed and puffed. No one even considered leaving the reading group for a trip down the hall.

Beth could have wasted a lot of energy trying to squelch the children's surface behaviors. Fortunately, Mrs. Jensen accurately recognized their difficulties in getting along and sitting still as symptoms of an undeniable need for movement. Her recommended discipline approach dealt directly with the cause of theproblem.

Mrs. Jensen knows her students well and is in a position to know the cause of behaviors such this: the reason why Allison, Jeffrey, and Randy had a problem sitting still. But the same behavior could have had a different cause. It is possible that the "troublemakers" might have been uncooperative due to their inability to read the material. Or the problem could have been just the opposite: The material lacked challenge for them. Similar disruption could have been caused by one child's attention-getting tactics. Often there are multiple causes, which create an even greater challenge for helpful adult intervention. Without information about the children involved, it is not possible to diagnose the problem accurately. Without an accurate diagnosis, discipline approaches are likely to go astray. Knowing students well enough to guess fairly accurately about the cause of problems involves establishing authentic relationships with the child and the parents (Greenberg, 1992).

UNDEVELOPED COMMUNICATION ABILITY

Let's look at hitting, kicking, biting, and spitting. Although these behaviors are unacceptable, they generally only indicate a need to learn more productive approaches for expressing needs and feelings. The common cause of this type of behavior among preschoolers is their lack of communication ability. Young children are still beginners with language (Vygotsky, 1962). They haven't yet had sufficient practice to find the exact words they need; and in times of stress, what they do know may fall apart (Gartrell, 1988). A child who is angry, frustrated, or otherwise upset often has trouble expressing those feelings in words. Instead, the child hits, kicks, bites, or spits to communicate.

Productive discipline does more than simply stop the behavior. It doesn't just let kids know what *not* to do; it teaches them what *to* do. Therefore, when lack of communication skills appears to be the cause of the behavior, adults need to help children express themselves with language. Teachers of young children can frequently be heard reminding them, "Please use your words."

Being around twenty-eight pseudo-siblings was just too much for Amy today. It seemed like anything she wanted to do didn't work out. The people on the other side of the easel jostled it and made her ruin her careful painting. When Amy built with the blocks, Kenji and Colette chose all the good shapes. Megan got to Amy's favorite rabbit dress-up costume first, and Tory wouldn't share the bristle blocks. Then Amy took an alphabet puzzle to a table, spreading it all out to mark her territory. Oblivious to her needs for privacy and ownership, Sam plopped his circus puzzle down on her table and proceeded to dump his pieces out. Several landed on top of Amy's. That was the last straw! She grabbed his pieces and threw them on the floor, glaring at the intruder. Confused, Sam said, "Those aren't your pieces." He leaned down and picked up his clown and seal pieces, placing them on empty table space. Amy pushed them roughly back toward him. Engrossed in his puzzle, Sam ignored her gesture. Where was that dancing bear piece? Oh! It had fallen way across the table when he'd dumped out the pieces. He leaned way over to reach it, his arm

Helpful discipline doesn't just let kids know what not *to do; it teaches them what* to do.

right in Amy's face. She couldn't stand it; she bit him! Surprised, Sam squealed in pain.

Dennis moved quickly to the scene. First he checked out the injury, putting his arm around the boy to comfort him. It wasn't a bad bite, but it sure had scared Sam, who kept repeating, "She bit me! She bit me!" On the defensive, Amy protested, "He was in my way!" While acknowledging her conflict, Dennis modeled a more effective way for her to communicate to Sam. "You want to be alone. You need to tell Sam that with your words. When you bite him, he only under-stands that he is hurt. You can tell him 'Please don't sit here. I feel like playing by myself.' Then he'll know what you want." Amy made an attempt, "I feel like you going away!" It wasn't a perfect "I message," but it was a beginning. Certainly, it was better than biting! Sam got the message. Dennis helped the boy scoop up his puzzle pieces and find another table. Then he alerted the other staff members to Amy's special needs so that they could help her find what privacy she could in their crowded setting.

When lack of language skill causes behavior problems, the proper discipline approach is to teach the missing skills. Possibly the most valuable communication skill is how to use an "I message" as described in chapter 7. Dennis was teaching Amy how to use "I messages" when he modeled better ways of expressing her feelings.

Another discipline approach might have been appropriate for this behavior if there had been a different cause. You may recall that we recommended in chapter 8 that a child who hurts another child should help the injured youngster. Do you know why that wouldn't be appropriate in this case? Remember, you select your discipline approach based on what you believe the child needs to learn. Dennis saw the need for communication skills here, apparently having cause to believe that Amy already knew that biting hurts. Additionally, a child who desperately needs time alone is not in the best condition to offer nurturing help right then. The choice of discipline approaches was based on the teacher's perception of the child's current intellectual and emotional needs.

UNDEVELOPED SOCIAL SKILLS

Learning the complexities of human interaction takes at least a lifetime. No won-der small humans with very little experience often have problems. To make mat-ters worse, society groups these inexperienced beings into crowds where they have to compete for limited space and resources. Some children don't face this test until kindergarten age, but many are thrust into preschool or group care at much younger ages. They are expected to "get along" by "sharing" the attractive toys and being "nice" about letting others infringe on their play territory. When children are unable to rise to these challenges, adults generally consider it a disci-pline problem. Those who understand discipline as teaching respond in one way, while those who view discipline as controlling behavior respond in another (DeVries & Kohlberg, 1987).

"Teacher, Leo won't let me have any little people!" complained Colette. The two children were playing at the same table with a set of miniature people and an airport setup. Leo was hoarding all of the small figures in his play space.

Joanne immediately came to the rescue. "Leo, you must share the people with Colette. All the toys at the center belong to everyone."

Learning the complexities of human interaction takes at least a lifetime.

Leo still wouldn't part with his pile of figures, so Joanne got firmer. "Leo, if you can't share, you must go to the time-out chair and think about being kind." Leo knew he was beaten. Either he had to give up some of the people, or he would lose out all together. Sullenly, he sorted out some of the least attractive figures and shoved them at Colette.

Sheri, the aide, watched this incident with interest. Because her hours at the center were from mid-morning to mid-afternoon, she noted the contrasting teaching styles of the morning and afternoon head teachers. Sheri had to admit that Joanne's style got the incident over with quickly, but children definitely got along better in the afternoon under Dennis's management system. After lunch, Sheri observed closely as Dennis handled a similar situation.

Kelsey and Joshua dragged the zoo box out to the sun room. Kelsey busied herself putting the cages together, while Joshua sorted out all the animals. There were two sets mixed up, and one was notably newer. By the time Kelsey had the zoo ready for occupancy, Joshua had decided that he didn't want to play with her after all. He was building his own cages with the Lincoln Logs. He had all the shiny new animals hoarded away in a basket next to him. Noticing that she only had the scuffed-up critters with broken legs, Kelsey protested, "You can't have all the good animals!" Joshua retorted, "I got 'em first!" The disappointed girl said tearfully, "But I was building the cages for them." "Well, I've got my own cages," he told her. Kelsey repeated her position, her voice rising, "But you can't have all of those good ones!" She grabbed at the basket, but Joshua snatched it out of reach and pushed her away.

Overhearing their disagreement, Dennis helped them think about their problem through reflective listening. "You both want the same animals," he began. Kelsey clarified, "He's got *all* of the good ones! All that's left are these old broken ones." Dennis continued, "You don't want to play with the older animals." "Yeah, they don't even stand up," she complained. Kelsey demonstrated by attempting unsuccessfully several times to get the three-legged zebra to stay up. Dennis acknowledged, "The ones with broken legs won't stand up." Addressing both children, he encouraged them to brainstorm solutions. "Well, what can you do with the old animals?" "Throw them away!" said the disgusted girl. Then she remembered that if they threw them away, she wouldn't have any. She restated her claim, "But I want half of the new ones!" Dennis invited Joshua's input: "What do you think we could do with these animals?" "Fix 'em?" the boy suggested, wondering if it were possible. "How would you fix the animals?" the teacher inquired. Joshua said knowingly, "You fix animals at the ventrananium!" His old dog had been hit by a car, and he knew all about animal doctors. "You're right. Veterinarians do help fix broken animal bodies," Dennis replied. "Could we have an animal hospital here?"

Eager to show off what he knew about vets, Joshua volunteered to transform his zoo into a hospital. Not sure she was satisfied with Joshua's solution, Kelsey asked, "But can I have some of the new animals?" "OK, but I want all of yours with the broken legs," insisted the boy. He had an idea about making legs out of paper straws from the collage box. They would look kind of like the bandage his dog had worn. Kelsey agreed, and they exchanged critters. Dennis doubted that the straw appendages would work, but that problem wasn't as important as the fact that the children had come up with a solution they could both accept. Someday the preschool would probably have to throw away the old animals, but he'd wait until everyone agreed to it.

Sheri could see that Joshua was feeling more cooperative at the end of this exchange than Leo had after being forced to share the airport people. Yet Dennis had had to spend several minutes working with the youngsters on the problem. Sheri found a chance to ask Dennis, "Why didn't you just tell Joshua to give some of the new animals to Kelsey instead of spending so much time with the children?"

Dennis was glad to discuss his approach with Sheri; she seemed to have a good rapport with the children, and he hoped she would stay in this job for a while. He explained that children don't learn to solve problems if a teacher solves problems for them. He also shared his view that forced sharing creates selfishness rather than generosity. He communicated his goals of teaching youngsters how to get along and helping them learn to consider the feelings of others. He told Sheri that he considered this knowledge one of the most essential parts of early childhood education; therefore, he was happy to spend his time working on it. However, he commented further on the time element, mentioning that he seemed to spend less and less time on arguments between youngsters as the year progressed. Sheri was inclined to agree; Dennis spent more time on individual problems, but Joanne had many more continuing problems to deal with.

Sometimes the problem seems to be about sharing toys or materials but actually has another source. As we explained in chapter 3, many young children don't know how to initiate play with another child (Ramsey, 1991). It is common for these youngsters to grab a possession away from someone they really want as a playmate. Sometimes they will punch or shove to get attention from someone they want as a friend. This behavior is a primitive way of saying, "I like you." Adults who don't understand young children will simply try to stop the behavior. Adults who realize the cause of the problem will help children learn more productive ways of making friends. It is difficult to stop unacceptable behavior unless you help children find another behavior to take its place. In the following example, Kyle learns something about seeing another child's viewpoint and uses one of the play entry approaches described in chapter 3.

They were finally getting a new boy at Midway Children's Center! If they had enrolled many more girls, they would have had to rename it "Midway Girls' Center." Kyle was especially excited. He was by far the biggest boy, and this new guy looked more his size. In his excitement about a potential playmate, he became quite forward, attempting to get the new boy, Aaron, to notice him. Walking by Aaron, Kyle made sure to bump him. In line for juice, Kyle socked the newcomer lightly on the shoulder to let him know he was behind him. But the more physical Kyle got, the more Aaron avoided him, intimidated by the jarring contacts. Fortunately, Dennis recognized Kyle's interest and helped him out. "You are glad we have a new boy at our center, aren't you, Kyle?" he opened. "Yeah, but he doesn't want to play with me," said the rejected boy sadly. "What does Aaron like to play with? Could you play next to him?" Kyle looked over at the block tower the big guy was building. He could build one that tall! He got up his nerve, went over, and grabbed some blocks off the shelves, starting a twin tower beside the new boy's. Aaron stopped working for a minute and watched Kyle with interest. He offered a shy smile, and Kyle beamed back! Their friendship had begun.

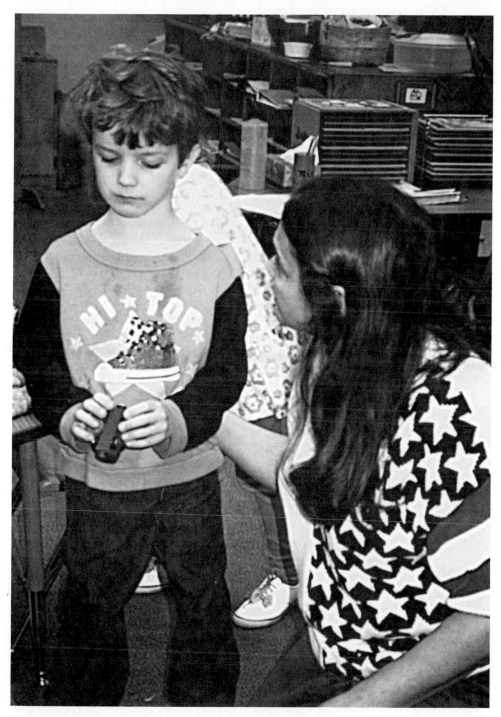

Sometimes children have problems because they don't know how to get a playmate.

EGOCENTRISM

Young children want their own way, and they want it now. Adults would actually like the same thing, but they have learned not to insist on it. Adults have learned that other people's wishes don't necessarily match their own. They have also learned that give-and-take is part of getting along with others. Young children need help in learning these things. In the meantime, their behavior often appears selfish and inconsiderate (Katz & McClellan, 1991) and is difficult to deal with. Many adults believe that such behavior should be punished, but those who understand child development know otherwise. Punishing selfish behavior doesn't make children more thoughtful; it only makes them more careful about being caught and resentful about sharing (Kamii, 1982). Youngsters will become more considerate and less selfish only when they are able to understand that other people have important needs and feelings, too. This understanding takes time to develop and requires experience in order to be learned. Constructive discipline gives children both time and experience.

> Katya jumped tirelessly on the mini-trampoline. Her obvious enjoyment attracted several other children. Of course, they all wanted a turn right now. Danny and Sam tried climbing on with Katya, even though it was clearly too small for two. Katya began yelling at the boys, reminding them of the one-person-only safety rule. Things were getting out of hand as Nancy, the assistant teacher, hurried over.

Young children naturally want their own way, and they want it now.

"One at a time," cautioned Nancy as she gently held Danny and Sam back from the trampoline. Bending down to the boys' eye level, Nancy assured them that she understood their desire to jump on the trampoline. Then she described the danger of having more than one child on it at once, pointing to the small center and the surrounding springs. She continued to talk to the boys, "Katya is using the trampoline now, and it ruins her fun if you get in her way. How would you feel if it were your turn and she tried to get on?" Nancy tried to help the boys understand Katya's feelings by encouraging them to imagine how they would feel in the same situation. It is hard for young children to think that way, but Nancy was understanding.

The teacher and the children worked on a way for everyone to get a turn. These kids like sign-up sheets for showing whose turn it is, so Nancy helped them get out the necessary materials. "But Katya is taking too long a turn!" How should they solve the problem of how long a turn each child gets? Nancy again helped the children problem-solve. She didn't take the role of decision maker, deciding how long a turn should be or telling children when their turn is up. Instead, she helped them review the options. Should children be allowed stay as long as they want, or should there be a set time? If the time is set, can it be the length of a song on a tape, or should they use an egg timer? With Nancy's help, the youngsters learned ways of resolving conflict. By the end of the school year, they automatically made a sign-up sheet and got the egg timer or a tape when such a problem occurred.

A similar situation involving a rope ladder was handled quite differently by another teacher. Contrast what children learned in each incident.

The rope ladder was an exciting new attraction at preschool. Many youngsters wanted to try it out, so the teacher had lined them up for taking turns—one time up and then off. By the time Kyle got there, the line was discouragingly long and he just couldn't wait. He plunged past those waiting in line and started to climb the ladder while the other children wailed their indignation. Teacher Joanne reacted quickly and firmly. She pulled him away, explaining that he would have to wait in line like all the others. Kyle began crying loudly. Needing to get back to supervising the line, Joanne asked Maureen to quiet Kyle. While Maureen was desperately trying to think of what to do, her eye fell on the gerbil cage next to Kyle. "I think you are making Pinky sad," Maureen told the crying boy. Kyle's attention was successfully diverted to the gerbil, and the problem was over.

Many people would consider Joanne's and Maureen's actions to be good solutions. Yet they did not help Kyle learn anything useful. Both teachers ignored his feelings of frustration, and Maureen eventually covered up his feelings by distracting him. Is this what we want to teach children about dealing with their own feelings? What about the feelings of the other children when Kyle crowded them? Neither teacher tried to help him understand the viewpoint of those who were waiting in line. Kyle needs help learning to deal with his own feelings and those of others. They are important realities that prepare a child to function effectively in society, whereas feigned concern about the gerbil's feelings is only a manipulative tactic.

A more productive approach to handling Kyle's problem involves only a subtle shift in the teacher's response. The teacher could have used the guidelines (provided in chapter 8) for implementing a related consequence. Instead of just pulling Kyle away, Joanne could have told him to leave *until* he decided to get back into line and wait his turn. This method gives him some power over his own situation and focuses his attention more clearly on the problem. Instead of just thinking about how mean the teacher is, he is free to think about how he can change his behavior to get a turn (Curwin & Mendler, 1988). A related consequence addresses the immediate problem but needs to be supplemented with other approaches. Kyle obviously needs help understanding the feelings of other children. Therefore, it would be useful for him to hear how they feel about his crowding. Kyle also would benefit from the security of knowing that he would get a turn eventually. The sign-up sheet and the egg timer used with the trampoline line would address the children's needs in this situation. A combination of causes calls for a combination of approaches.

OTHER IMMATURE PERCEPTIONS

Young children often get fact and fantasy mixed up (Piaget, 1965). Many adults get very angry when they believe a child is "lying." However, as explained in chapter 3, the problem may be more a result of being young than one of immorality. Nevertheless, not telling the truth is unacceptable behavior in our society. Children still need to learn how to sort out truth from untruth. They also need to learn why the truth is preferable. Effective communication strategies can help us teach both.

> Sam constantly bragged about his amazing exploits, patterned after those of cartoon superheroes. Dennis didn't want to call Sam a liar, but he did want the child to learn. Therefore, he responded with an active listening comment that read between the lines: "It sounds like you wish you were big and strong and could do all those things." This response got Sam onto a reality track for the rest of the conversation.
>
> When Sam told these stories to his preschool friends, they weren't so kind. They argued, "You did not!" Sam's reaction was to argue back and defend his incredible statements. Dennis decided Sam needed more specific feedback. He took the child aside and kindly but frankly told him, "Your friends can't believe you when you tell them things they know can't be true." Dennis continued with more information. "If you tell people things that aren't true, they might not

believe you when you tell them the truth." Sam needed time to digest this idea, but Dennis was there to assist his growth over time. Dennis's goal was to help Sam sort out the difference between *real* and *pretend* without losing his joy in pretending.

Almost everyone has an experience with "stealing" as they grow up. Taking what doesn't belong to you is a serious crime in our society. Many adults believe they must harshly punish children for stealing to save them from a life of crime. Parents and teachers with more knowledge of young children realize the need for helping them learn about ownership (Curwin & Mendler, 1990). Punishment may stop kids from taking something if they think they may get caught, but it won't help them understand why it is unacceptable to take what isn't theirs. Related consequences will help children learn this concept and also increase the likelihood that they will respect others' ownership, even when no one is around to enforce it. A consequence for stealing involves making restitution by replacing what was taken. In the following example, Tory is helped to understand why taking the scissors is a problem, but he is allowed to return them without confrontation.

Amy complained that there weren't any scissors left. Dennis was surprised. Only two people were cutting, and there should have been three pairs of scissors. He checked the cubbies and noticed a bunch of cut-paper creations in Tory's. Thinking Tory might have inadvertently scooped up the scissors with his work and stuffed them into his cubby, Dennis picked through the pile. As he moved Tory's backpack aside, Dennis felt a scissors shape pressed against the cloth. A pair of scissors had been stuffed deep into the pack. There was a chance the pair was Tory's own from home, but it wasn't likely. Perhaps he just wanted a good pair of scissors at home.

Rather than putting the boy on the defensive or making him feel guilty by accusing him of stealing, Dennis called a brief class meeting. He announced that one pair of scissors couldn't be found; now there weren't enough for the school. Dennis expressed confidence that they might show up. He concluded, "If anyone finds them, please put them in the lost-and-found basket in the back hallway." Tory looked self-conscious and trapped when Dennis began the meeting. But the final comment brought some relief to his face. No one could see the lost-and-found basket from the classroom. It was back by the cubbies! He could sneak those scissors into it, and no one would see.

An hour later, Dennis glanced in the lost-and-found basket. There were the scissors. He brought them back into the classroom and put them on their tray. Seeing Tory eye them, Dennis offered, "Would you like to use them?" As the child eagerly reached for them, Dennis inquired, "Do you have a good pair of scissors at home?" "Nope," Tory frowned. Dennis replied, "I'll tell your parents where you can buy this kind. OK?"

CONCLUSION

This chapter provides only a few examples of the problem situations children encounter simply because they are young. Sometimes the problem requires only your respectful acceptance of the nature of young children, such as when you are dealing with wet pants or spilled juice. If youngsters can be part of fixing the problem, it helps them feel good about themselves. Sometimes the problem requires you to change your expectations to match the abilities of young children, such as adjusting your plans when youngsters can't sit still any longer. At other times you can help children's growth by teaching them a strategy for making friends or a skill, such as modeling self-expression through "I messages." Adults can significantly aid children's social maturation by helping them try to understand another child's viewpoint, which is part of learning to negotiate solutions for interpersonal conflicts. Effective guidance for young children also involves knowing when behavior that looks like lying or stealing is really only a reflection of a child's point of view.

When you are searching for the cause of a discipline problem, be sure to consider lack of maturity as a possibility. Remember, your role as the teacher is to allow youngsters the time they need to grow as well as to provide the experiences they need to learn. It may help you to cope if you can also remember that it isn't their fault when they are inept.

FOR FURTHER THOUGHT

1. A problem to solve: Jason grabs the ball that Tanya and Eric are playing with and runs away laughing. The other two children are hurt and indignant.
    a. Describe the probable cause of the problem.
    b. Describe the guidance approach that addresses that cause.
2. A problem to solve: Frequently, Kris "accidentally" tips her chair over during quiet reading time, disrupting her first-grade class.
    a. Describe the possible causes.
    b. Describe the adult responses that address the causes.
3. Analyze actual behavior problems and guidance approaches in a setting where you know the children. Cases in which you are the adult providing the guidance will probably prove most instructive.
    a. Describe the situation.
    b. Based on your knowledge of the children involved, state the probable cause.
    c. Describe the adult intervention that addresses that cause.
    d. Describe the children's response to intervention.
    e. If the approach was not helpful, was it unsuccessful because it did not address the actual cause or because one intervention was not enough?
    f. If a different cause is suggested, plan a different strategy for next time.

REFERENCES AND RECOMMENDATIONS FOR READING

Books

BIBER, B. (1984). *Early education and psychological development.* New Haven: Yale University Press.

BREDEKAMP, S. (1987). *Developmentally appropriate practice in early childhood programs serving children from birth through age 8, expanded edition.* Washington, DC: National Association for the Education of Young Children.

CURRY, N. E., & JOHNSON, C. N. (1990). *Beyond self-esteem: Developing a genuine sense of human value.* Washington, DC: National Association for the Education of Young Children.

CURWIN, R. L., & MENDLER, A. N. (1988). *Discipline with dignity.* Alexandria, VA: Association for Supervision and Curriculum Development.

CURWIN, R. L., & MENDLER, A. N. (1990). *Am I in trouble? Using discipline to teach young children responsibility.* Santa Cruz, CA: Network Publications.

DEVRIES, R., & KOHLBERG, L. (1987). *Constructivist early education: Overview and comparison with other programs.* Washington, DC: National Association for the Education of Young Children.

KAMII, C. (1982). Autonomy as the aim of education: Implications of Piaget's theory. In C. Kamii, *Number* (pp. 73–87). Washington, DC: National Association for the Education of Young Children.

KARAN, S. L., & ZIGLER, E. F. (EDS.). (1987). *Early schooling: The national debate.* New Haven: Yale UniversityPress.

KATZ, L. G., & McCLELLAN, D. E. (1991). *The teacher's role in the social development of young children.* Urbana, IL: ERIC Clearinghouse Document, ED313168.

PIAGET, J. (1965). *The moral judgment of the child.* New York: The Free Press.

RAMSEY, P. G. (1991). *Making friends in school: Promoting peer relationships in early childhood.* New York: Teachers College Press.

VYGOTSKY, L. J. (1962). *Thought and language.* Cambridge: MIT Press.

Periodicals

GREENBERG, P. (1992). Ideas that work with young children. How to institute some simple democratic practices pertaining to respect, rights, responsibilities, and roots in any classroom (without losing your leadership position). *Young Children, 47*(5), 10–17.

KEMPLE, K. M. (1991). Preschool children's peer acceptance and social interaction. *Young Children, 46*(5), 47–54.

OKEN-WRIGHT, P. (1992). From tug of war to "Let's Make a Deal": The teacher's role. *Young Children, 48*(1), 15–20.

RICHARD, N., & HOFWANN, D. (1991). The adult's role in play: A tool for self-evaluation. *Child Care Information Exchange, 79,* 44–45.

Papers

GARTRELL, D. (1988). *Developmentally appropriate guidance of young children.* St. Paul: Minnesota Association for the Education of Young Children.

HILLS, T. W. (1987). *Hothousing young children: Implications for early childhood policy and practice.* Urbana, IL: ERIC Clearinghouse Document, ED294653.

KATZ, L. G., & McCLELLAN, D. E. (1991). *The teacher's role in the social development of young children.* Urbana, IL: ERIC Clearinghouse Document, ED331642.

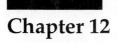

Chapter 12

Unmet Needs

Like a baby's cry, a young child's actions can signal a variety of unmet needs. Although they now have some words, young children may not be articulate enough to communicate their problems. Often they may not even be consciously *aware* of what they need. What's more, even if they do know what they need and can verbalize it, they may not have any idea of what to do about it. Thus, the adult's role is threefold: first, to help identify the need(s); next, to help the child learn to communicate them; and finally, to facilitate problem solving so that the needs can be met. This chapter discusses some typical emotional and physical needs that cause problems if left unmet.

PRIVACY NEEDS

Adults as well as children often have difficulty properly identifying their own need for privacy. General grumpiness is frequently a sign of a need to be alone. In the following example, careful teacher observation identified this cause of a child's antisocial behavior. Then the youngster was helped to figure out how to get his need met.

> Denali was being unusually aggressive Monday morning at Midway Children's Center. Even his favorite playmate, Colin, received a rough shove when he tried to entice Denali to play with the new dinosaurs in the sandbox. Nancy took note and began to observe. Denali chose one activity after another. But whenever other children tried to join him, he'd hurt either their bodies or their feelings until they went away. Tory held his own next to Denali in the book corner, telling him to quit kicking. But Denali didn't stop.
>
> Nancy joined them, sitting across from Denali. She matter-of-factly said, "You're kicking Tory." Denali retorted, "I don't want him here." "Have you told him that with your words yet? He needs to hear what you want." "Go away!" Denali growled at Tory. Tory refused, protesting, "This is a three-person place!" Denali frowned. "You want to be alone," Nancy verbalized for him. "Where are there one-person places in our center?" Denali thought for a minute; then he remembered, "The resting mat and the easel!" Nancy continued, "You can take your book to the resting mat, or you can paint by yourself. What do you want to do?" He chose the mat and read undisturbed for most of the morning.

POWER NEEDS

Sometimes the more you try to get a child to do something, the more resistance you meet. She *won't* put her boots on, he *won't* eat, and nap time is a constant fight. Such behavior is often a symptom of a child's healthy desire to have some control over his or her own life (Curry & Johnson, 1990). Arising conflicts can easily turn into fruitless power struggles. If the adult in charge insists, "You have to

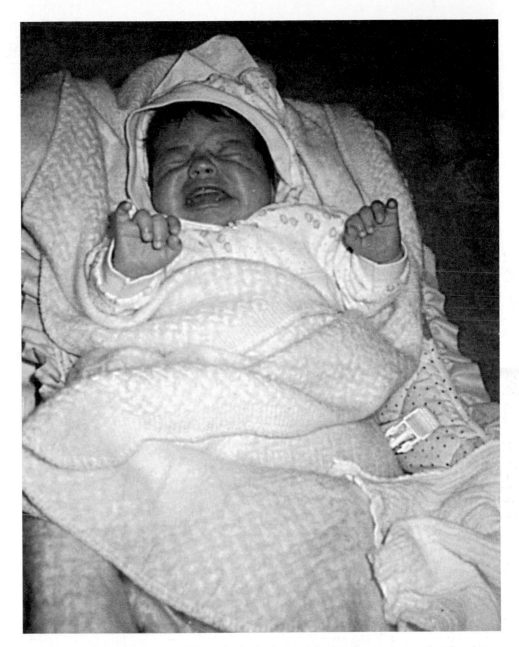

Figuring out the cause of a child's misbehavior is important in the same way that figuring out the reason for a baby's cries is important: A solution depends on the problem.

eat your lunch," the child insists, "I'm *not* hungry!" A limitation like "No, you can't go outside without your boots. There are puddles under the swings" evokes the response, "I *hate* those red boots!" To the statement, "Your mother still wants you to take a nap," the child replies, "I'm *not* tired!"

The problem may not be about hunger or boot color at all, and the child may actually be tired enough to sleep like a log. These responses may be expressions of the need for personal power. Recognizing this need, the attending adult can, within reason, give the child as many opportunities for choice as possible (Katz & Chard, 1989). She must eat. But which food does she want to eat first, her apple or her sandwich? How does she want to eat her apple, like a worm nibbling through or around and around like a circling caterpillar? He must rest. But which nap story would he like, *Rumpelstiltskin* or *Strega Nona*? Does he want a back rub or to be rocked? She must wear her boots to play in the swings with the puddles under them. But if she wants to play in the fort or the playhouse, she can race out to them in her shiny shoes.

These are *real choices*, both desirable to the child and acceptable to the adult. They give children a chance to satisfy their need for control in a world governed by many rules they don't yet understand. And by allowing them some control at levels appropriate to their age, you will find that children are much more able to allow you to control decisions that must be made by adults. As they experience the desired power, they also develop valuable problem-solving skills. The following situation is an example of a child's being allowed some power, choice, and opportunity for problem solving.

The youngsters at the children's center were going outside to play, and they were excited to get out after being cooped up indoors by bad weather. The joyful hustle and bustle of coats and boots was interrupted by Angelina's wail. She threw her boots across the floor and her coat on top of them. Then she sat crying and hitting her heels on the floor. Sheri, the aide in charge of helping everyone get ready, asked another staff person to help with the other youngsters and went over to Angelina to see what the problem was. It turned out that the little girl had new shoes, and she wanted to wear them instead of taking them off and putting her boots on.

Sheri explained carefully to Angelina that her new Care Bear shoes would get ruined if she wore them out in the mud. Angelina continued to cry and say that she wanted to wear her new shoes outside. Sheri tried reasoning with the child while upholding the rule about not going outside without boots, but Angelina kept crying loudly. Suddenly Sheri remembered what she had learned from the head teacher, Dennis, about giving children choices. Sheri changed her tactics and asked Angelina what she thought she might do to protect her shoes if she kept them on.

Angelina's sobs ebbed as she began to talk about some ideas and possible solutions. Sheri stayed with her as the others trooped outdoors with another adult in charge. Finally Angelina decided to wear some big boots from the emergency supply box, which were large enough to fit over her beautiful new shoes. She was pleased with this solution and happily marched outdoors in the giant boots. Later, Angelina asked Sheri for help. She had decided to change into her own boots, explaining that it was hard to run in the other pair. Sheri noticed that Angelina's concern about wearing her new shoes seemed to evaporate once she had an opportunity to make a decision for herself.

OWNERSHIP NEEDS

"Amy won't share!" This cry is familiar to all who spend their days with preschoolers. In the chapter 11, we explored both undeveloped social skills and egocentricity, both of which contribute to sharing problems. However, it is also important to consider whether or not it is necessary for a child to share at this time. Adults as well as children have a need for ownership of possessions and territory. Notice that office workers want their own designated spaces, and the contents of each person's desk are personal and private. Adults are not required to share with others the personal items they bring from home to make work more comfortable. Yet we routinely demand more generosity from young children. The need for ownership must be balanced with social expectations for sharing (Curry & Johnson, 1990).

Dennis addressed the problem of personal possessions at preschool by designating a large box as the "precious place." Youngsters who brought things from home that they didn't want others to touch could

A child's need for ownership can sometimes be more important than sharing.

put their belongings there and be assured that they would be undis-
turbed. It was a child's decision when and if to bring something out
for the group to enjoy.

Mrs. Jensen found that putting a child's name on a personal
possession helped children share. She figured out that having the
item labeled as their own fulfilled the need for ownership and freed
youngsters to be more generous. First graders enjoyed labeling,
which became part of their emerging literacy. They began using the
approach for staking temporary claim to class materials as well. Thus,
when Eric was working on a jigsaw puzzle and had to leave it and go
out for recess, he placed a sign on it that said, "Do Not Tuch. Eric."
The children in the class respected such written notices, and they
solved many potential conflicts.

Both these teachers defend children's temporary or permanent ownership
rights. Rather than making children selfish, this defense of their rights actually
helps them to be more generous (Hendrick, 1988). When children have their
ownership rights respected, they learn how to respect those of others. When they
are not busy defending their rights to an item, they are more likely to give it up
voluntarily.

ATTENTION NEEDS

Often, behavior labeled disruptive can actually be a plea for attention—a cry for
help! You may know kids who get attention by showing off, and you have probably seen others who seem to seek a reprimand for misbehavior deliberately. Even
negative attention, after all, is attention (Cairns, 1986).

The desire for attention is a legitimate need, yet it is often difficult to meet
that need adequately in large group settings. Ratios of ten or more students to
one teacher can make it difficult for even the most conscientious child-care
worker to give enough personal attention to each individual. Public school classes
of twenty or twenty-five children create an impossible challenge. There *is* a limit
to how many children you can fit into your lap at once! Levels of need vary
among children, depending on their personality types and their stages of development. Levels also vary from day to day, and they are often related to rest and
stress levels. In addition, sometimes home life can fail to provide adequate attention.

A teacher's awareness of current home factors can provide valuable information, even about children from the best situations. A parent's absence or
increased work hours, newborn siblings, or even visiting houseguests can create a
need for extra attention. In the following case, teachers combine information
from home with observations at school to solve the mystery of Alex's behavior.

Alex was really being a handful at Midway Children's Center this
week. His moods swung between angry and giddy, as he alternately
had temper tantrums or played the clown—and always at the most

A teacher's awareness of current home factors can provide valuable insights, even about children from the best of homes.

inopportune times! Just as teachers had the whole group organized and ready to head out on a field trip, Alex threw a fit because he couldn't be a teacher's partner. Maureen, one of the teachers, was confused. Last week Alex had been proud that he was finally old enough to have the helper-friend position: holding a younger child's hand on outings. Why was it so important now to be with the teacher? Later, at circle time, he seemed to be out to sabotage every activity she initiated. Maureen finally asked her aide Sheri to remove him. The only place to take him was to the small group story area, but he seemed content in that more intimate setting.

At lunchtime Alex was unusually silly, too. Because he was making it difficult for others at his table to eat, he was moved to a table for two with a teacher. Maureen noted that he seemed pleased with this consequence.

After nap time, Maureen invited Alex into her lap for a wake-up cuddle. She asked him how things were going. In the course of the conversation, he volunteered, "I want Uncle George to go home." Maureen asked him what would be better when Uncle George left. She found that the extended visit was making Alex have to compete for his dad's attention. He was tired of it! Knowing that Uncle George was going to be with Alex's family for a while longer, Maureen made a note to suggest to the father that he take some "just with Alex" time each day. And she made a point of giving the boy some extra one-on-one time herself. At that night's meeting, she also advised the rest of the staff of the boy's special need for extra attention. They decided to invite Alex to the smaller group activities for a while so he could receive more individual attention.

In some cases, disruptive behavior for attention is not a temporary problem. Some youngsters have a well-learned pattern of trying to get attention and status by disrupting class. No doubt you remember these class clowns from your school days. Their behavior is a sad symptom of low self-esteem and a cry for help (Grossman, 1990). These children need to unlearn their counterproductive strategies; but as long as their disruptive behavior gets attention, they will continue it. Helping a youngster unlearn a behavior is sometimes called the *extinction* of that behavior. In order to extinguish an unacceptable behavior, you must *never* reinforce it. We consider behavior modification acceptable when it means ignoring inappropriate behavior. This action helps correct mislearning by extinguishing previously reinforced unacceptable behavior (Curwin & Mendler, 1990). Chapter 9 in this book describes behavior modification and explains that occasional reinforcement may actually entrench the behavior more firmly than consistent rewards do. But in the following example, a teacher manages not to reinforce negative behavior.

A group of children was listening to a tape recording of a book about birds and were following along in their own copies of the book. The children were enjoying the tape and the book; the vibrant and detailed illustrations helped hold their interest. Then Jeffrey quit listening and began to open and close his book loudly. The other children complained that he was making too much noise and they couldn't hear. Mrs. Jensen went over to Jeffrey and quietly asked him to please stop disturbing the other children. As soon as she walked away, he began the same behavior and got the same complaints from the other youngsters. Refusing to give attention to the behavior this time, Mrs. Jensen said nothing to Jeffrey but instead calmly walked over and turned up the volume on the tape recorder a little so that the others could still hear. Jeffrey's eyes showed his surprise. Because he was no longer getting any attention from his classmates or teacher, he began to follow the text again. Afterward, he had many comments about the birds in the book.

It takes time and patience, but eventually behavior learned through reinforcement will stop once the rewards of attention stop. Mrs. Jensen was able to respond effectively to the cause of Jeffrey's behavior because she had made a special effort to understand him and his problems. She knew that Jeffrey not only needed to have his inappropriate behavior ignored, but also needed to have his desire for attention met in another way. Mrs. Jensen did want to give Jeffrey the attention he craved, but not in response to inappropriate behavior. She had been working with his parents on the problem and was making an effort to notice him when he was working well in school. Rather than make an issue over this minor incident, she appreciated that his inappropriate behavior was happening less and less frequently.

While ignoring inappropriate bids for attention may be the best approach for some children's growth, there are many other children who may be inadvertently ignored. It is easy to overlook some very quiet children. The too-quiet ones cause more serious concern than the too-loud ones because they have given up. They have quit trying to get their needs met. They may appear blank or unhappy, uninvolved in activities, and generally unsuccessful. Sometimes these children assume victim roles, but more often they seem to fade into the background. You may find yourself wishing that they would disagree with something actively, get upset, or show *some* strong emotion—even if it's disruptive! The source of this kind of problem generally lies outside the school. Chapter 13 discusses ways of getting help for children with more serious unmet needs.

NEEDS FOR SUCCESS AND CHALLENGE

Youngsters who don't complete school assignments often get into trouble. Children who don't participate in planned activities in preschool worry both teachers and parents. There are reasons for their behaviors. Forcing a child to comply or punishing noncompliance does not address the reasons. The traditional loss of recess for not completing work is a classic example of counterpro-

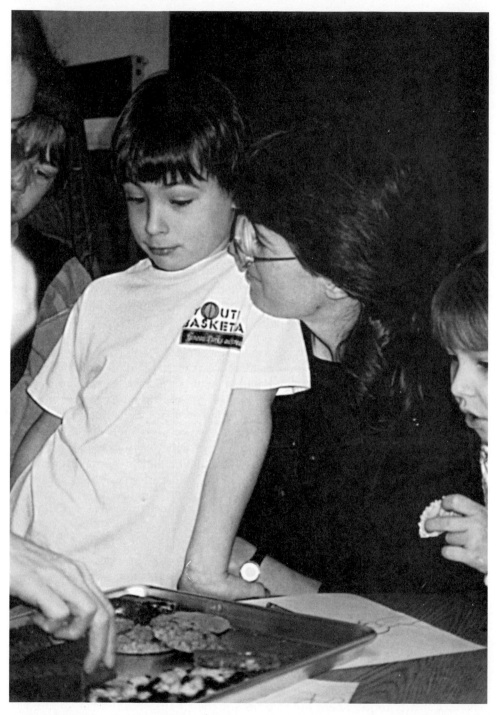

There are many reasons for children's behaviors. Forcing a child to comply does not address those reasons.

ductive discipline. What should you do instead? The answer depends on the cause of the behavior.

> ## OBSERVATION GUIDE FOR SCHOOLWORK PROBLEMS
>
> ❑ Does the child look upset or anxious when confronted with the task? Or does she appear merely distracted?
>
> ❑ Is she interested in something else instead? If so, what is she interested in?
>
> ❑ What kinds of tasks go uncompleted? Does she only avoid writing, for example, or does she avoid any work?

You will get clues to the cause by observing the child's specific behaviors and by noting the circumstances surrounding the problem. Does the child look upset or anxious when confronted with the task? Or does she appear distracted? Is she interested in something else instead? If so, what is she interested in? What kinds of tasks go uncompleted? Does she only avoid writing, for example, or does she avoid any work? Depending on the answers to these kinds of questions, you may decide that the child lacks the ability to succeed at the task, or you might decide that she is not sufficiently challenged by it. You may discover that she does her math just fine but can't read the material to complete her science work. Each of these different findings suggests different responses. The goal is to address the problem in such a way that you help the child find success and satisfaction in her work. Treating each child as an individual is an important key in meeting this goal.

If Jimmie won't read because the book is too hard, one useful response is to help him find a book at his level. Another response would be to help him improve his reading skill by inviting a volunteer to read to him daily. Perhaps reading in partnership with a friend who is a little more skillful would be more fun as well as more productive.

If Joel is acting up at reading time because he is bored, find a more appropriate challenge for him. Help him find material at his level that is related to topics of personal interest.

If Ashley never uses the large-muscle equipment at preschool because she is afraid, help her find activities that will increase her confidence in her physical abilities. Perhaps helping her make friends with Kelsey, who is more physically active, would encourage her. Ashley spends a lot of time in the playhouse area; suggest large-muscle activities that fit in with her pretend play.

The need for success coupled with the need for appropriate challenge continues as the young child matures (Curry & Johnson, 1990). Finding the right balance for each child is essential to avoiding the problem behaviors caused by either boredom or frustration. Instead of assuming that children are misbehaving when they don't match our expectations, it is more helpful to examine the appropriateness of our expectations first.

NEED FOR SECURITY

We usually equate security with safety. Part 2 discussed safety in terms of both physical and emotional security. Essential to a safe and secure environment are clear, consistent limits in both the physical and emotional realms. While adults generally focus on their obligation to keep children physically safe, children's behavior deteriorates if they lack emotional security (Katz & McClellan, 1991).

Although children can be extremely kind to one another, we also see instances of cruelty. Children sometimes suffer greatly from the thoughtlessness of other youngsters at school. Because their emotional security is being seriously threatened, these children are unlikely to thrive and grow in that setting. Young children are just beginning to develop their sense of how to treat other people. While allowing children as much opportunity as possible to learn through experience, we must not allow them to learn at the expense of their peers.

> Megan had a turned-in foot, and she wore leg braces at night. Doctors suggested giving the foot a few years to correct itself before they tried surgery. The problem wasn't very noticeable until she tried to run. Then her foot folded under whenever she turned too tight a corner, and she would usually fall. Megan's sensitivity about her foot was demonstrated by her elaborately contrived reasons for why she had planned to fall. She generally avoided running games, but one morning at Midway Children's Center she couldn't resist joining Alex and Corrie in a freeze-tag frenzy. After Megan fell several times, the boys noticed her difficulty and began to tease—laughing when she fell, taunting "Humpty Dumpty sat on a wall, Humpty Dumpty had a great fall. . . . " After a particularly hard fall, she broke into tears.
>
> Teacher Nancy stepped in, calling the boys over to her. She said, "Your friend Megan has fallen. Is she OK?" They looked at Megan, grinning. Alex sneered, "She's OK. She always falls. She's just a Humpty Dumpty!" "I am not!" wailed Megan. Nancy decided this situation was an opportunity for the boys to work on developing some empathy. First, she firmly assumed her authority role and stopped the name-calling. "I cannot allow you to call Megan any name but her own. It hurts feelings to call names. Now let's see if she's really OK. Alex, can you help her up?"

For children to feel secure in a group, they need to know that others will not be allowed to harass, humiliate, or threaten them. When adults observe such behavior, they need to interact to help the perpetrator recognize how the other child's feelings are being affected. It is time for the adult to accept an authority role and set limits. Nancy firmly stated that name-calling was *not* acceptable and told the boys why. She and the boys will determine positive alternatives through discussion.

Substitute teachers often get treated badly, too. They have a difficult time because youngsters must test this new person's limits. If the usual adult in charge is wishy-washy about limits, children will constantly test that person, too. Testing behavior may appear "naughty," but it is actually an effort to learn what is acceptable in a given situation (Curry & Johnson, 1990). This knowledge provides youngsters with the security of clear expectations. Just as they need safety limits set, children need to have clearly communicated and firmly held behavioral expectations. Although they naturally push against their limits, their tests help them find out where the boundaries are and if those boundaries are flexible.

Teachers who strive for mutual respect with children, will involve youngsters in determining appropriate limits and help children understand the reasons for limits. It is wise to have much freedom for individual decisions and choice, but that freedom must have clearly defined limits that protect everyone. Mrs. Jensen, for example, is firm about kindness and safety for all people and animals in her classroom. She also insists on responsible treatment of equipment and materials. Her expectations can be condensed into three easy guidelines: Be kind. Be safe. Be careful.

CLASSROOM GUIDELINES

Children need limits as well as freedom. These guidelines are easy for young children to learn: Be kind. Be safe. Be careful.

A child having a tantrum may also be a child who needs the security of limits. Children need the emotional security of knowing that someone will help them keep themselves under control. When they experience anger, they can actually terrify themselves with their rage and rapidly escalating emotions. Because they have not yet learned how to take personal time to calm down, they can be overwhelmed by the strength of their feelings and be unable to escape them. Your intervention can actually be a relief, reassuring them that you not only won't let them hurt others, but also won't let them hurt themselves. Calmly holding a child close and offering comfort will help some youngsters calm down. Others need to be left alone so as not to reinforce the tantrum through attention. However, children must be protected from doing damage to themselves, to others, or to their environment. As they fight the endless struggle to get control of their own actions, children are comforted by the reminder that there are limits outside of themselves.

Children need clear, consistent limits in order to feel safe and secure.

NEEDS FOR LOVE AND ACCEPTANCE

Asking teachers to love all the children in their care may be unrealistic; however, at least one of the *American Heritage Dictionary*'s (1992) definitions of love sounds possible: "a strong enthusiasm for another." It *is* reasonable to expect a teacher to have an enthusiastic approach toward children. This enthusiasm can be demonstrated by efforts to create an environment and a program that continually attempt to meet the needs of all the children enrolled. Your efforts are a way of showing love, whether you actually *like* a child or not. What is important is that you accept all children as they are. By respecting each child's unique position and potential, the teacher's role is to care for, guide, and encourage all the children as they grow. Some children are just hard to like. Much as you try not to have favorites, you must admit that some kids (and adults too) are just a lot more pleasant to be around than others.

> Sandy was yelling at the other children again. Miss Wheeler wished once more that Sandy hadn't been placed in her room. What a nuisance she was, always getting into fights with the others. She also constantly talked out of turn but never would answer a question when called on. As if those difficulties weren't enough, Sandy lost everything. She never had a pencil, never knew where her reading book was, and always lost her lunch box. Miss Wheeler had tried everything. It seemed that Sandy was constantly taking time-out for interrupting or fighting. And Miss Wheeler had finally begun taking everything away from Sandy that she might lose. Sandy's only reaction was to pout and look like she was going to cry, but Miss Wheeler thought it was an act because there were never any tears. Now look at the child! She was crawling under the table instead of sitting on her chair. What next?

Miss Wheeler clearly doesn't like Sandy, and neither do the child's classmates. Her behavior gets constant rejection from others. As a result of this rejection, Sandy has learned that she is a bad girl. The more she believes this lesson, the more she acts accordingly. As strange as it may sound, her reaction is normal and human. People who feel unlovable tend to act unlovable, which makes them feel worse and act worse (Rabiner & Cole, 1989). What a vicious cycle! The only hope for Sandy is to break the cycle by introducing experiences that teach her good things about herself. It won't be easy to change her self-image. At first, she will be so uncomfortable with positive feedback that she will act worse (Miller, 1990). This behavior is the normal reaction of a person with low self-esteem: It is unsettling to be treated in any way incompatible with one's own self-image. Therefore, Sandy's first response to good feedback will be to act worse in order to show others who she really is. It takes dedication and perseverance to help a child unlearn a negative self-image. Planting a positive image in its place is essential to a child's success in life.

The following example shows how adults can start the process by gaining a more positive perspective on a child.

> At one staff meeting of Midway Children's Center, everyone was complaining about a certain boy who was exhibiting particularly undesirable behavior. To relieve the negative focus, director Caroline suggested an exercise. She asked everyone to think of just one thing they really liked about Leo. Some were embarrassed to find them-

selves struggling at first to come up with a positive point. Gradually, though, they each brought to light one part of the child they could genuinely say they liked. Musical himself, Dennis said he liked Leo's singing. Even though Leo was usually disruptive during music time, at least he was on key! Nancy liked his eyes. Sure, they were constantly darting around, checking to see if anyone was observing his mischief. But Nancy had to admit they were bright, beautiful brown eyes, just like her mother's. Maureen respected his self-assurance. He may have been bossy, but at least he was capable, an attribute Maureen valued. As the list grew, the teachers felt themselves coming to a new appreciation of the boy they had been complaining about earlier. It didn't erase their irritation with his behavior, but it did put that behavior into a little more positive perspective. They were then in a better frame of mind to brainstorm about ways to help him.

The children who are hardest to like are the ones that need your acceptance the most (Katz & Chard, 1989). Their unmet needs for love may be acute, causing behavior that is extremely demanding. If you feel unable to meet their needs, they can become an irritation and a drain. Or they can become a challenge! It depends on your attitude.

It can be exciting to work with difficult children; while they may take the most out of you, they are also potentially the most rewarding. You will be delighted when a child who usually hits in anger progresses for the first time to venting that anger verbally. At that important moment, you can see the results of your coaching. A habitually disruptive child who makes it through a whole day, or even a whole hour, without having a negative impact on the group can give you hope for humanity! It also allows you to congratulate yourself on helping that child channel energies more productively.

CONCLUSION

When children have behavior problems caused by unmet needs, effective teachers help them get those needs met in acceptable and productive ways. Accurately determining when a child has an unmet emotional need and responding to that need can eliminate much unproductive discipline effort. Additionally, you can make a difference in a child's whole future by intervening in the early years and not allowing the problem to escalate.

As you work at helping children get their needs met, you will come to appreciate the obvious "problem children." They are literally crying out for help; you can't ignore them. But they are also generally the survivors.

FOR FURTHER THOUGHT

1.   A problem to solve: Several children in your child-care center refuse to help at cleanup time before lunch.

     a.   What is one possible cause? Describe the guidance approach that addresses it.

     b.   What is another possible cause? Describe the guidance approach that addresses it.

2.   A problem to solve: Jenny keeps forgetting to put her papers into her cubby. At the end of the day a mad scramble ensues, often accompanied by tears, while everyone searches for Jenny's papers.

     a.   What is one possible cause? Describe the guidance approach that addresses it.

     b.   What is another possible cause? Describe the guidance approach that addresses it.

3.   Analyze actual behavior problems and guidance approaches in a setting where you know the children. Cases in which you are the adult providing the guidance will probably be the most instructive.

     a.   Describe the situation.

     b.   Based on your knowledge of the children involved, state the probable cause.

     c.   Describe the adult intervention that addresses that cause.

     d.   Describe the children's response to intervention.

     e.   If the approach was not helpful, was it unsuccessful because it did not address the actual cause or because one intervention was not enough?

     f.   If a different cause is suggested, plan a different strategy for next time.

REFERENCES AND RECOMMENDATIONS FOR READING

Books

BEATY, J. J. (1990). *Observing development of the young child* (2nd ed.). New York: Merrill/Macmillan.

CAIRNS, R. B. (1986). Contemporary perspectives on social development. In P. Strain, M. Guralnick, & H. Walker (Eds.), *Children's social behavior (pp. 3-47).* Orlando, FL: Academic Press.

CURRY, N. E., & JOHNSON, C. N. (1990). *Beyond self-esteem: Developing a genuine sense of human value.* Washington, DC: National Association for the Education of Young Children.

CURWIN, R., & MENDLER, A. N. (1990). *Am I in trouble? Using discipline to teach young children responsibility.* Santa Cruz, CA: Network Publications.

DEPAOLA, T. (1975). *Strega nona.* Englewood Cliffs, NJ: Prentice-Hall.

GRIMM, BROTHERS. (1967). *Rumpelstiltskin.* New York: Brace and World.

GROSSMAN, H. (1990). *Trouble-free teaching: Solutions to behavior problems in the classroom.* Mountain View, CA: Mayfield.

HENDRICK, J. (1988). *The whole child: Developmental curriculum for the young child* (4th ed.). New York: Merrill/Macmillan.

KATZ, L. G., & CHARD, S. C. (1989). *Engaging children's minds: The project approach.* Norwood, NJ: Ablex.

KATZ, L. G., & McCLELLAN, D. E. (1991). *The teacher's role in the social development of young children.* Urbana, IL: ERIC Clearinghouse Document, ED313168.

KELLERMAN, J. (1985). *When the bough breaks.* New York: Atheneum.

MILLER, D. F. (1990). *Positive child guidance.* Albany: Delmar.

SABATINO, D. (1991). *A fine line: When discipline becomes child abuse.* Summit, PA: TAB Books/McGraw-Hill.

Periodicals

EDER, R. A. (1989). The emergent personologist: The structure and content of 3 1/2, 5 1/2, and 7 1/2-year-olds' concepts of themselves and other persons. *Child Development, 60*(5), 1218–1228.

GREENBERG, P. (1992). Ideas that work with young children. How to institute some simple democratic practices pertaining to respect, rights, responsibilities, and roots in any classroom (without losing your leadership position). *Young Children, 47*(5), 10–17.

RABINER, D., & COLE, J. (1989). Effect of expectancy inductions on rejected children's acceptance by unfamiliar peers. *Developmental Psychology, 25*(3), 450–457.

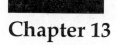

Chapter 13

Family-based Special Needs

Even the best intentions and discipline practices sometimes do not meet all children's needs. Children from dysfunctional families, those whose families are in temporary crisis, or youngsters who are victims of abuse or neglect all have special needs that can cause serious behavior problems. The demands of these children can tax the most skilled teachers.

When you believe that the cause of a child's misbehavior lies outside the classroom setting, you may need to get help in identifying the problem base. Once the probable cause for behavior difficulties is determined, you may be in a good position to get the child some much-needed help. In addition to working in partnership with parents, teachers should not hesitate to call on available resources such as school counselors (when available), other teachers, and even outside specialists accessible through service agencies in the community. Remember, too, that one of your roles is to be an advocate for the child when appropriate. This role may include connecting the family with professionals who can help.

Children with family-based specials needs can sometimes be overwhelming for a classroom teacher. You might decide you need training in special techniques, or you may choose to request additional assistance in your classroom. Depending on the seriousness of the behavior difficulties, an appropriate range of services may be recommended by professionals who come on team to help you work with the child. With more severely emotionally disturbed children, a *system of care* may be implemented—"a comprehensive spectrum of mental health and other necessary services which are organized into a coordinated network to meet the multiple and changing needs" (Stroul & Friedman, 1986, p. iv). Such systems are "child-centered, with the needs of the child and the family dictating the types and mix of services provided" (p. vii).

Remember, it is not a sign of weakness on your part to ask for help. It is a realistic response to demands beyond your current expertise or capabilities, and acknowledging these limitations can be the beginning of improving your skills through training and resources. Sometimes finding a solution involves moving children to an environment where they can more readily get their special needs met, such as a class with a lower ratio of children to adults. This move doesn't mean you have failed with the child; on the contrary, your concern and follow-through have opened doors of much-needed assistance.

CHILDREN ASSUMING SURVIVAL ROLES

Many thousands of children in the United States live in dysfunctional families who are often, but not always, struggling with alcoholism. According to the Children of Alcoholics Foundation, "alcoholism is a family disease. Its primary victim is the alcoholic, but the family and children suffer its ravages as well. Seven million American youngsters under the age of eighteen live with parental alcoholism. Each and every day each of these children must cope with emotional turmoil, stress, erratic and irrational behavior, and often physical as well as psychological pain" (Califano, 1990, p. 8). As a teacher of these children, you will be working with the symptoms of this overwhelming disease.

Children growing up in these families often assume roles and behavior patterns that help them cope with the pressures of their situations.

Joey, the class clown, was "on stage" as usual, pleased to have an audience for his goofiness in the housekeeping center. Unfortunately, it was cleanup time, and his antics were distracting everyone from the task at hand. Wishing for once that Joey could be serious and accept her request to calm down, Mrs. Jensen half-heartedly told him that it was time to clear the tea table. The boy glared at her for a second and then replied in a tense voice, " Sure, I'll clear it!" With that, he began pushing the play dishes off the table and throwing them to the floor with great gusto. Then, standing defiantly amid the scattered plastic, he swaggered, "So, what else do ya want?" Mrs. Jensen couldn't decide immediately how to react to his outburst. Giving herself time to consider, she dispersed the crowd that had gathered excitedly around the scene, sending those who were finished cleaning up to the lunchroom.

As the room emptied, she returned to Joey, who was making ineffectual attempts to clean up. He piled the dishware into precariously balanced stacks, delighting as they collapsed when he tried to pick them up. Caught up in his silliness, he was oblivious to her presence. She listened to his running commentary as he scolded himself mockingly: "Joey shouldn't throw dishes! No, no, Joey shouldn't throw. Daddy throws. Joey shouldn't throw!" Mrs. Jensen decided to try reflective listening. She matter-of-factly acknowledged his comment: "Sometimes your dad throws things." He darted a defensive glance at her face, trying to figure out whether she was criticizing his father. Finding her calmly receptive, he admitted, "Sometimes." But he shrugged his shoulders to try to downplay the admission. The teacher opened again: "Sometimes you throw things when you're mad." (This incident was not the first.) Joey retorted, "Not at home! Daddy gets really mad. He gets really mad at Mom, too!" Then the boy's face contorted into a worried frown. He'd never told anyone about his family's fights before. He retreated to the safety of silliness. "Oops!" he giggled as he attempted another impossible pickup, the dishes crashing once more to the floor. Mrs. Jensen accepted his obvious closure of the conversation and returned her focus to helping him clean up.

When all the children had gone to lunch, Mrs. Jensen wrote a documentation of Joey's scene. As she reviewed the list of incidents she had recorded so far this semester, the pattern of violence and silliness appeared over and over. Then she looked through Joey's parent file. Four attempted parent conferences had failed to happen. The parents hadn't even called to cancel; they just never showed up. And they always sounded irritated when she called to reschedule. They hadn't come to parent night either, although Joey had excitedly told her several times that his dad had promised to be there. As she scanned the

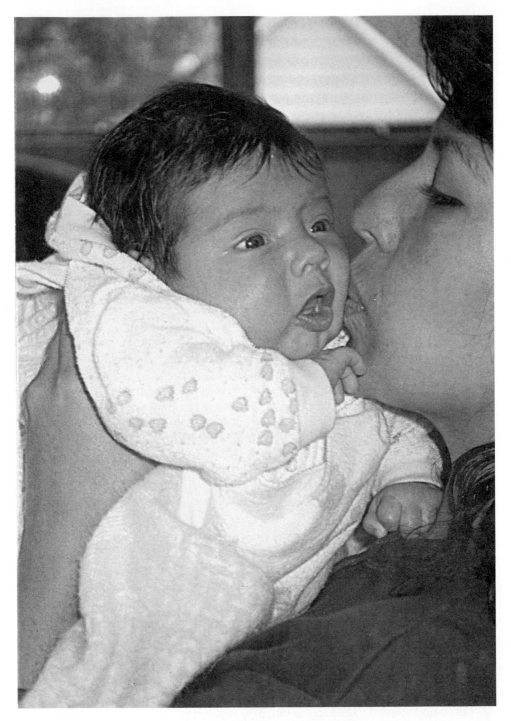

Not all children are lucky enough to have this kind of start in life.

rest of Joey's files, other pieces, such as his frequent absenteeism, started to fit together into a pattern she had seen before in families with alcohol problems. She decided to visit the school counselor to see if there were any additional clues from Joey's kindergarten year. She also found some reading materials that contained excellent classroom guidelines from the National Association for Children of Alcoholics and put the brochures into her bag to review that night.

Joey has adopted a survival role: the dysfunctional family's *mascot* or clown. His mask of silliness is an effort to take his difficult life, and himself, less seriously. His inappropriate humor and bizarre attention-getting attempts are symptoms of his struggle to cope. Even his anger is a valid cry for help, an understandable rage at the unfairness of his life.

Typically, children of alcoholics adopt a survival role or a combination of several. The *super-coper* assumes a great deal of responsibility, far beyond what is appropriate to his age level; he is seven going on seventeen. This tactic works for him at home, as he tries to keep his unstable household functioning. At school, however, it often causes him to clash with his peers because he has a great need for control and is often very rigid and bossy. The *scapegoat* adjusts to the family scene by accepting blame; negative attention at least acknowledges that she is alive! Her low self-image sets her up for victimization by more powerful classmates, as she seemingly attracts conflicts. The *lost child* role may be the least disruptive in class because invisibility is the skill these children have mastered at home. They are usually withdrawn and antisocial at school, and they often have trouble differentiating between fantasy and reality.

These coping mechanisms—alone or in combination—as well as other survival patterns of coping can interfere with a child's ability to live a full life. They can also interfere with basic problem-solving and social-skill development, which often translates into behavior difficulties in the classroom.

Children from dysfunctional families, whether the problems stem from alcoholism or other causes, have little opportunity to model and practice appropriate interpersonal relationships at home. As a teacher of these children, you can make a big difference. The National Association for Children of Alcoholics (1989) publishes some basic classroom guidelines that can help you meet the special needs of these children. (See p. 240.)

Children from families with special needs can have emotional, behavioral, and social difficulties that require much extra attention. They may exhibit high anxiety, lack of self-control, aggression, or withdrawal. Carefully document your observations, and share your concerns with the family. If you need help understanding and working with these children, do not hesitate to contact other professionals for consultation and assistance.

CHILDREN COPING WITH FAMILY CHANGES

When a child's family experiences a death, the loss of employment or housing, separation, divorce, or another crisis, the child's behavior is often a barometer of

DEALING WITH CHILDREN FROM DYSFUNCTIONAL FAMILIES: GUIDELINES FROM THE NATIONAL ASSOCIATION FOR CHILDREN OF ALCOHOLICS

1. Teach words and concepts that express feelings and emotions, acknowledging all feelings without labeling them as right or wrong.

2. Teach children to talk positively about themselves and others and to feel comfortable about accepting compliments.

3. Praise or criticize the behavior, not the person.

4. Teach appropriate ways to express anger and other feelings; show that anger will not result in loss of love, affection, and friendship.

5. Teach that it is OK to think of yourself and to say no.

6. Be consistent and predictable.

7. Establish clear expectations and boundaries that are enforced consistently and fairly.

8. Establish a warm, open classroom climate where children can feel safe; convey to each child a sense of your personal concern and caring.

9. Invite a person knowledgeable about particular problems in dysfunctional families to speak to students or to provide in-service training for school staff.

10. Provide age-appropriate readings on the subject for children.

her stress. Even events that may not be viewed as negative can be terrific strains on a sensitive young person: the birth of a new sibling, a grandmother who comes to live with the family, a remarriage, or the transition from one working parent to two.

A ten-year study of children living with divorce, conducted by J. S. Wallerstein and J. B. Kelly (1980), recognized some common symptoms of children in such stressful situations: anxiety, depression, regression, asthma, allergies, tantrums, daydreaming, overaggressive behavior, withdrawal from relationships, poor school performance, frequent crying or absence of emotion, and difficulty in communicating feelings. The researchers recommend that if these symptoms persist, the child may need counseling. Teachers who recognize that these behaviors may be possible side effects of the child's difficult family situation are able to respond with compassion and sensitivity to the child's special needs. Expectations for social and academic performance may need to be temporarily reduced. Close communication with the parents is essential, and referrals to supportive resources may be necessary.

Millions of children across the country are struggling with the adjustments and traumas of grief and loss caused by divorcing parents. Even during an amicable separation or at the end of an abusive situation, divorce can still be a painful process for everyone. Besides going through the grief of losing a parent, the child may not have the full emotional support of the emotionally strained remaining caregiver. These children need help as they move through the natural stages of mourning: disbelief and then anxiety, anger, sadness, depression, and eventually, if given reassurance, acceptance of the divorce. Candy Carlile, in her article "Children of Divorce: How Teachers Can Help Ease the Pain" (1991), recommends tolerance for behavioral changes. Such changes may occur immediately or gradually appear.

> Caroline, the director of the children's center, shared the information that Alex's parents had approved for general staff knowledge: They were going to divorce. The father had moved out of the house that weekend and would be leaving town to go to school in a few months. Experienced staff members braced themselves, well aware of the possible ways a divorce process can affect a child. Alex was quite a good-natured boy, somewhat demanding at times but generally pleasant to work with. They wondered aloud how and when it would sink in that his dad was leaving, and how he would react. Time passed, and everyone was relieved to see that he seemed to have accepted the divorce in stride. His dad left town, and still Alex gave no visible response except to become a bit clingier. Dennis mentioned this behavior at a staff meeting, suggesting that the boy might be moving from disbelief (denial) into anxiety.
>
> Still, no drastic changes in Alex were noted until after winter vacation. Disagreeable and contradictory, he just couldn't get along with anyone. He reverted to shoving and hitting instead of using his words when anyone did something he didn't like. He even regressed to biting on two occasions, a reaction he had not used since he was two years old, more than a year ago. He was like a walking time bomb, primed to be set off by anyone unlucky enough to get in his path. As staff members new to the field complained irritably about how difficult Alex was being, the more experienced caregivers encouraged them to be patient with the boy. Emphasizing that his anger was a natural reaction, they assured the newcomers that Alex would likely pass through this stage. The center staff made special efforts to provide opportunities for Alex to talk about feelings and learn how to work through his anger. During story time, they read fictional books dealing with the topic of divorce, which drew Alex's rapt

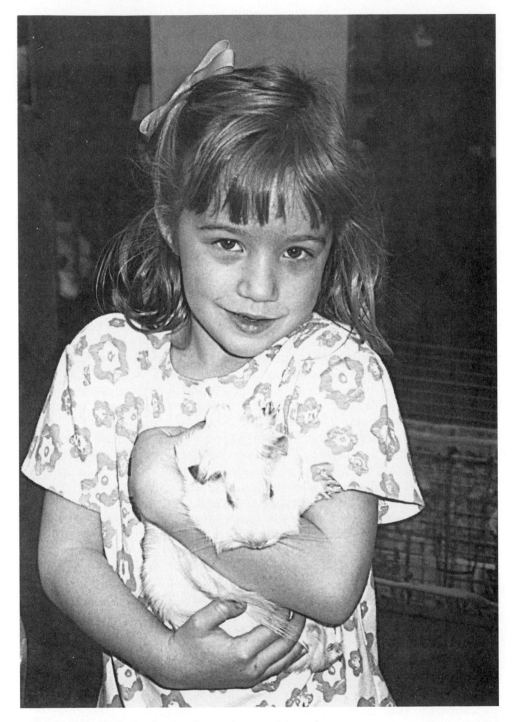

Changes in a child's family situation create special needs.

attention. Puppets, dolls, and unstructured art projects became his favorite activities. He also became a regular in the home center, where he role-played episodes of angry, fighting parents as well as idealistic, traditional family scenes.

Gradually, Alex's aggressive situations became fewer and fewer. In fact, he was hardly interacting at all, negatively or positively. He became notably reserved and quiet, quite a change from the bundle of explosives the center had carefully handled in midwinter. Now the staff sensed a growing sadness and dejection. When his mother volunteered the new information that Alex's dad wasn't going to be back in town that summer after all and that Alex had recently heard about this change of plans, Dennis better understood the boy's new mood. He also learned that Alex had moved three times that winter as his mother searched for affordable subsidized housing on her reduced income. Again, the staff accepted his special need for extra reassurance; he needed to know that they were really there for him. The preschool became his secure haven as well as a place to learn how to accept and work through his feelings and to build relationships. Years later, when he moved on to public school, his mother thanked Caroline for all the support and acceptance she and her son had received during that difficult first year. They were both coming through the divorce all right, and she was very grateful for everyone's help.

In about a year, 80 to 90 percent of children recover from the initial shock of divorce (Klavan & Jellinek, 1988). Parental hostility and bitterness may continue even after the divorce, however, and the child may continue to suffer. There may also be resultant hardships such as life-style changes and financial stress. In addition, the child may be faced with two households and daily or weekly transitions between them. Differences of opinion about child rearing can become volatile issues between estranged parents; therefore, consistent expectations and limits at school can become a vital stabilizing factor for the child. A nurturing, supportive, and understanding classroom environment can be the safest place in a child's life while the family goes through the initial crisis and the continuing stress.

Death in a family can have similar effects on a child. As with divorce, the timetable for a child's grief and loss may be unpredictable. Youngsters may have difficulty understanding the permanence of the loss, but it is important, as always, to be honest with them. Sugarcoating death with terms like "gone to sleep" or "gone on a long trip" can not only create fears about sleeping or traveling but also mislead children, which can seriously damage their future ability to trust. It is also important for the adults around them to be truthful about their own feelings. Pretending not to be sad is deceptive and confusing; children's senses tell them one thing while adults feign another. Be sure to communicate with the parents so that what you say in school is consistent with what is happening at home. And if the child initiates conversations on the subject, be willing and available to listen to those fears and feelings. Other children may also experi-

A nurturing, supportive, and understanding classroom can be the safest place in a child's life while the family goes through the initial crisis and the continuing stress.

ence fears about their loved ones when they hear about a classmate's loss. If you do not feel prepared to discuss the subject of death, seek out advice; doctors or counselors may be helpful. And, as in any time of crisis, be sensitive to the special needs of the child, understanding that behavior patterns may swing wildly for a time. Your consistent base may be the only stable point when a child's world spins temporarily out of control.

Of course, even when there is no sudden event or change in a child's life, a continually strained home situation can greatly affect the child's ability to function in the classroom. Whatever the cause of stress in a child's life, it is important for the teacher to communicate with the parents closely and to reach for assistance when needed.

ABUSE AS THE CAUSE OF BEHAVIOR PROBLEMS

For some children, physical, emotional, or sexual abuse is a pervasive element of their existence. You are highly likely to work with children who are being abused now or whose behavior is shaped by past experiences of abuse. Though abuse may occur outside the family, statistics reveal that most does not. It, too, is most often a family-based problem.

The child who is aggressive in your classroom because he is a victim of abuse at home needs your guidance. As the child learns alternatives to violence, the pattern of aggression may begin to fade. But to break the cycle of abuse, there must be intervention; and everyone involved must receive help and education. Therefore, it is important to report the problem by calling on professionals and their resources to begin the process of help and healing.

> Sheri listened as Tory loudly accused Sam of destroying his block construction. But the way Sam saw it, Tory had abandoned the area to go on the swings. Sam had assumed that Tory was done, so he was using the blocks left behind to build his own creation. Because Sam seemed to be using his words fairly well to explain his misunderstanding, Sheri watched them try to work it out. But she was distracted for a minute when Katya asked for help with her shoelaces, and she didn't notice Tory's escalating anger. Next thing she knew, Tory was undoing his belt, pulling it out with a flourish, and threatening, "I'm gonna show you! You don't touch my stuff!" Luckily, Sam did a quick crab-walk scramble to get out of the way, and Sheri reached Tory before the second thrash of the belt.
>
> This wasn't the first time Tory had tried this tactic, and Sheri was well aware of how dangerous he could be! Last time it happened, she had explained to him that belts were only used for keeping up pants. Then she had modeled words for him to express his anger. Sheri responded similarly this time, but she also told him that she couldn't feel safe about his belt anymore today. She replaced it with a twisted scarf.
>
> Unfortunately, Sheri suspected that Tory's belt wasn't the real problem. This morning she had seen welts on his back when he yanked his coat over his head. She put that together with the nightmares he often had during nap time and the way he'd wince and put up his arm in defense sometimes when his uncle reached for him. In fact, he often pulled away when anyone reached for him, especially adult males. Sheri decided it was time to file an abuse suspicion report.

Behavioral indicators of physical and emotional abuse are similar. Both may cause sudden or pronounced new fears as well as behavior extremes of either passivity or aggressiveness. Physically abused children are likely to be afraid to go home and wary of any physical contact as well. Emotionally abused youngsters are prone to depression and low self-esteem. Eating disorders, begging or stealing food, or refusing to eat may also signal physical or emotional neglect. A sexually abused child generally exhibits sophisticated or unusual sexual behavior or knowledge and may engage in excessive masturbation. Extremely clingy behavior may also be associated with sexual abuse. Behavior problems can be expected as a result of any abuse or neglect situation.

Maltreated children generally suffer in silence, their trust of adults damaged to the point that they cannot seek out anyone to comfort and help them. Sometimes physical symptoms bring the abuse to light, such as unexplained bruises, welts, burns, nonorganic failure to thrive (illness and/or delayed development with no apparent physical cause), pronounced fatigue, restraint injuries, discharges from genital areas, unexplained gagging, or difficulty walking or sitting due to injury. But behavioral indicators are more subtle symptoms of abuse and neglect. Although they can easily be attributed to many other possible causes, the intensity or the combination of behaviors will alert a professional to the possibility of abuse or neglect.

Published lists of abuse indicators should, of course, be used with caution, but combinations of symptoms may be significant and should be reported. When you observe a combination of "red flag" behaviors or physical symptoms, do not hesitate to file a report. Even though your concerns may prove unfounded, you must report, just in case your suspicions are correct. Remember, you are not an investigator or a judge, and it is not up to you to prove abuse. Teachers and caregivers not only have a professional responsibility to work as advocates for children, but they are also mandated by law to report suspicion of abuse or neglect to the appropriate agency. Make sure your center or school provides adequate training and support for this important role. Together, teachers and other professionals can stop the heartbreak of abuse and get the child and family the help they need (Broadhurst & MacDicken, 1979).

CONCLUSION

Each morning, as your classroom fills with children, remember that you are receiving members of families. When their families' special needs cause serious problems for children in your care, you are in a unique position to help. In this very responsible role, a teacher must show an educated awareness of the possibilities and a willingness to reach for assistance and support. Sometimes working with children who have family problems can be difficult, but the rewards are potentially high. As you come to a clearer self-awareness of your capabilities and when you need to reach for help, you will find new directions for growth. In the process, you will build your network of resources. Often, you will find that you can genuinely make a difference in the life of a child who is from a family with special needs.

FOR FURTHER THOUGHT

1. Every school district, community, and state has different resources to assist special-needs children, their families, and the educators working with them. Choose one of the potential causes of behavior problems mentioned in this chapter. Research the individual, professional, and institutional assistance available to you. For example, possible resources for dealing with a death in the family include the following:
   a. Family: accessible support system of relatives
   b. School counselor
   c. Library: stories on the subject
   d. Agencies: hospice organizations, mental health services, social service programs

   Note the networking between resources; when contacting one, are you referred to another? Determine the specific expertise of each resource. Start your own resource reference file by requesting telephone and address contacts, reading list suggestions, and brochures or publications.

2. As an early childhood professional, you will probably work with abused or neglected children eventually. Because you are required by law to report suspected abuse, you need to know how. Research methods of reporting abuse: time requirements for reporting, numbers to call, report forms, confidentiality options, response-time expectations, and potential follow-up responsibilities.

3. Many problems can be prevented. Early-childhood professionals are increasingly asked to help protect our nation's children from abuse through education for empowerment. How do you feel about this role expectation? Specialists trained to teach children basic concepts about "good touch/bad touch" and "secrets you don't have to keep" may be available to do talks in your classroom or center. Would you be comfortable having these subjects introduced to children in your care? Why or why not?

4. When a child first *discloses*, or voluntarily shares a piece of information about abuse, it is essential that the person the child has chosen to take the risk of telling responds appropriately. What reactions might make the child feel able to talk and continue to reach for help? What responses might make the child feel unsafe or not accepted? What listening skills discussed in previous chapters might help a child feel that a hard-to-tell story is heard nonjudgmentally?

REFERENCES AND RECOMMENDATIONS FOR READING

Books

BIENENFELD, F. (1987). *Helping your child succeed after divorce.* Claremont, CA: Hunter House.

BROADHURST, D., & MACDICKEN, R. A. (1979). *Early childhood programs and the prevention and treatment of child abuse and neglect: For workers in Head Start, family day care, preschool, and day care programs.* (DHEW Publication No. OHDS 79-30198). Washington, DC:

U.S. Department of Health, Education, and Welfare, National Center on Child Abuse and Neglect.

GROSSMAN, H. (1990). *Trouble-free teaching: Solutions to behavior problems in the classroom.* Mountain View, CA: Mayfield.

NATIONAL ASSOCIATION OF CHILDREN OF ALCOHOLICS. (1989). *It's elementary: Meeting the needs of high risk youth in the school setting.* Washington, DC: National Association of Children of Alcoholics.

WALLERSTEIN, J. S., & KELLY, J. B. (1980). *Surviving the breakup.* New York: Basic Books.

Periodicals

CARLILE, C. (1991). Children of divorce: How teachers can help ease the pain. *Childhood Education, 67*(4), 232–234.

CAUGHEY, C. (1991, May). Becoming the child's ally: Observations in a classroom for children who have been abused. *Young Children,* pp. 22–28.

DAVIS, R., ALLEN, T., & SHERMAN, J. (1990). Children of alcoholics: The role of the teacher: Strategies for helping. *Prevention Express, 9*(2), 6–7.

KLAVAN, E., & JELLINEK, M. (EDS.). (1988, September). The single parent. *Good Housekeeping,* p. 126.

SWAN, A. M. (1992). Children's literature and alcohol: Being aware. *Childhood Education, 69*(1), 10–14.

WASSERMANN, S. (1992). Professional teachers deal with children "in trouble." *Childhood Education, 68*(4), 232–233.

Reports and Papers

BLUME, S. B. *Report on the conference on research needs and opportunities for children of alcoholics.* New York: Children of Alcoholics Foundation.

CALIFANO, A. (1990). *Children of alcoholics in the medical system: Hidden problems, hidden costs.* New York: Children of Alcoholics Foundation.

TURNER, J. (1988). *Child discipline and world peace.* Presented at the annual conference of the National Association for the Education of Young Children, Anaheim, CA. ERIC Clearinghouse, ED304226.

STROUL, B., & FRIEDMAN, R. (1986). *A system of care for severely emotionally disturbed children and youth.* Washington, DC: Child and Adolescent Service System Program/Georgetown University Child Development Center.

Chapter 14

Children Experiencing Disabilities

Children suffering from serious chronic illnesses, those with learning disorders, and those with physical difficulties experience temporary and permanent disabilities that present special challenges to their teachers and caregivers. In current practice, special-needs children are included in regular classrooms and preschools rather than segregated in special education classrooms; therefore, you can expect to have these children in your care. A special education teacher may be available to assist you part of the time but will probably not remove the child from your classroom. The goal is to provide the least restrictive, most normal environment for learning. An understanding of these children's limitations as well as their potential will help you develop reasonable expectations and choose appropriate guidance and teaching methods.

FETAL ALCOHOL SYNDROME/EFFECTS

More and more teachers are working with children who experience disabilities resulting from alcohol in their prenatal environment. The child in the following example exhibits typical signs of *fetal alcohol syndrome*, which can affect physical, mental, and behavioral capabilities. The damage done by alcohol to Netta while she was in the womb severely impairs her life's potential.

> When Netta's day-care provider recommended that she have a Wechsler Preschool and Primary Scale of Intelligence (WPPSI) IQ test, her parents agreed, although they were understandably uncomfortable with the idea of testing a four-year-old. The results made them even more distressed. The two-part verbal and performance test found Netta's IQ to be borderline; her skills ranged from a year below average in visual tasks to several years below her age level in "areas requiring attention to auditory input." In other words, she had extreme difficulty concentrating and dealing with any level of abstraction. She was also found to be easily distracted, both auditorily and visually. Her parents listened, stunned, as the psychologist recommended an educational program for "children like Netta." According to him, *if* she were able to be in a regular school, she would need lots of external structure and a distraction-free environment, possibly a study booth separate from the other children. He also commented that Netta was easily stimulated and unable to inhibit herself. He warned that "children like this," unable to control themselves or be sensitive to others, often had great difficulty socially.
>
> Netta's parents were defensive. They had never had their child lumped into a category before, and they refused to believe the test results. But many painful years and difficult experiences later, a knowledgeable doctor finally put all of Netta's symptoms together. Then they received the full prognosis: fetal alcohol syndrome (FAS). Devastated, they began to grieve for the adult they had hoped their child would become.

Netta's mother is not an alcoholic. She simply didn't know the facts: Drinking alcohol is potentially harmful all through pregnancy, and even light drinking can damage the unborn child (Funkhouser & Denniston, 1985). In fact, the surgeon general advises pregnant women and nursing mothers not to drink any alcoholic beverages at all (American Council for Drug Education, 1991).

FAS is a medical diagnosis made by physicians trained to recognize a combination of congenital birth defects caused by prenatal exposure to alcohol. Common symptoms are growth deficiencies, facial malformations and other physical irregularities, and central nervous system effects that may include seizures. There may also be varying degrees of major organ system malformations. Besides producing physical deformities, fetal alcohol syndrome is the leading cause of mental retardation (Children of Alcoholics Foundation, 1990). Any of these characteristics taken by itself does not identify FAS; but when in combination and with a history of maternal drinking, these symptoms may indicate a diagnosis. When the physical symptoms of FAS are not all present but behavior and neurological effects exist, the child may have *fetal alcohol effects* (FAE).

COMMON FACIAL MALFORMATIONS IN FAS CHILDREN

❏ Small head circumference

❏ Flattened midface

❏ Sunken nasal bridge

❏ Flattened, elongated philtrum (groove between nose and upper lip)

❏ Thin or flattened upper lip

❏ Small, far-set eyes

❏ Short nose

❏ Outer-ear anomalies

❏ Excess tissue on eyelids

FAS and FAE children often have similar behavioral and cognitive characteristics. Infants and young children may have poor sucking response, failure to thrive, high distractibility and hyperactivity, delays in walking and language development, delayed toilet training, difficulty following directions, temper tantrums, inability to screen out irrelevant stimuli, sleep disturbances, speech delays, and hearing loss. They generally have little patience and do not have the ability to keep their bodies still or to concentrate. It is exceptionally difficult for

Many pregnant women don't know that prenatal exposure to alcohol can cause a combination of birth defects called fetal alcohol syndrome (FAS).

them to think through a problem and its possible consequences or to come up with a reasoned decision.

School-age children with FAS/FAE may have the following characteristics: low ceilings for academic achievement, poor impulse control, poor social judgment, fearlessness, developmental delays, imperviousness to verbal commands, concentration/attention problems, and restlessness. Their slow cognitive pace can make it difficult to complete classroom tasks, and struggling to function with their various disabilities can quickly exhaust them. Their inability to predict consequences makes it hard for them to understand and accept rules; it can even translate into nonmalicious acts of lying, cheating, and stealing. Social rules regarding touching and body distance are also difficult for them to relate to. This trait, in combination with their generally friendly, affectionate, and easily influenced natures, makes them very vulnerable to abuse. These children often exhibit challenging behaviors due to an inability to communicate effectively (Pacer Center, 1990). They can be easily overstimulated because of an impaired ability to filter external stimuli.

One frustrating characteristic of FAS children is an inability to learn from their mistakes. In *The Broken Cord*, an insightful book by Michael Dorris, the author describes his FAS son:

> [This was] his greatest problem, the day-in, day-out liability with which it was hardest for the world to cope. . . . He could not, cannot, project himself into the future: "If I do x, then y (good or bad) will follow." His estimation of consequences was so hazy that it translated into an approach to action so conservative that it appeared to be stubborn. He existed in the present tense. . . . each leap was off a cliff and into an unknown depth . . . and so he tended to dig in his heels. And when he did venture forth, sometimes tentatively, sometimes with the brashness of having nothing to lose, he made wrong choices, saw only part of the picture" (Dorris, 1989, p. 201).

This inability to learn from experience, to see cause and effect, or to understand possible consequences is perhaps the most wearing attribute of FAS/FAE students. Because they are incapable of figuring out *why* things are done one way or another, they do not internalize limits. No matter how many times they are told a rule or an expectation, they are likely to operate outside the established boundaries simply because they cannot relate their actions to another's perspective. For this reason, they need extensive one-on-one guidance and often require a classroom aide. This assistance is also necessary because they usually have an extremely hard time not only learning to read and write but also performing basic life skills such as tying their shoes. Not being able to look ahead and see the benefit of learning, they have very little motivation or desire to work at mastering skills. As FAS/FAE students cope with these factors beyond their control, they may become stubborn, sullen, defiant, resistant, aggressive, rigid, and disruptive. They also may feel socially isolated and depressed and develop a sense of hopelessness.

Your job, of course, is not to diagnose. But as a professional and an advocate for children, you should be able to recognize possible characteristics; and you are required to follow up on your observations and concerns. Early diagnosis facilitates the essential early introduction of services and prevents increased difficulties—and costs—in childhood, adolescence, and adulthood.

COCAINE AND CRACK EFFECTS

Marcy's mother didn't know she was pregnant yet when she celebrated her birthday with a gift from her best friend: some cocaine. Not a regular user, she was surprised at how briefly the euphoria lasted. Unfortunately, for the tiny fetus inside her the effects would last a lifetime. The effects of cocaine on babies can be devastating, whether the mother uses the drug once or is a regular user.

> As he watched her wander aimlessly around the classroom, Dennis worried about Marcy. She seemed completely unable to organize her own play. Just choosing a toy seemed to be more than she could manage; and when she was included in a group, she simply couldn't focus on the play activity. She was too easily distracted by any environmental noises or movements. Her poor language skills, at a "baby-talk" level that seemed younger than her three years, often caused her to be ostracized by her peers. For that matter, she made very little effort to communicate at all, rarely using any gestures. And Dennis couldn't remember the last time he had heard Marcy laugh; there was a flat, unemotional quality to the child. What feelings she did exhibit, such as irritability or anger, came on rapidly and changed with unnerving force. One moment she might be eerily quiet, the next loudly crying. Any unexpected change in the center routine or environment threw Marcy into a screaming fit. Unable either to comfort herself or be comforted by others, she might wail full force for fifteen minutes and then shut it off completely in a moment.
>
> Marcy also had difficulty with problem-solving tasks such as the puzzle she had weakly attempted that morning. She just didn't seem to have the ability to look at the pieces and imagine any plan of attack. After dumping them into a heap as she'd seen her neighbor do, she sat immobile, staring blankly at the pile. Several times Dennis had modeled the trial-and-error approach, but one try was about Marcy's limit. Frustrated, she would throw the puzzle base across the room. Part of the problem was her minimal fine-motor skills; just picking up the pieces was a major effort. But Dennis sensed that the problem was more serious. For example, he occasionally noticed odd eye movements when Marcy was in a staring spell. There were just a lot of unusual features in this child. He decided to check his perceptions at the next staff meeting. Could there be something seriously wrong with Marcy?

Marcy shows classic symptoms of fetal cocaine damage. Her aimlessness, staring spells, blanking out, unusual eye movements, poor language and social skills, flat emotions, irritability, and distractibility are notable features. Others are impulsiveness, avoidance of eye contact, aggressiveness with peers, and failure to seek or respond to praise or even recognition from adults. These children have difficulty with transitions and changes of routine. They are hypersensitive to touch and surroundings. Easily overexcited, they are unable to calm themselves down and have difficulty regulating their own behavior. Physical characteristics include gross-motor clumsiness, poor fine-motor dexterity, and difficulty following movement with their eyes. In the classroom, they constantly test the limits, insisting on doing things on their own terms. They often don't respond to even simple requests, partly because of an inability to understand or follow verbal directions.

How can you best work with these children? First, as with any children, become knowledgeable about their individual needs. Dennis began by recognizing the different aspects of Marcy's difficulty at the preschool. After he discussed his observations with the staff, Dennis and the center's director met with Marcy's parents. As a result, they took her to a physician and a psychologist who diagnosed the cocaine-affected syndrome. When the child's problems were more clearly identified, the staff worked with Marcy's parents and professional consultants on how best to meet Marcy's special needs with appropriate environmental and teaching strategies. In Marcy's case, the strategies meant special attention to routine, reduction in stimulation, forewarning of transitions, and support from an assigned aide during those transitions. The strategies also included extra help with self-expression by constant verbal modeling.

Marcy's teachers also had to adjust their expectations to match her capabilities. And as they learned more about the child's problems, they also learned to adjust expectations of themselves as her caregivers. Sheri, the school aide, admitted that she had been quite unnerved by Marcy's screaming spells and had felt personally inadequate because of her inability to soothe the child. Now she knew that it wasn't her failure but rather Marcy's personal difficulty. Sheri found herself much more able to cope. She could just be there for the child as a calm support, however long it took, without becoming anxiety-ridden herself. Other staff members reported that they, too, had become more comfortable working with the child now that they were aware of her special needs.

Whenever children are diagnosed with FAS, FAE, cocaine-affected syndrome, ADD, or other conditions, there arises the danger that other people will primarily relate to the children according to those labels. As does every child in your care, each individual has special needs, strengths, and weaknesses. Be on the lookout for positive attributes as well as specific problems. For example, in the brochure *Fetal Alcohol and Drug Affected: A Guide for Classroom Teachers* (Alaska Staff Development Network, 1991), descriptions of classroom performance, behavior, history, and dynamics—all of which can be intimidating—are followed by a list of the common characteristics associated with these children. The list describes the children as tactile, friendly, spontaneous, trusting, humorous, loyal, determined, committed, caring, kind, affectionate, curious, creative, persistent, athletic, fair, involved, affectionate to animals, fond of gardens, artistic, energetic, musical, highly verbal, imaginative, happy with younger children, compassionate, cooperative, great storytellers, and hard workers. But the brochure also points out that such "characteristics often extinguish/mutate in a gradual erosive process without appropriate identification and support" (Juneau School District, 1991, p. 12).

Individualized Plans

Because parents want to maximize their child's life potential, some may be in a state of denial about how much they can reasonably expect from both you and

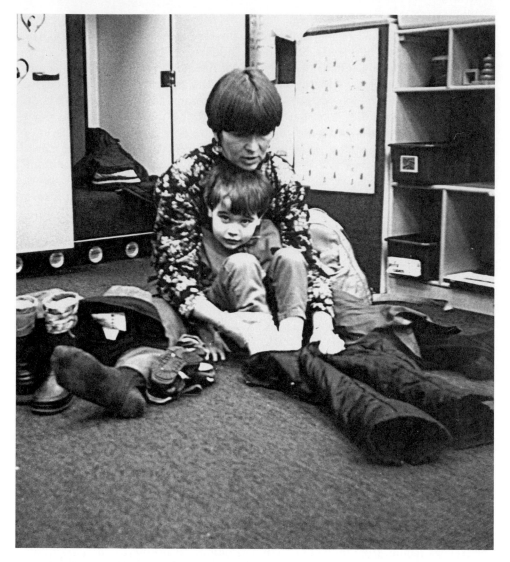

Sometimes children require special attention, such as individual assistance when they make the transition from one activity to the next.

the child. Guilt-ridden and yearning to see progress, they may try to encourage teachers to overlook symptoms. In such cases, it can be to your benefit and theirs if you connect them with resources that will help them better understand the physical, psychological, and social needs of their child.

If a child in your care experiences severe difficulties, the special education staff may work with you and the child's parents to draw up an Individual Education Plan (IEP). Based on evaluations by experts, this plan provides some guidance about reasonable expectations for the child. Brainstorming with the experts about how you can best implement the IEP can be a good starting place for increasing your knowledge about working with children who are experiencing disabilities.

In some states there are agencies that also facilitate the ongoing process of providing an Individual Services Plan (ISP) for children who have multiple needs. This is a holistic approach, taking into account all aspects of the child and the situation. When drawing up an ISP, an agency works to coordinate all the possible sources of assistance, including family and friends as well as medical, vocational, educational, psychological, safety, and economic services. The goal is to develop cooperatively an individualized plan of services to support the child's needs in the best way possible.

CHRONIC ILLNESSES AND PHYSICAL DISABILITIES

Modern medical science and technology has brought new hope for children who are born with serious birth defects, develop cancers, or experience organ failures. Operations, medications, therapies, and transplants have changed many conditions; some that were formerly listed as terminal are now considered life-threatening chronic illnesses (Ruccione, 1983). Children with these conditions may lead quite normal lives, which includes attending regular schools between stays in clinics or hospitals. But they may have physical limitations that the teacher needs to be aware of. If you teach or care for such a child, consult with the parents and possibly with the doctors involved. You also need to ask about medications and possible side effects; inquire about therapy methods being used and learn about any precautions, limitations, or requirements. Beyond this knowledge, it is important with special-needs students to see them first and foremost as children, with the illness or handicap as secondary. You may be tempted to feel sorry for them or to treat them differently, giving them excessive attention, making allowances, or giving in when they misbehave. However, this special treatment is a disservice to the child, who may become overly demanding and unpleasant to be around.

> Nancy set Heather's snack down in front of the child, who made a face and whimpered, "I don't like rice cakes." Nancy calmly responded, "We are having rice cakes with peanut butter for snack time today. There is also apple juice coming." Used to getting her own way at home, Heather escalated her complaint: "I won't eat this! I don't like it!" Nancy accepted her choice, thinking the girl wouldn't get too hungry without it. She remembered what a big lunch Heather had eaten. "You don't have to," she said evenly, moving around the table to serve the other children. Indignant, Heather raised her voice to the command level she used when she expected people to give in to her: "Give me something else! I don't like this!" Nancy was used to Heather's attempts at ordering people around, and she resisted reacting.
>   The girl's outburst brought some disconcerted stares from the children seated around her, but Heather didn't back down. Then Kelsey, always hungry, meekly asked, "If you don't want it, can I have

it?" "No, it's mine!" snapped Heather. With that she wadded the rice cake up in her napkin and tossed it into the garbage with a flourish. Ashley mimicked her mother's admonition: "You shouldn't waste food!" "Can if I want to," taunted Heather, as she stomped away from the snack table. It was hard for Nancy to see the small girl's unhappiness. She wanted Heather's time between rounds of chemotherapy to be as pleasant as possible. However, Nancy knew it was important for this child to make choices and learn from her experiences, just as it was for every other child.

Heather's appearance is disturbing to some people. Her sparse new crop of hair, which is growing in after chemotherapy, and her extreme frailty give her an otherworldly effect. Children at the preschool occasionally voice concern about "catching" what Heather has, fearful of losing their hair, too. Classmates of children with chronic, noncontagious illnesses often need to be reassured that they will not get sick from playing together. You may want to ask the parents or medical professionals to help you explain the child's condition to the group in the best way possible. Parents of other children may also need reassurance.

Heather has been having cancer treatments as long as she can remember; she no longer questions the facts of her situation, such as the limitations on her activities. Her social and behavior problems are more a result of how other people have related to her—people who have been overprotective and servile. For children who have only had physically limiting conditions for a short time, the problems are related more to frustration because they are no longer able to do what they once could. Anger at the limits imposed by a handicap, such as a lost limb, may be expressed in temper tantrums; the children understandably resent the hardships of their altered life. Disabled children may also be embarrassed and self-conscious about their differences. Teachers sensitive to these disability-adjustment traumas need to validate the children's feelings as they work through the initial shock, depression, and anger. At the same time, teachers can provide supportive encouragement to help the children adjust to their situation. When modifications to the environment or alternative ways of doing things are needed, the children themselves can also help to problem-solve.

Randy hated his wheelchair. His arms hadn't built up much strength yet, and the big, clunky contraption was very hard for him to maneuver. Because it was too rainy to go outside, Nancy and the children were laying out an obstacle course all over the classroom. Taking care to modify each element so that Randy could participate if he chose to, the teacher explained to the other children why the tarp tunnel had to be wider and the tricycle slalom had to have a more gradual turning radius. Some parts were harder to modify for Randy, such as the trampoline and the hopscotch.

She asked Randy and the other children for suggestions. They proposed that he go around the trampoline ten times instead of jumping ten times, and he could throw beanbags onto the hopscotch

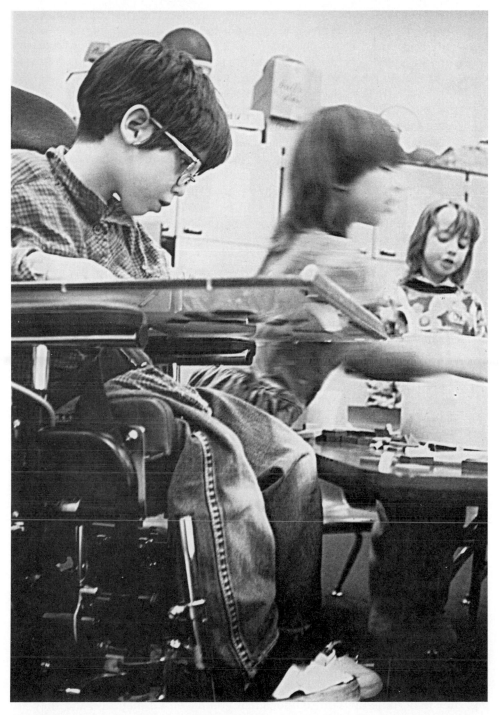

Children with serious congenital disabilities, other disabilities, or illnesses may attend regular schools.

numbers instead of stepping on them. Satisfied that the course was challenging for everyone and possible for Randy, Nancy started the music tape and let the children go at it. "She'll be coming 'round the mountain when she comes" seemed a perfect background for the trail of scrambling, hopping, jumping, and tumbling children.

Everything was going fine until Randy entered the tunnel. One of the tie-down lines attached to the piano leg had loosened. Somehow it got caught in his wheel, and he started pulling down the tarp. The kids behind him cried out, "Hey, you're ruining the tunnel!" Randy backed up, but he was ensnared and just pulled down more of the tarp. He tried spinning the wheelchair around to escape, but the tarp had immobilized him. Christie wailed, "He ruined our tunnel! He pulled it down!" Beet-red with embarrassment, Randy impulsively turned on the girl. He threw a beanbag at her, shouting, "Shut up!" Then, venting his frustration, he threw the rest of the beanbags angrily at the wall.

Nancy intervened, quickly checking on Christie. Finding her surprised but unhurt, she turned to Randy who was yanking angrily on the tarp to no avail. He was starting to work himself into a fit (he'd had quite a few since his debilitating car accident). Nancy said, "That really made you mad when the tarp line got caught in your wheels." Sensing that she understood his feelings, the boy replied, "I couldn't help it. This stupid thing can't do anything!" Nancy accepted his frustration by saying, "It sure is hard to have to do things differently, especially when they don't work out." As she helped him untangle the tarp, she admitted, "I guess we didn't have it set up quite well enough yet. How could we make it work for you? You were doing the rest of the obstacle course really well. Didn't you get dizzy going around the trampoline? I didn't think you'd be able to do that!"

As the boy refocused for a moment on something he had accomplished well, he calmed down. Nancy handed the freed tarp line to him and asked, "Where should we tie this to keep it out of your way?" Eager to help fix the tunnel, Randy rolled himself over to the piano leg and tied knot after knot until he ran out of rope. Nancy figured the time it would take her to untangle that huge knot was well worth it, as she watched Randy and Alex take off together to race around the trampoline again.

Creative modifications such as Nancy's can make programs and activities accessible to children experiencing disabilities. Remember, you don't have to reinvent the wheel. Reach out to resource personnel, co-workers, and the child's parents when you need support. Libraries and bookstores can also be sources of helpful information. Whenever possible, include the children in your brainstorming; they may come up with solutions that you haven't thought of, and they are also much more likely to be enthusiastic and motivated about their own ideas. No matter what chronic illness or physical disability the children are experiencing,

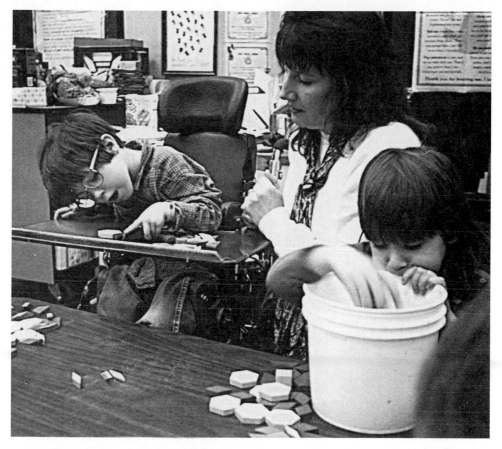

Creative modifications and supportive encouragement can make programs and activities accessible to children with disabilities.

remember to emphasize their abilities, something you need to keep in mind with all special-needs children. As you do with all children, focus on the child as a whole: emotionally, cognitively, physically, socially, and spiritually.

ATTENTION DISORDERS

Many teachers face attention disorders in the classroom. They include the disruptive behaviors associated with hyperactivity, attention-deficit disorder (ADD) or attention-deficit hyperactivity disorder (ADHD), minimal brain dysfunction (MBD), and hyperkinetic syndrome. Actual diagnosis of any of these disorders includes a complex process of observation, testing, and child interview, with the extremeness of a child's behavior working as the definitive factor. Being labeled with an attention-deficit disorder can be damaging to a child's self-esteem and to parents' and teachers' expectations for the child; therefore, any conclusions should be carefully determined by professionals.

Children with ADD and ADHD can be very impulsive, acting without consideration of consequences. They often have short attention spans and are thus unable to concentrate on a task long enough to complete it. They switch from one activity to another without gaining satisfaction or focus, and they also have great difficulty organizing themselves and their work. Lacking goal direction, they are easily frustrated—another reason for why they seldom complete work. Because they are easily distracted, they have trouble paying attention to the task at hand and have difficulty redirecting attention to their original task once distracted. On the other hand, they may become so intensely involved in an activity that it is extremely hard to redirect their attention during transition times. They are often restless and fidgety, constantly in motion even when surroundings are quiet and calm. They may call out information without being asked, often interrupt others, and either talk or make odd noises incessantly. ADD children have difficulty establishing and maintaining friendships because of their inability to control their behavior, which causes serious problems with social relationships (Parker, 1988).

Mrs. Jensen had received much solid advice from the school counselor about how to help Timmy, who had been diagnosed with ADD. She had moved his seat closer to hers, in a low-traffic and relatively distraction-free area of the classroom. She had reduced the extraneous materials in his work area, and his parents had provided a desk organizer that had a place for paper, pencils, glue, and books. She worked with Timmy on a chart of reminders about what to do at different points in the day. She also posted the large classroom schedule, which had been made with the whole group, next to Timmy's seat. She quietly referred to it in advance of each transition to forewarn the boy, knowing he had difficulty with change.

Rather than insisting that he complete his school assignments—an impossible goal—Mrs. Jensen helped Timmy celebrate his efforts in that direction. In this way, the focus was on his successes rather than his failures. Recognizing the difficulty that Timmy had in listening effectively, Mrs. Jensen made a special effort to make eye contact and sometimes gentle physical contact, such as a hand on his shoulder, when she gave instructions. She also gave him verbal clues about when it was time to listen and stated the purpose for listening: "Listen now while I give you the directions for the leprechaun game." She also made sure that her instructions were clear and simple. If there were several steps, she broke them down one at a time for Timmy, giving him each direction only as he became ready for it.

Mrs. Jensen noticed that Timmy frequently sought out solitude in the one-person reading nook. He seemed to be able to cope better with the bustle of the classroom after a time away from all that stimulus. His teacher took her cue from the child and began to encourage him to seek a private spot when he began getting agitated.

Her efforts did help Timmy function with the academic expectations of the classroom, but he still had constant problems with social relations. He seemed unaware of even common courtesy. When she tried to read a story to the group, he incessantly interrupted. His exuberance and lack of self-control made his classmates more and more irritated with him. But Timmy just looked confused by their irritation, unable to recognize that his interruptions were bothering them. Concerned that his relationships and self-image were suffering, Mrs. Jensen returned to the counselor and specifically asked for suggestions for ways to address these problems. The counselor reassured her that Timmy was not breaking these rules out of active resistance to her. Instead, he had a lack of ability to make connections either between expectations and actions or between actions and consequences. Thus Timmy needed frequent reminders, without irritation or reprimand.

The counselor suggested that when Timmy did break a rule, Mrs. Jensen could quietly remind him of the rule and the reason for the limit. If there was a related consequence, the counselor recommended that Mrs. Jensen simply explain the connection and consistently follow through with it. He also reminded her not to expect Timmy to necessarily learn from the experience; the child would probably repeat similar inappropriate behavior. The lack of progress wouldn't be due to her failure to teach but to Timmy's inability to process the relationships in his world. ADD children lack the internal dialogue that normally helps children work through experiences and construct an understanding of what is expected of them.

Reassured that she was doing the best she could, Mrs. Jensen resolved to accept Timmy as he was and try to give him as positive an educational experience as possible. The more she knew about his special needs, the more effective she became as his teacher. Her classroom was still disrupted often by Timmy's difficulties, but she felt less overwhelmed and exhausted by his demands, thanks to her increased knowledge.

ADD children do not outgrow this chronic disorder, which commonly persists into adulthood (Wender, 1987). However, they often can be helped to instruct, monitor, and evaluate themselves at some level, both in academics and in social situations (Kirby, 1986). ADD just means that it will always take unusual effort for them to do what comes naturally for most people. One of the best things an educational setting can do for these children is to see that they experience some success. With awareness and effort, the classroom teacher can help these children begin to develop positive attitudes and skills that will last them a lifetime (Buchoff, 1990).

CONCLUSION

Because early-childhood educators do not diagnose disabilities, we have not presented a totally inclusive list of the physically and emotionally disabling problems that can cause behavior difficulties or a complete inventory of the details involved with each situation. Instead, we have tried to introduce you to the complexity of behavior problems that may be caused by certain types of special needs. This introduction is designed to alert you to situations requiring special assistance.

As you work with special-needs children such as those discussed in chapters 13 and 14, you will become aware of your own reasonable limitations. Remember to speak up when you need help, and keep communication open with the family. Do not hesitate to reach out to other teachers, counselors, doctors, and human-services specialists.

Although many of the conditions we have described will cause children to experience physical, social, and educational disabilities throughout their lives, teaching methods and supportive services can improve children's quality of life. You may or may not be able to see immediate results after your repeated efforts, but "in the long run, a baby's caretakers and [the child's] learning environment are as important as the mother's prenatal drug use for healthy growth and development" (Cook, Petersen, & Moore, 1990). You are in a position to make a difference.

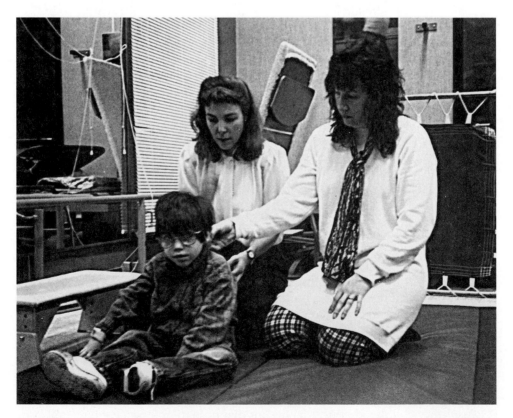

Consulting with specialists can help teachers learn how to meet children's special needs.

FOR FURTHER THOUGHT

1. Think about how you would feel if a child in your classroom were diagnosed with a long-term, possibly life-threatening illness. What would you be most uncomfortable about? What could you do to help yourself feel more confident?

2. Children experiencing disabilities often receive support services that require closer progress tracking and accountability than you may be used to. Would you feel threatened or irritated by this expectation? Whom could you turn to for assistance? Research various documentation methods and decide which ones seem best for recording targeted goals effectively and efficiently.

3. Think about your favorite activity with young children in a group setting. Now consider a child with FAS/FAE who is trying to engage in this group activity. What possible difficulties can you foresee? Next, consider children with other disabilities: hearing, vision, mobility, ADD. How could you modify the activity to meet the special needs of each of these children?

4. Parents of children diagnosed with learning disabilities may be in a state of denial, which sometimes leads to unrealistic expectations for the child and for you. Role-play a parent conference about a cocaine-affected child; one person (or a couple) should act the part of a disappointed or angry parent(s), and another should play the teacher. If possible, have a neutral observer for this exercise.

    Afterward, analyze the teacher's responses. Did you become defensive about your teaching skills? Were you tempted to play down the reality of the child's difficulties in an effort to appease the parent's discomfort? How did you feel at the end of the conference? How did the parent feel? If you were not comfortable with the conference, think about alternative responses and counsel with your observer. Now plan a follow-up conference. Set goals of what you want to communicate and how. Try again!

REFERENCES AND RECOMMENDATIONS FOR READING

Books

Dorris, M. (1989). *The broken cord.* New York: Harper & Row.

Grossman, H. (1990). *Trouble-free teaching: Solutions to behavior problems in the classroom.* Mountain View, CA: Mayfield.

Kirby, E. A. (1986). *Understanding and treating attention deficit disorder.* New York: Pergamon.

Macht, J. (1990) *Managing classroom behavior: An ecological approach to academic and social learning.* White Plains, NY: Longman.

Pacer Center. (1990). *Let's prevent abuse: A prevention handbook for early childhood professionals and families with young children.* Minneapolis: Pacer Center.

Parker, H. (1988). *The ADD hyperactivity workbook for parents, teachers, and kids.* Plantation, FL: Impact Publishing.

VILLARREAL, S., McKINNEY, L. E., & QUACKENBUSH, M. (1992). *Handle with care: Helping children prenatally exposed to drugs and alcohol.* Santa Cruz, CA: ETR Associates.

WENDER, P. (1987). *The hyperactive child, adolescent, and adult: Attention deficit disorder through the lifespan.* New York: Oxford University Press.

Periodicals

BORDNER, G. A., & BERKLEY, M. T. (1992). Educational play: Meeting everyone's needs in mainstreamed classrooms. *Childhood Education, 69*(1), 38–40.

BOS, B. (1992). Welcoming all abilities: What will happen? *Child Care Information Exchange, 88*, 26–28.

BROWN, M. H., ALTHOUSE, R., & ANFIN, C. (1993). Guided dramatization: Fostering social development in children with disabilities. *Young Children, 48*(2), 68–71.

BUCHOFF, R. (1990). Attention deficit disorder: Help for the classroom teacher. *Childhood Education, 67*(2), 86–90.

CARTER, M. (1992). Sensitizing teachers to the concerns of parents. *Child Care Information Exchange, 88*, 37–39.

COHEN, S., & TAHARALLY, C. (1992). Getting ready for young children with prenatal drug exposure. *Childhood Education, 69*(1), 5–9.

FIALKA, J. (1992). Advice to professionals who must conference cases. *Child Care Information Exchange, 88*, 40.

FUNKHOUSER, J., & DENNISTON, R. (1985). Preventing alcohol-related birth defects. *Alcohol Health and Research World, 10*(1), 54.

GRIFFEL, C. (1991). Walking on a tightrope: Parents shouldn't have to walk it alone. *Young Children, 46*(3), 40–42.

KRANOWITZ, C. (1992). Every body's different: Talking about special schoolmates. *Child Care Information Exchange, 88*, 29–30.

ROBINSON, M. (1992). Parenting a child with special needs. *Child Care Information Exchange, 88*, 31–34.

RUCCIONE, K. (1983). Acute leukemia in children: Current perspectives. *Issues in Comprehensive Pediatric Nursing, 6*, 329–363.

STRIMPLE, K. (1992). Linking parents to professionals: The director's role. *Child Care Information Exchange, 88*, 35–36.

Catalogs, Reports, and Papers

ALASKA STAFF DEVELOPMENT NETWORK. (1991). *Fetal alcohol and drug-affected children.* Research and resource catalog.

AMERICAN COUNCIL FOR DRUG EDUCATION. (1991). *Drugs and pregnancy—It's not worth the risk.* New York: American Council for Drug Education.

COOK, P., PETERSEN, R., & MOORE, D. (1990). *Alcohol, tobacco, and other drugs may harm the unborn.* Rockville, MD: U.S. Department of Health and Human Services.

Chapter 15

Analyzing Discipline Problems

You have read about many approaches to discipline and many causes of discipline problems. In case the information is whirling around in your head and you're not sure what to do with it, this final chapter presents guidelines for how to put it all together in a usable fashion. However, it is not a recipe for no-fail discipline, but rather assistance in the difficult task of analyzing discipline problems and matching them with appropriate discipline approaches. Each child and each situation is unique, requiring your professional judgment about discipline.

KEEPING GOALS IN MIND

The first step in exercising your judgment is to examine your goals for discipline. Chapter 1 discussed the importance of keeping long-term goals firmly in mind as you plan discipline strategies; and this book has emphasized the long-term goals of enhancing self-esteem, self-discipline, and moral autonomy. It is crucial that no discipline approach damage a child's growth in these areas. This book has attempted to explain how inappropriate expectations as well as inappropriate forms of discipline counteract progress toward these long-term goals.

Short-term goals are also important, although meeting them must not conflict with long-term goals. There are certain behaviors that are so disruptive or dangerous that they must be stopped immediately, leaving the teaching aspect of discipline for the next step. If children's actions put them into danger, it is essential to act quickly and decisively. Talking directly to the children involved is much more productive than yelling directions across a room. An emergency situation may require a warning shout, which will be useful if the teacher's voice is usually calm and controlled. However, teachers who routinely raise their voices in an effort to control a group will find that a raised voice quickly loses effectiveness.

FINDING THE CAUSE OF THE PROBLEM

If the situation is not an emergency, or if the emergency is over, you are free to think about the most appropriate discipline approach for long-term goals. This step requires a search for the cause of the discipline problem. Discipline that deals only with the symptoms rather than the causes of behavior problems is doomed to failure; the problem behavior will continue to surface until the reason for that behavior is addressed. But the cause of a problem is not always obvious, and it may take serious study and even some trial and error to get at the root of the matter. The chart in figure 15-1 may help you in the process of analyzing a discipline problem.

Typical Childlike Behavior

As you start to search for the cause of a behavior problem, ask yourself whether the offending behavior may simply be typical of that child's stage of maturation. Some adults don't realize, for instance, that a two-year-old is not being naughty when she wets her pants. These adults might punish the child or try bribing her

No discipline approach should ever damage a child's self-esteem or growth toward self-discipline and moral autonomy.

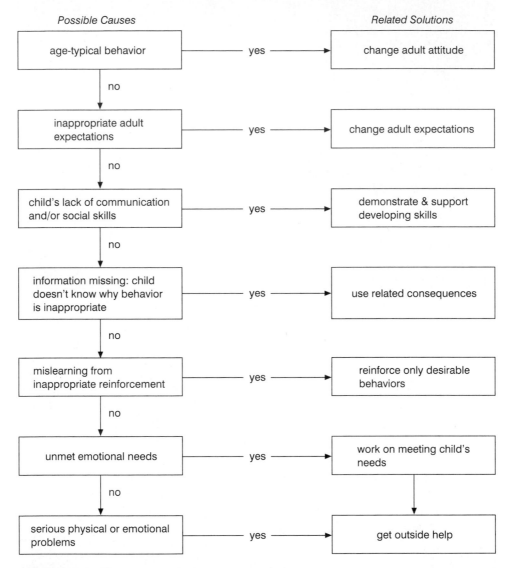

FIGURE 15-1. Matching problem causes to solutions.

in efforts to change this behavior, unaware that a two-year-old who isn't potty-trained is exhibiting maturationally normal behavior. The child can't change the behavior until she is older. Chapters 2 and 3 as well as chapter 12 offer other reminders of age-appropriate child behaviors that may frustrate adults. Your soul-searching may reveal that the "problem" is actually adult intolerance or a misunderstanding of childlike behavior (Curry & Johnson, 1990). In that case, the cause of the problem is the adult's attitude; therefore, that attitude, not the child's behavior, needs to be changed.

Inappropriate Adult Expectations

The next step in finding the cause of a behavior problem involves examining whether or not inappropriate adult expectations may have created the problem. Chapters 4 and 5 describe many common ways in which well-meaning teachers and caregivers accidentally cause discipline problems. Adults create problems when they require young children to sit still and be quiet for more than a few minutes, to wait with nothing to do, or to engage in learning activities designed for older youngsters. The National Association for the Education of Young Children offers guidelines for appropriate programs (Bredekamp, 1987) and curriculum (Bredekamp & Rosegrant, 1992) that teachers can consult to make sure discipline problems are not being caused by an inappropriate environment. If you suspect that the environment is causing children to react negatively, the solution is to change the situation rather than try to change the children. This preventive discipline approach saves both teachers and children a lot of trouble.

Lack of Knowledge

Once you have satisfied yourself that you are accepting children at their maturational level and providing an age-appropriate environment, you can go on to look for other causes of discipline problems. Perhaps the problem results from children's lack of knowledge about how to behave or about the results of certain actions. Young children have a lot to learn about how to get along socially as well as cause-and-effect relationships. If you suspect that lack of knowledge is causing the problem, a discipline approach that provides needed skills or information is indicated.

Communication Skills

Chapters 6 and 7 present ways of helping children learn social skills and effective communication techniques. Adults can demonstrate desirable modes of self-expression and of interacting with others (DeVries, Zan, Reese-Learned, & Morgan, 1991). They include the use of "I messages" and problem-solving techniques to teach children effective conflict resolution (Gordon, 1989). Teachers can also help children find words so that they can share their views and feelings with their peers, thus decreasing egocentricity. Teaching children in these ways are effective discipline strategies that promote lifelong harmonious social interaction.

Understanding Why

Chapter 8 explains how natural and related consequences help youngsters to understand why certain behaviors are undesirable. Adults often have trouble allowing children to learn from experience because of the desire to protect them. Although you do need to keep children from harm, you don't want to protect them so much that they lose the opportunity to learn. Finding out that you get cold if you don't dress for the weather or that you get hungry if you don't eat are valuable educational lessons. They are examples of natural consequences (Dreikurs, 1964). Related consequences are adult-imposed, but they link the behavior to a result that demonstrates why the behavior needs to be changed. Too often, adults expect children to learn from lectures and forget that experience is the best teacher (Piaget, 1965). Natural and related consequences are effective forms of guidance that help children gain knowledge, and that knowledge guides youngsters in self-regulating their behavior.

Inappropriate Learning

Sometimes children have learned the wrong things. Chapters 9 and 12 describe how youngsters often get attention for undesirable behavior and how this attention encourages the behavior to continue. These children have learned to get their emotional needs met in counterproductive ways. In this case, the needed discipline approach involves reteaching. Children need to unlearn old ways of getting attention and learn new ones (Curwin & Mendler, 1990). Judicious use of

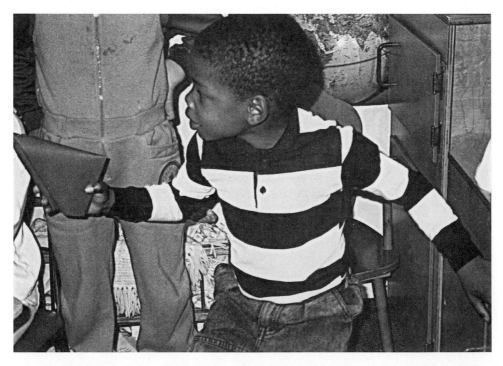

The cause of a behavior problem is not always obvious. It may take serious study to get to the root of the matter.

behavior modification techniques guides teachers in ignoring undesirable behaviors and reinforcing desirable ones.

Unmet Emotional Needs

If you are sure the child knows better but still is acting out, you need to look further for the cause. Sometimes undesirable behavior is motivated by children striving to feel OK in spite of experiences that have left them with emotional deficits (Curry & Johnson, 1990). Strong survival instincts motivate these youngsters to try to get their needs met, and they frequently act out in extremely disruptive ways that show misguided efforts toward "wholeness." But other youngsters with emotional deficits give up and retreat into their shells. The latter may be easier to deal with but are ultimately an even greater cause for your concern and attention.

Chapter 12 discusses how unmet needs in such areas as trust, pride, love, and power can contribute to discipline problems. If unmet needs are the cause of the problem, a truly effective discipline approach must involve attempts to help children get those needs met. These attempts may be made in conjunction with other approaches that will make the symptoms more manageable, such as temporary behavior modification or related consequences. It is important to keep the cause of the problem in mind, however, and continue to work on helping the child get needs met.

Problems beyond the Classroom

Teachers frequently find that a child in their care has a problem that they cannot adequately address. Chapters 13 and 14 discuss sources of help for children with severe problems. In some cases, the child's entire family must be helped in order to benefit the child. There is a limit to what can be expected of teachers and caregivers, and they must insist on outside expertise for these situations.

WHOSE PROBLEM IS IT?

Another way to analyze a discipline problem involves asking yourself, "Whose problem is it?" Thomas Gordon (1989) suggests the usefulness of separating those problems that belong to the child from those that belong to you, the adult. When you know whose problem it is, you have a start on how to solve it (see figure 15-2). To find out who owns a problem, look at who is bothered by the behavior.

Your Problem

If the child is perfectly content with the situation and you are the unhappy one, the odds are that you own the problem. If you are bothered by children's messiness, exuberance, or lack of logic, you definitely own the problem. These characteristics are part of being young and aren't likely to change until children are no longer so young. This type of problem leaves you with only one reasonable solu-

YOUR PROBLEM	CHILD'S PROBLEM
DISCIPLINE APPROACHES	DISCIPLINE APPROACHES
Change expectations	Natural consequences
Change situation	Related consequences
Express "I message"	Active listening
Remove yourself	

MUTUAL PROBLEM

Problem solving

FIGURE 15-2. Whose problem is it?

tion: Change yourself. Perhaps you can increase your understanding of young-sters to the point of increasing your acceptance of them. For some teachers, the solution is to find work with older children.

Common examples of discipline problems that belong to the teacher include children's taking blocks out of the block area, leaving the group at circle time, or talking out of turn. The child exhibiting the behavior certainly is not bothered by it, and rarely are other children offended by these situations. If the problem is the teacher's, then the teacher is the only one motivated to find a solution.

Solutions to Your Problem

When you own the problem, you have several options. One is to change your expectations so that you no longer perceive the behavior as unacceptable. For example, you may decide to allow blocks to be used in other centers as long as they are eventually returned to the block storage area. You may also decide to allow children a choice about attending circle time, as long as they don't disturb those who are participating. You might even decide to allow more informal talk-ing and not require raised hands.

Your options also include changing the situation to prevent the problem from recurring. You may decide to locate the block center next to the pretend-play area because the blocks so frequently get taken for use in playhouse scenar-ios. You may decide to shorten circle time and make it more lively so that chil-dren's attention won't wander. You might decide to encourage more small group rather than large group activities, thereby reducing the need for formal turns in discussion. All of these solutions involve creating a more developmentally appro-priate learning environment for young children, as discussed in chapters 4 and 5.

If you cannot overlook the behavior or change it by modifying the situation, then you still have other options. If the child is capable of changing the behavior, you might find an "I message" effective (Gordon, 1989). Matter-of-factly telling a youngster, "I can't read this book when you climb on my back," provides infor-mation about the situation and your wishes. It does not suggest that the child is being "bad," nor does it reinforce the behavior with undue attention. If you have

Another way to analyze a discipline problem involves asking yourself, "Whose problem is it?"

established caring relationships with the children around you and have respected their feelings, they are likely to respect your feelings expressed as "I messages." Saying "I don't like to be hit" may be the way for you to deal with another problem. This approach also demonstrates to children how they can deal with some of their own interpersonal problems.

If that method doesn't work, you still have options. If you have tried the other approaches without success, you may decide that the behavior has a cause that needs attention. As Lillian Katz suggests, if you have tried the same discipline approach more than two or three times with the same child and it hasn't worked, you can assume it isn't going to be effective for that child (Katz & McClellan, 1991). Perhaps you need to investigate the possibility that the cause of the problem includes mislearned approaches for getting attention, as described in chapters 9 and 12. In that case, the option of walking away from the offending child not only can meet your needs, but also can address the cause. When you withhold attention from inappropriate bids, you help the child unlearn the misguided behavior. There are some behaviors, however, that are too disruptive or dangerous to ignore. These instances may be good times for related consequences that teach why certain actions cause problems. These strategies try to make the problem also belong to the child by getting the child involved in a solution.

The Child's Problem

Many times the problem does belong to the child in the first place, but the adult takes it on. We describe this situation in chapter 8 when we introduce the mother who repeatedly brings the child's forgotten library book to school. Remember, children won't see a need to change behavior that is not causing a problem for them. Therefore, it is crucial that we acknowledge when the problem belongs to the child. Natural and related consequences get the adults out of the way and let the child experience the problem. These approaches quickly teach youngsters what behavior needs changing. Through natural and related consequences, children experience the problem, understand its cause, and are motivated to solve it.

When a child has an emotional rather than a physical problem, reflective listening (described in chapter 7) is useful. When you listen carefully and reflect back a child's words, you are not taking over the problem and offering solutions (Gordon, 1989). Rather, you are being a supportive sounding board to help the child arrive at his or her solution. This approach helps children learn to own their problems and demonstrates an effective communication technique for them. Reflective listening respects children's ability to solve their problems, which not only enhances their self-esteem but also provides practice in autonomous decision making.

Mutual Problems

Sometimes a situation arises that makes lots of people unhappy. But even if it only makes two people unhappy, the problem does not belong to just one person. Perhaps a group of youngsters can't start their math game because they can't agree about who should have the first turn. Now mutual problem-solving skills are required: It is important to find a solution that is acceptable to everyone involved. Chapter 7 describes how to brainstorm solutions and look for one that pleases all participants. This process may be a formal and time-consuming operation with a large group, or it may be a quick negotiation between two youngsters or between an adult and a child. Using this process solves many discipline problems, and teaching it to children provides them with a lifetime tool (Kriedler, 1991).

TAKING TIME FOR DISCIPLINE

Some teachers and parents want solutions too fast. They don't want to take the time to work through problem solving. They provide their adult solutions instead of listening reflectively, and they even force desirable behavior through fear or coerce it through rewards. These adults are short-circuiting the learning process that defines constructive discipline. Instead of helping children become autonomous and self-disciplined, this quick-fix attitude makes them dependent, rebellious, and sneaky (Kamii, 1984).

Time for Children to Learn

Teaching desirable behavior is a process of helping children learn a complex set of concepts and skills. Adults need to understand that children's exploration of behavior and social interaction is as natural for them as their exploration and manipulation of a new toy or another interesting object. Children need to try out

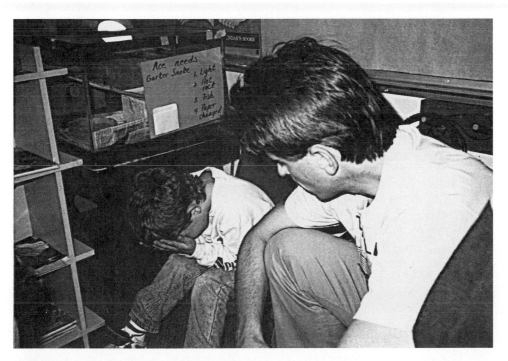

Quality solutions to problems can't be rushed.

certain behaviors to see how they work in relation to themselves and others. Given sufficient practice and time, youngsters will discover through their explorations that there is a logical pattern or consequence of actions. Children need to experience repeated connections between their behaviors and the reactions of those around them. As they reflect on these experiences, they construct their knowledge of productive behaviors, which eventually allows them to self-direct their actions as morally autonomous people. Such an important process does not happen quickly. Understanding gradually evolves as the child internalizes experiences and information over time. But the results are important enough to be worth waiting for.

Time for Cool-downs

It is hard to quit rushing. Sometimes teachers hurry to implement effective teaching techniques in a discipline situation. Perhaps two children are fighting. You know that they need to use their words to express their feelings and then negotiate a solution through problem solving. It is tempting to immediately start in on this important teaching as you separate the antagonists. But they are red-faced and short-breathed and still swinging. Will they hear your voice of reason right now? A wise teacher allows a cool-down time before trying to teach more acceptable social skills.

Time for Adults to Plan

Adults usually don't give themselves time for discipline. Behavior modification, with its emphasis on immediate feedback, has contributed to the common view that discipline must be instantaneous. Therefore, adults see a child doing something unacceptable, and they feel pressured to respond immediately. But thoughtful, reasoned responses on any subject take time. None of us does our best thinking without reflection time. Many teachers and parents confess to using discipline approaches they don't like simply because they couldn't come up with a better one *at the time*. It rarely occurs to them to allow sufficient time for effective planning in the area of discipline.

If you discovered a child had a language development problem, you would study the situation and consult others as you carefully planned proper intervention strategies. However, when the subject to be learned has to do with proper behavior, adults tend to act without thinking. Next time you are confronted with a discipline problem that you don't have an immediate answer for, try telling the child or children involved that you need time to think about this. Such a response demonstrates the seriousness of the situation and also models the use of thoughtful reflection in problem solving. Of course, for ongoing and predictable discipline problems, it's possible to plan ahead and have a guidance plan ready to implement.

We learn so effectively through the role models in our lives. Unfortunately, most of us have learned some highly inappropriate discipline methods from our own childhood. When we react quickly instead of thoughtfully, these old models may influence our actions. The automatic response generally corresponds with the one our own teachers used. If we want to implement better ideas about effective discipline, then we must make a constant effort to override our automatic responses with rational ones. Be careful and take your time.

THE ROLE OF RESPECT

Few of us experienced discipline with respect in our childhoods. American mainstream society values children but demonstrates little respect for them. Many of us experienced punishment and behavior modification. Adults in our lives also criticized us when they wanted to improve our behavior. The idea that criticism helps people to improve is widespread. Yet, in fact, it discourages us, and it does not improve behavior. When children's efforts result in feedback about their shortcomings, they are discouraged. Discouragement leads to quitting, not to trying harder. Alternatively, encouragement (described as an alternative to praise in chapter 9) leads to trying harder.

Respect accepts the child as a child, not as an imperfect adult. Respecting children means that we provide situations in which they can thrive while still acting their age. It also means that we give them as much choice as possible. When we respect youngsters, we don't force or coerce them to bend to our will. However, that attitude doesn't mean they are allowed to run wild and be undisciplined. Respect for children guides us in helping them learn effective behaviors and understand the reasons for them. When we respect children, we help them to respect themselves. The resultant self-esteem combines with self-discipline skills to create morally autonomous people—something our society needs more of.

CONCLUSION

The teacher with the knowledge and the caring to implement this sophisticated approach to discipline deserves society's high respect. Few observers realize how much effort and thought goes into a smoothly functioning program for young children. Teachers make hundreds of important initial decisions about the environment and the program, and they must make hundreds more daily as they implement their plans and keep youngsters constructively involved. We hope that this book is helpful to your own professional growth toward implementing the best possible approaches to discipline for young children.

FOR FURTHER THOUGHT

1. Think about your goals for guidance and discipline. Do you feel clear about what you hope to accomplish?
2. Analyze an actual ongoing discipline challenge using the chart in figure 15-1 and the accompanying explanation as a guide. Does this analysis help you to consider your own possible role as a cause of discipline problems? Have

you discovered a cause you had not previously considered? Have you discovered a need for outside help? Does this analysis approach help you to match guidance approaches to the causes of discipline problems?

3.   Analyze another discipline situation using the chart in figure 15-2. Have you been unsuccessfully trying to get children to take responsibility for your problem? Have you been inadvertently taking responsibility for theirs? Does this analysis help you to match your responses to the situation more effectively?

4.   Practice taking your time with responses to undesirable behavior. Give yourself cool-down time and planning time. What are children's reactions? Do they seem to learn from your example? Are your interventions more effective?

REFERENCES AND RECOMMENDATIONS FOR READING

Books

BREDEKAMP, S. (1987). *Developmentally appropriate practice in early childhood programs serving children from birth through age 8, expanded edition.* Washington, DC: National Association for the Education of Young Children.

BREDEKAMP, S., & ROSEGRANT, T. (EDS.). (1992). *Reaching potentials: Appropriate curriculum and assessment for young children.* Washington, DC: National Association for the Education of Young Children.

BUZZELLI, C. A. (1992). Young children's moral understanding: Learning about right and wrong. *Young Children, 47*(6), 47–53.

CURRY, N. E., & JOHNSON, C. N. (1990). *Beyond self-esteem: Developing a genuine sense of human value.* Washington, DC: National Association for the Education of Young Children.

CURWIN, R. L., & MENDLER, A. N. (1990). *Am I in trouble? Using discipline to teach young children responsibility.* Santa Cruz, CA: Network Publications.

DREIKURS, R. (1964). *Children: The challenge.* New York: Hawthorne Books.

GORDON, T. (1989). *Teaching children self-discipline: At home and at school.* New York: Random House.

KATZ, L. G., & McCLELLAN, D. E. (1991). *The teacher's role in the social development of young children.* Urbana, IL: ERIC Clearinghouse Document, 313168.

LANE, D. (1990). *The impossible child.* Staffordshire, England: Trentham Books.

PIAGET, J. (1965). *The moral judgment of the child.* New York: The Free Press.

Periodicals

DEVRIES, R., ZAN, B., REESE-LEARNED, H., & MORGAN, P. (1991). Sociomoral atmosphere and sociomoral development: A study of interpersonal understanding in three kindergarten classrooms. *Moral Education Forum, 16*(2), 5–20.

GOFFIN, S. G. (1989). How well do we respect the children in our care? *Childhood Education, 66*(2), 68–74.

GREENBERG, P. (1992). Ideas that work with young children. How to institute some simple democratic practices pertaining to respect, rights, responsibilities, and roots in any classroom (without losing your leadership position). *Young Children, 47*(5), 10–17.

KAGAN, S. L. (1989). Early care and education: Beyond the schoolhouse doors. *Phi Delta Kappan, 72*(2), 107–112.

KAMII, C. (1984). Autonomy: The aim of education envisioned by Piaget. *Phi Delta Kappan, 65*(6) 410–415.

KRIEDLER, W. J. (1991, Spring). Dispute resolution in education: Creating "peaceable class-rooms" in elementary schools. *Forum: National Institute for Dispute Resolution*, pp. 5–8.

O'BRIEN, C. (1992). Between the cereal and the potato chips. *Childhood Education, 68*(4), 236–238.

Papers

TURNER, J. (1988). *Child discipline and world peace.* Presented at the annual conference of the National Association for the Education of Young Children, Anaheim, CA. ERIC Clearinghouse Document, ED304226.

INDEX

ABOUT THE AUTHORS

MARJORIE V. FIELDS

Dr. Marjorie V. Fields has been teaching in the field of early-childhood education for twenty-five years. First she taught kindergarten, then first grade, and finally teachers themselves. Thanks to her own children, she became actively involved in cooperative preschools and various types of child care.

Marjorie has a doctorate in early-childhood education with research in parent involvement. She is active in early-childhood professional organizations at both local and national levels. Currently national vice-president of the National Association of Early Childhood Teacher Educators, she has also served on the national governing board for the National Association for the Education of Young Children. For several years she was a member of the early-childhood review panel for NCATE accreditation of schools of education.

Marjorie has previously published books and articles applying the constructivist theory to emergent literacy. She is the primary author of the widely used teacher education textbook *Let's Begin Reading Right*, and she has also written a book about literacy for parents titled *Literacy Begins at Birth*. She has published articles in professional journals such as *The Reading Teacher*, *Childhood Education*, and *Principal*.

This book on guidance and discipline is the outgrowth of nearly twenty years of reading and thinking in conjunction with developing and teaching an early-childhood discipline course. Marjorie credits her two sons, one now in college and the other recently graduated, with helping her learn what is most important about child guidance and discipline.

CINDY BOESSER

Cindy Boesser has worked in the field of early-childhood education for seven years. In a private, nonprofit preschool/day care center, she worked in all positions—from aide to teacher to co-director to administrator. At a university child-care center, she was on a team that planned and implemented a full-day program including after-school integration of older children. The variety of experience that Cindy brings to the book has given her a wealth of examples to draw from. Her awareness of the nitty-gritty details of classroom and center environments makes for believable scenarios illustrating many different discipline approaches.

Cindy's "you are there" writing style earned her a nine-month contract from an Alaskan newspaper to work as a correspondent in Moscow during the historic winter of 1991–1992. Her specialty was sharing the lives of people in the former U.S.S.R. with American readers, with the goal of reminding her readers that news and history are made up of real people with real personal struggles. She applies a similar approach to the anecdotes in this book.

Cindy appreciated the opportunity to co-write a much-needed textbook on constructive guidance with her mentor, Dr. Marjorie V. Fields. She also thanks the many co-workers and parents who have generously shared their expertise over the years. Foremost, however, she credits the hundreds of children she has had the pleasure to be with as they guided her in her own development as an early-childhood educator.

ISBN 0-02-337285-0